Pat Garrett

From a sketch by José Cisneros.
Reproduced by permission.

UNIVERSITY OF OKLAHOMA PRESS : NORMAN

PAT GARRETT

The Story of a Western Lawman

LEON C. METZ

By Leon C. Metz

John Selman: Texas Gunfighter (New York, 1966)
Dallas Stoudenmire: El Paso Marshal (Austin, 1969)
Pat Garrett: The Story of a Western Lawman (Norman, 1973)

Library of Congress Cataloging in Publication Data

Metz, Leon Claire.
    Pat Garrett: the story of a western lawman.

    Bibliography: p.
    1. Garrett, Patrick Floyd, 1850–1908.
I. Title.
F801.G3M47   363.2′092′4 ₁B₁   72–9261

ISBN: 0–8061–1067–8

Permission has been granted by the University of Arizona Press to publish a revised portion of a chapter entitled "Pat Garrett: El Paso Customs Collector" which appeared in the Winter, 1969, edition of *Arizona and the West*.

To Sam

who tagged along when the trails were dim and hard to follow

Acknowledgments

My first thanks go to the librarians, without whom no researcher could function. I extend my appreciation to Baxter Polk, University Librarian at El Paso, and to his excellent staff, Barbara Blair, Wallace Brucker, James Cleveland, Rosemary Corcoran, Jesse Duggan, Yvonne Greear, Kenneth Hedman, Simeon Newman, Bernice Le Mense, Martha Prather, Sibyl Rhodes, Inez Schweer, Frank Scott, Gloria Thomas, Mildred Torok, Edward Weir, Jacqueline Willingham, and Anne Wise. My gratitude also to Librarian John Wayne Smith of the El Paso Public Library and his staff, Shelah A. Bell, Emma Evans, Virginia Hoke, and Lizabeth Davis; to Myra Ellen Jenkins and Max Cox of the New Mexico State Records Center and Archives; to Archivist Chester Kielman at The University of Texas at Austin; to Archivist Roy Sylvan Dunn of Texas Tech University; to Arrell M. Gibson and Jack Haley of the University of Oklahoma Archives; to Mrs. Aloys Gilman, Assistant Librarian of the Iowa State Department of History and Archives; to Librarian David Kelley and his staff of the University of New Mexico Library; to Librarians James Dyke and Mildred Barrett of the New Mexico State Library; to Belle Wilson and Nora Henn of the Lincoln County Museum at Lincoln; and Harwood Hinton of the University of Arizona.

For friendly and helpful advice by mail and in person, I am deeply grateful to Eve Ball, Nona Barrick, Ed Bartholomew, Ramon Adams, Cecil Bonney, the Reverend Albert Braun, Frank Brito, Ruby Burns, Burrel Oral "Snooks" Burris, Frank Burris, Jack Carter, Nick Carter, Mrs. C. Claberon, Phil Cooke, James Cox, Lenore Dills, Hiram Dow, James L. Dow, Robert C. Dow, Raymond Dwiggans, Jeff Dykes, Bruce G. Eaton, G. Adlai Feather, Florence Fenley, Helen Garrett Fitch, Arthur Fountain, Tully Garner, Wilma A. Garner, Jarvis Garrett, Pauline Garrett, Mrs. M. W.

vii

Greer, J. Evetts Haley, Lorraine R. Haut, Carl Hays, Carl Hertzog, Peter Hertzog, Harwood Hinton, W. H. Hutchinson, Emmett Isaacs, Sue Ives, William H. Keleher, Randolph Lay, Dee Linford, R. L. Madison, Fred M. Mazzulla, John L. McCarty, Robert McCubbin, Cliff McKinney, Millard G. McKinney, Bill McGaw, Ruby Moore, Robert N. Mullin, Lee Myers, David Myrick, Dorothy Jensen Neal, Simeon H. "Bud" Newman, G. F. O'Neal, Edward Penfield, Baxter Polk, Sidney Redfield, Peggy Richards, Dawn Richie, Colin Rickards, Bud Rutherford, James D. Shinkle, Charles Skelton, J. J. "Jack" Smith, Joe H. Smith, C. L. Sonnichsen, Mrs. Tommy Powers Stamper, David Stratton, Rex Strickland, Mary Taylor, Mildred Torok, Ralph Vandewart, George Virgines, Dale Walker, Willis Walter, Herman B. Weisner, Victor Westfall, Mrs. Hugh White, Mrs. Rose White, Belle Wilson, Mrs. Ellis Wright, and Hal Cox.

Those who patiently spent hours typing and retyping the manuscript were Robin Fuller, Esperanza Monroy, Gilda Peña, Rachel Peña, Delia Reyna, and Mildred Torok.

People with the patience to read all or portions of the manuscript were my wife, Cheryl, Maryl Curry, Robert N. Mullin, S. H. Newman, C. L. Sonnichsen, Mildred Torok, and Dale Walker.

And a special note of thanks and appreciation to my wife and our four children and to Robert N. Mullin, C. L. Sonnichsen, Mildred Torok, and Dale Walker, all of whom saw me through some very difficult and trying times with this manuscript.

LEON C. METZ

El Paso, Texas

Contents

Illustrations

Pat Garrett

MAP

Pat Garrett

A Start Toward Fame

Pete Maxwell's low adobe house was peculiarly quiet as Sheriff Pat Garrett and his two deputies, John Poe and "Tip" McKinney, crept along the wooden porch that wrapped around the sides and front of the dwelling. Only minutes before, stationing themselves in the peach orchard brush outside Celsa Gutiérrez' place south of the Maxwell house, the lawmen had listened to the raucous scraping of fiddle music as almost everyone in Fort Sumner, New Mexico, stomped and clapped at the *baile*.

While watching the Gutiérrez house from their cover, they had heard nearby whispered voices speaking in Spanish and had silently observed a man, his face obscured beneath a broad-brimmed hat, walk swiftly toward the orchard fence, vault it, and disappear into the night. They did not know then that it was Billy the Kid, but they were reasonably certain that the youth was somewhere in town.

While Poe squatted on the splintery Maxwell porch and McKinney slouched against the weathered picket fence, Pat Garrett moved furtively across the south porch toward Pete Maxwell's room and through the door, which sagged open against the hot weather.

Inside, adjusting his eyes to the darkness of the bedroom, Garrett sat on the edge of the mattress and gently shook Maxwell's shoulder. Half-awake, Maxwell began mumbling replies to Garrett's questions about the Kid's whereabouts.

Outside, Poe and McKinney, motionless but alert, watched a lone, slight figure nonchalantly wander down the path toward them, yanking up his trousers and adjusting his suspenders as he walked. They were unperturbed, for neither man knew Billy the Kid in person and figured the advancing stranger to be a friend of

Maxwell's. The last thing on their minds was actually bumping into the Kid on the Maxwell premises.

The Kid stepped onto the porch and was instantly aware of the two men standing in the shadows. Automatically he drew his six-shooter and called out "Quien es? Quien es?" The question was not answered because both men were too surprised to speak. McKinney in particular was stunned by the sight of a gun barrel practically touching his shirt buttons. He stood up quickly and almost toppled over when his spur caught in a loose board. As he struggled to regain his balance, Billy noticed that he carried side arms, something few Mexicans wore. Puzzled, the Kid sprang across the porch and backed into Maxwell's room, saying, "Pete, who are those fellows outside?" He stepped to the end of Maxwell's bed, laid his hand on the covers and repeated the question in Spanish, "Pete, quien es?"

For the first time he noticed someone else sitting there, unrecognizable in the darkness because of the high-crowned sombrero that Garrett wore. Jumping backward, frightened, confused, and uncertain, the Kid cocked his revolver and hoarsely whispered once more, "Quien es?" And again, "Quien es? Quien es?"

The moment had arrived—midnight, July 14, 1881—that provided Pat Garrett with his modest niche in history and a considerably larger one in legend. Before he heard the Kid's worried question in the blackness of the Maxwell room, he had already lived a moderately long life—especially for a peace officer—and he was to live for twenty-seven strenuous years more. Still, at Fort Sumner on that midnight, he reached a turning point.

Did Pat have to shoot the Kid in Pete Maxwell's bedroom? Was he a traitor for killing a boy who had been his friend? Was the victim actually Billy or someone else? These questions have caused campfire and barroom arguments for nearly a century, and they deserve honest answers.

To examine the events which brought Pat Garrett to this turning point, it is necessary to go back to a winter night, December 13, 1852, in Chambers County, Alabama. A wild storm hammered on the door, and the frosty chill sent premonitions of death through the brittle bones of Patrick Floyd Jarvis, Pat's grandfather, for whom Pat had been named. Carefully the old man scratched out his last will and testament. To his wife, Margaret, he left the Negro slaves Fanny and George, plus all of his real estate—property which he did not itemize or describe except in a passing manner.

Jarvis possessed little, but with what he had he proved loving and generous toward his family. To his daughter Sarah, who had married James Gray, he gave Bacchus and July, two Negro slaves. In the event of the deaths of the Grays the slaves were to pass on to any grandchildren. To Elizabeth, his older daughter and the wife of John Garrett, he left three slaves, Big Ben, Little Ben, and George. The same stipulations applied.

To his grandson Pat he specifically awarded the slave George in case anything should happen to Elizabeth. The old man also gave Pat his personal possessions—rifle, saddle, and bridle. Thus the two-year-old toddler came into possession of equipment destined to become as much a part of him as his long legs.[1]

Patrick Floyd Jarvis Garrett was born on June 5, 1850, in Chambers County, Alabama. His father, the amiable John Lumpkin Garrett, was a farmer and a senior member of the extremely close-knit Jarvis-Garrett family, which began to unravel in 1852 when Jarvis died. The yarn strung out completely a few months later when the remaining family members moved to Louisiana. Mrs. Jarvis failed to survive the trip, and was buried beneath the wiry brown grass of Dallas County, Alabama.

In 1853, John Garrett purchased the Louisiana plantation of John Greer and settled in Claiborne Parish, the largest and richest upland district in the state.[2] Pat was then almost three.

Growing like a wild briar, Pat early developed proficiency as a pathfinder and crack shot by stalking the squirrel, quail, and pheasant flitting through the oak, pine, hickory, gum, and walnut trees. Cottontail rabbits thumped through shadowy tunnels in the heavy brush, and crows cawed in frustration across the low, green hills when the boy sent them scattering from a carefully laid ambush.

The Garretts considered themselves prosperous. Their plantation, approximately eight miles east of present-day Homer and two miles west of Antioch, covered eighteen hundred acres, although the property waxed and waned as various portions were either purchased or sold. Overseer J. Y. Coleman often supervised the loading of sixty-five mule-drawn wagons carrying produce and cotton to market.[3]

[1] J. J. "Jack" Smith to author, December 2, 1970.

[2] Pearl Smith, *Historic Claiborne*; Pearl Smith, *Historic Claiborne '65*; Walter Prichard (ed.), "The Parish of Claiborne," *Louisiana State Historical Quarterly*, Vol. XXI, No. 4 (October, 1938), 1110–1215; *Claiborne Guardian*, June 8, 1881.

[3] J. G. Garrett, nephew of Pat Garrett, interview with author, August 31, 1967,

No records exist to tell what part young Pat played in the business of his family's little empire. He did admit to doing the usual farm chores: plowing, hoeing, and breaking up red dirt clods. He also clerked in the plantation store.[4]

How much of a formal education Pat obtained is open to question. The state's educational system was one of the worst in the Union and remained that way long after Garrett had left. He did have some formal schooling, however, for, while his surviving letters do not reveal any writing talent, they do indicate a literate, practiced hand, something his wife could not have taught him in later years because she was Spanish and little versed in the rudiments of proper English. To those who sneer at Pat's "illiteracy," it is relevant to mention that he served two counties as sheriff, and even in those pioneer days a lawman had to read more than wanted posters. He helped shape both the Republican and Democratic parties in New Mexico and Texas, received a presidential appointment as customs collector in El Paso, Texas, and was the author of a book—even though very little of the actual writing was his. His daughter Pauline claimed that he read frequently and kept a small library.[5]

Pat took an interest in the education of his younger brothers and sisters.[6] During the late 1800's he journeyed back to Claiborne Parish nearly every summer. A favorite visit was to his former one-room, log schoolhouse, complete with wooden shutters across the windows, ax-hewn seats, a huge fireplace, and a long writing desk extending the entire length of the room. "Public Friday" was the yearly day on the schoolground. Parents and friends flocked from all over the state to observe the students' progress. Pat always sat in attendance when he could make it. People remember how he would squeeze his long legs under the desk, rub his mustache,

---

Haynesville, La. Garrett is the authority for the figure eighteen hundred acres. Official records do not show the plantation as being larger than eighteen hundred acres, but these documents are incomplete.

[4] *El Paso Herald*, August 24, 1905.

[5] Pauline Garrett, interviews with author, May 17, June 27, 1967, Las Cruces, N. Mex.

[6] According to the Claiborne Parish, La., census of 1860, the following persons resided in the Garrett household: John L. Garrett, age thirty-four, Elizabeth Garrett, thirty; children Margaret J., twelve; Patrick F., ten; Elizabeth Ann, eight; Sarah M., five; Susan L., three. Three other children were born after 1860 but before 1867, the time of the mother's death. They were John L. Garrett, Jr., Alford (Alfred?) J. Garrett, and Hillary W. Garrett.

try to appear comfortable, and stare at his younger brother Hillary, who, with numerous flourishes, recited the following stanzas:

> We must educate
> We must educate
> Or sad will be our plight
> From the cradle to the grave!!![7]

If little is known of Garrett's formal education, his religious education is an even greater puzzle. Ordinarily a small southern community boasted of one sect (Protestant) and two churches (Methodist and Baptist).[8] Anyone holding different religious views came under suspicious scrutiny. Baptisms were held in a large spring behind the Baptist Church. Whether or not Pat ever allowed its icy waters to close over his head is not known. Probably he did not. Very early in life, even before he left Louisiana, he began to question established religion, a fact that his mother did not live to learn.

She was born Elizabeth Ann Jarvis on September 28, 1829, in Georgia. Apparently she married John L. Garrett there and bore him eight children. Not even a physical description lived after her, and death came on March 25, 1867, at age thirty-eight.[9]

John Lumpkin Garrett's life is only slightly better known. Most of the details are folklore handed down from one generation to the next and not matters of public record. His birthplace was either Georgia or Alabama, and he was allegedly born on August 13, 1822.[10] Pat claimed that he was a colonel in the Confederate Army, but the Garrett descendants presently living in Louisiana dispute this claim. According to them he did not serve in the military because of poor health and because "the community asked him to stay and take charge of things" during the Civil War.[11]

During the ensuing northern occupation of Louisiana, Governor James M. Wells, backed by northern bayonets, appointed local officers favorable to his administration. Before leaving office in 1867, Wells called a constitutional convention, which meant that

---

[7] J. J. Smith, district clerk of Claiborne Parish, to author, July 21, 1967. Smith was quoting from an interview he had had with his mother, Mrs. James Patrick Smith, on May 23, 1967, at Homer, La. Mrs. Smith was ninety-one years old at the time of the interview. She had known Pat Garrett when she saw him and had had a very close relationship with his brothers and sisters.

[8] Southern Louisiana is and was predominately Roman Catholic.

[9] Probate Book B, 523, Claiborne Parish, Homer, La.

[10] Genealogy furnished by Mrs. Walter L. Haney, Arvada, Colo. There is a discrepancy of about two years between the genealogical sheet and the 1860 census.

[11] Jarvis G. Garrett, interview with author, August 31, 1967.

delegates had to be elected. Blacks, who were the predominant voters, elected Bill Meadows and W. Jasper Blackburn. Meadows was a black man, and on the evening before he left for the convention nightriders came calling and lynched him.

Shortly afterward the Yankees confiscated a large amount of Garrett cotton, causing the Garretts to flounder and stumble deeply into debt. John Garrett began drinking heavily, partly because of his poor health and partly because of carpetbagger and scalawag abuse. One day in a rage he shot down a northern sympathizer who was standing on the courthouse steps. The man lived and fortunately left the county without pressing charges.[12] Though the elder Garrett never went to trial, his health soon began to fail, and on February 5, 1868, he died of unknown causes.

A battle quickly ensued for the remnants of his estate. John Garret had foreseen the difficulties that his death would bring. He had only one son-in-law, Larkin Randolph Lay, who had married eighteen-year-old Margaret. Lay was born on June 23, 1836, in Fayette County, Georgia, and at the time of his father-in-law's death he was a saloon owner in Shongaloo—a notorious Louisiana brothel community near the Arkansas line (today a ghost town). Garrett did not like the match his daughter had made, and so he passed over Lay and chose his friend Hillory B. Shellman to administer the estate.[13]

Upon John's death Shellman disappeared, and a stranger named William B. Maxey took his place. Maxey did not relish a fight, however, and gave ground to Lay, who officially became the administrator on December 9, 1868. A week later Lay asked the court for permission to sell the Garrett land and possessions.[14] The disintegration of the Garrett plantation began.

Somewhere in this whirlwind of court actions and grief Pat Garrett and Lay became embittered toward each other. Garrett resented Lay's handling of the property settlement, and Lay's position must have been uncomfortable at best. Before he could make peace he was charged with selling the Garrett possessions. There is no way of telling whether he personally gained from the transactions. No evidence of fraud exists.

Someone had to take charge and handle the mounting number of creditors' claims. According to the court records John Garrett

[12] *Ibid.*
[13] Probate Book B, 523, Claiborne Parish, Homer, La.
[14] *Ibid.*

8

left debts in excess of thirty thousand dollars. An inventory showed total assets at slightly over twenty-one thousand dollars. The Garrett holdings were undeniably in poor financial shape.[15]

The seven unmarried Garretts took their losses hard. Lay was blamed for their misfortunes, and all of them refused to live in his home. Pat, quick-tempered and high-strung, threatened to kill his brother-in-law.[16] Out of deference to Margaret he refrained, but trouble could only result if he stayed. The alternative was to leave Louisiana. He rode away on January 25, 1869, and a decade passed before he forgot and forgave.

[15] *Ibid.*
[16] J. G. Garrett, interview with author, August 31, 1967.

2.

The Buffalo Range

Pat Garrett's wanderings for the succeeding ten years are significant, for during those years his character, honed and sharpened in Louisiana, was finely edged by the blistering sun of Texas and New Mexico. Similar to thousands of others drifting west, he was a wayfarer on the highways of the western frontier. Events hardened and shaped him. He never changed, except that he evolved from a lanky, quick-tempered youth uncertain of the future into a lanky, quick-tempered young man, following a dream of fame and empire. Bodies might be scattered across his path, but he intended to follow it.

Oddly enough, our first knowledge about his life in the West may simply be a case of mistaken identity. In March, 1875, a Pat "Garrity" was indicted for "intent to murder" in Bowie County, Texas.[1] No further details exist. Garrity broke jail and vanished as completely as the court records that were long ago destroyed by fire. Garrity could have been Garrett, for along the frontier names were habitually slurred or mispronounced and clerks rarely bothered, or cared enough, to double-check their spelling. As for the murder charge, there are rumors that Garrett killed a black man in either Louisiana or Texas.[2] Perhaps the lynching of Bill Meadows is relevant here, as is the fact that the Bowie County line snuggles tightly against the Louisiana border on a direct path from Claiborne Parish into Texas. There are stories that Louisiana and Texas law officers trailed Garrett onto the Great Plains, where they either lost the trail or turned back out of regard for their own safety.[3]

[1] *Fugitives From Justice In Texas, 1878,* 155.
[2] Mrs. Helen Garrett Fitch (granddaughter of Pat Garrett) mentions that there is a family legend that he killed a black man back in east Texas. Mrs. Fitch, interview with author, August 31, 1970, Las Cruces, N. Mex.
[3] Eve Ball to author, May 18, 1967, June 1, 1967.

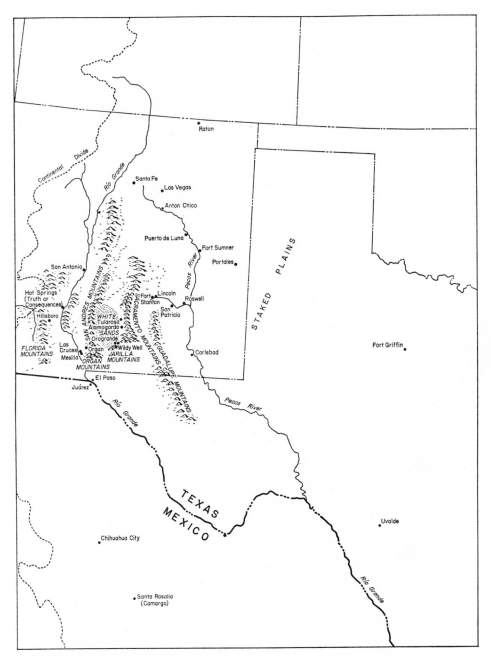

Pat Garrett's country

Garrett's version of events after leaving Louisiana (a version that makes no mention of the Garrity affair) is that he labored on a dirt farm in Dallas County, Texas. "I went into partnership with the owner," he said, "and my share was to grub the ground and clear the land. I got mighty homesick before the crop was in, but I stayed with it."[4] One growing season convinced Garrett that farming held no future for him, and he switched from the cotton fields to cow ponies. A Dallas County rancher offered him a job, and the tall youth picked up his personal belongings, jumped into the buckboard, and bounced along to new opportunity. Near Eagle Lake, Texas, the boss assigned him to a large cattle herd just starting north. Controversy exists now over whether Pat turned at Denison, Texas, and headed for the buffalo range or continued on into Kansas.[5]

By the middle of the 1870's he was in Tarrant County, Texas, making the acquaintance of a remarkable young Georgian named Willis Skelton Glenn, generally called Skelton by his friends because he regarded Willis as "sissyfied." Glenn was born about 1847 (plus or minus a couple of years since he himself was not sure of the exact date), moved into Louisiana as a gangling youngster, and joined the Confederate Army when he was fifteen. After serving with distinction, he took his discharge at war's end and moved to Mount Pleasant, Texas, where he grew cotton. From there he traveled around the state, speculated in land, and drove stock to Kansas. In 1874 he judged market conditions perfectly and drove a herd of longhorns to Florida, returning to Texas the following year with a remuda of horses.[6] Before long he began to consider the buffalo business a profitable enterprise, and by coincidence he met a tough, bearded fellow named Pat Garrett, who, with money in his pockets from his cattle driving and farm-product sales, happened to be studying the buffalo business himself.

Pat Garrett, Skelton Glenn, and Luther Duke, an obscure Ken-

---

[4] *El Paso Herald*, December 13, 1901, August 24, 1905; Jeff Dykes to author, August 5, 1967.

[5] In his biography of Wyatt Earp, Stuart Lake quotes Earp as saying that Garrett rode north to Dodge City, Kans., with ranchers Tobe Driskill and Ed Morrison. The cowboys tried to tree the town, forcing Earp and Doc Holliday to arrest them. Since the incident happened in 1878, Lake does not explain how Earp would remember Pat Garrett when the lanky cowboy had absolutely no reputation as yet, and there is no valid reason why Earp should distinguish him from hundreds of other ordinary cowmen that the "Marshal" daily encountered. Stuart Lake, *Wyatt Earp: Frontier Marshal*, 168–69.

[6] Skelton Glenn manuscript, University of Texas at El Paso Archives.

tuckian, pooled their resources and agreed on a buffalo-hunting partnership. Tagging along was Joe Briscoe, a youngster whom Garrett had met in Fort Worth. In October, with winter's frost already turning the heavy grass a dirty brown, they lumbered out of Fort Worth in a rickety buckboard, heading west across the high plains for Fort Griffin, almost three hundred miles away.

Fort Griffin in the 1870's was the epitome of all frontier sin towns. Its population of two or three hundred was primarily a migratory assortment of bullwhackers, stagedrivers, drifters, cowpunchers, soldiers, outlaws, ranchers, gamblers, prostitutes, and thieves, who cursed, brawled, drank, gambled, whored, slept, and died in its narrow, blood-slick streets. Honest and peaceful citizens ordinarily avoided the town. Buffalo hunters were everywhere, either leaving for the hunt or coming in for fresh supplies. Robes and hides were stacked by the thousands on every vacant lot. In Fort Griffin alone during August, 1877, over two hundred thousand hides changed hands.[7] Stale buffalo blood oozed and seeped into the ground and was tracked into every business house and shack in the village. Millions of flies droned everywhere, and the stench was so terrible that it would have driven anyone but a buffalo hunter out of his senses.

The military had opened up the territory. In 1867, Fort Griffin (first called Camp Wilson) was established on the Clear Fork of the Brazos River. For a while the cavalry pursued Kiowas and Comanches, thereby making the plains fairly safe for buffalo hunters and cattlemen. By the middle of the 1870's the Indians had been corraled on reservations, and the soldiers switched from fighting Indians to brawling among themselves in the village of Fort Griffin (often called Hide Town or The Flats), where there were plenty of toughs to accommodate them. Many of these young sluggers were cowboys whiling away time before heading north along the Western Cattle Trail.

The community organized a vigilante committee, and a month rarely passed that Fort Griffin was not the scene of two or three lynchings. Sheriff John Larn, suspected of rustling and murder, was shot to death in his own jail by masked men. Prostitutes with colorful names, such as Lottie Deno, Mollie McCabe, Long Kate, Big Billy, and Swayback Mag, were ordered by the "Tin Hat Brigade" to close their riverside houses or run more honest establishments.

[7] Carl Coke Rister, *Fort Griffin on the Texas Frontier*, 161–96.

What killed Fort Griffin, however, was not its wickedness or even its brutality. It died because of the railroads. The main line of the Texas and Pacific rolled sixty miles south of Hide Town through the tent city of Abilene. Fort Griffin had one more chance to live, and thus began a struggle with its neighbor, Albany, over which would get the branch line of the Texas Central. When that went to Albany in 1881, it spelled the end of Fort Griffin. Today the town is gone. All that remains are a state park, a few browsing longhorns, and the ruins of an occasional building.

When they arrived in Fort Griffin, Garrett and his friends rode straight for Frank Conrad's store, "a rambling house crowded with merchandise."[8] Conrad was the town banker, as well as the leading businessman, and he did not push Garrett's party to buy. Instead he encouraged them to look around and choose carefully. He had seen shoestring outfits before, and he paid little attention as his customers lifted harnesses from the wooden pegs, tested the leather for stitching and suppleness, and then moved on to saddles, knives, and other necessities.

Guns particularly interested Garrett. As the outfit's hunter, he wanted a reliable weapon. The Springfields were too military. Sharps had been experimenting for years beginning with the .50-caliber model with an octagonal barrel that fired a 380-grain bullet. Hunters had complained about the wind drift, and Sharps modified it to a .44-caliber, which failed because the cartridge case leaked and created an eye hazard when the rifle was fired. Undaunted, the company dropped to a .40-caliber, but the bullet did not contain enough lead to knock down a buffalo. So Sharps moved back to a .45-caliber and gave it 380 grains of lead, 120 grains of powder, and a straight cartridge case instead of a bottlenecked one. Most of the hunters accepted this weapon, even though in the final analysis the rifle was too good. It killed so easily that within a few seasons the hunters had literally shot themselves out of work.[9]

Pat carefully picked up the heavy guns, testing each for suitable heft and feel, swinging the long-barreled cannons to his shoulder with a practiced, smooth motion that brought the right eye and the front sight into perfect alignment. Finally he settled on the

[8] Phin W. Reynolds to J. R. Webb, January 27, 1947, J. R. Webb Papers, R. N. Richardson Collection, Hardin-Simmons University, Abilene, Texas.

[9] Glenn manuscript, University of Texas at El Paso Archives; Rex W. Strickland (ed.), "The Recollections of W. S. Glenn, Buffalo Hunter," *Panhandle Plains Historical Review*, Vol. XXII (1949), 15–64.

Winchester because of its portability and purchased one for fifty dollars. Glenn and the others preferred Sharps, for which they paid fifty-six dollars each. They also gathered up a thousand rounds of cartridges at eight cents a round, six kegs of powder at ten dollars a keg, and eight hundred pounds of lead at eleven cents a pound. Bacon and beans, staples of the buffalo hunters diet, were inexpensive, but tobacco cost one dollar a pound, coffee twenty-eight cents a pound, molasses two dollars a gallon, flour eight dollars for a hundred-pound sack, and corn seven dollars a bushel.[10] Hunters used a lot of corn. Part of it they fed to their animals, but most of it they distilled into liquor.[11]

After settling up with Conrad, the hunters purchased two common ponies worth about thirty dollars each, according to Garrett.[12] In the saloons they hired two drifters who were down on their luck. Nick Buck[13] said that he could skin with the best and Grundy Burns introduced himself as a cook. The three partners, along with Briscoe and the two itinerants, loaded up the wagons and headed for the buffalo range.

Briscoe had been with Garrett for several months. No one knew much about him, only that he had drifted into Texas from Louisiana, leaving a sister who was taking her vows in a convent. In contrast to Pat Garrett, young Joe was a strong and practicing Catholic who kept a small crucifix dangling around his neck. Glenn preferred someone with more experience than Briscoe, and he tried to block the youth's participation. Garrett's arguments carried, however, and Briscoe stayed with the group. Under Garrett's watchful eye, he learned that not every buffalo was necessarily to be killed—that a hunter had to choose and pick carefully. For instance, a buffalo robe worth three dollars earned the hunter about twenty-five cents, whereas a one-dollar hide brought him only a nickel. The hunter also cut out the tongue, hump, and tallow while the kill was still fresh. Otherwise the hide would stink for months, and its value would be reduced.

A remarkably good hunter like Pat Garrett could kill from sixty

---

[10] These are the prices that Glenn claimed were paid for equipment and supplies. See Case Nos. 1892 and 1893, Court of Claims of the United States, Indian Depredations, *Willis Skelton Glenn v. The United States and the Comanche Indians*, National Archives, Washington, D.C.

[11] *Ibid.*, testimony of Henry F. O'Beirne, May 17, 1893. O'Beirne claimed that the hunters also used a lot of barley costing three dollars a bushel.

[12] *Ibid.* Glenn claimed that the horses were worth more than $150 each.

[13] Nick Buck also seems to have gone under the alias Nick Ross.

to one hundred buffaloes in a day. Sometimes he shot so many animals that the skinners could not keep up. A good knife man could handle between sixty and seventy-five during daylight hours. Though he worked harder than the hunter—and certainly smelled worse—his pay was generally five cents less a hide. Moreover, he had to kill the cripples and calves that the hunter had overlooked.

The skinner carried a heavy, two-foot-long stick to prop up the front section of the dead animal. Commencing with the underjaw, he cut a straight line from the brisket to the root of the tail. After ripping the hide both ways as far as he could, he cut another slash from the hoof to a point near the brisket. Then the hides were easily peeled off, and the bodies were left to rot in the sun. Glenn wrote that he had "seen their bodies so thick after being skinned, that they would look like logs where a hurricane had passed through a forrest."[14]

The Garrett-Glenn party started in the Double Mountain country, an area of rolling grasslands about one hundred miles north of present-day Abilene. By November, 1876, buffalo hunting had become poor, and Glenn had left for Camp Reynolds, a way station for hunters, to have a gun repaired.

The clammy weather depressed everyone, particularly Garrett, who had not been able to purchase pants long enough to cover his skinny legs and consequently had tied an extra length of buffalo hide onto his trousers. On damp days the hides soaked up moisture and added walking weight, chapping his calves and making an annoying slap every time he moved. On one particular morning the hunters were sullen and sarcastic. Buck stared moodily across the prairie, even though he could not see very far. Not that it mattered; his thoughts seemed far away from the buffalo business.

For over an hour Burns had been trying to start a fire with damp wood and buffalo chips. Finally he got a small, flickering flame going and started breakfast. He hustled about, paying little attention to Joe Briscoe, who was approaching from an arroyo that had captured some rain runoff. Joe carried a few pieces of washed clothing, and his fingers throbbed, a penalty he paid for sloshing them in the nearly frozen water. With one hand slipped inside his heavy buffalo coat and tucked under a warm armpit, he thrust the other aching hand toward the cook's fire in an effort to dry a neckerchief, all the while mumbling—more to himself than to anyone else— about the impossibility of getting anything clean.

[14] Glenn manuscript, University of Texas at El Paso Archives.

Garrett, trying to obtain some small comfort from the fire as well, growled words to the effect that no one but a damned Irishman would be stupid enough to wash anything in that muddy water.

Briscoe immediately took offense, although he should have known that he could not whip his six-foot-five-inch tormentor. He rushed forward, and, as he crossed the muddy area separating them, Pat knocked him down, the process being repeated so many times that Garrett became ashamed of himself and tried as gracefully as he could to get out of the fray. But Joe would have no part of quitting. Stung by the disgrace of being hammered about and further humiliated by an opponent who felt sorry for him, Briscoe picked up an ax and tried to separate Garrett's head from his shoulders.

Several times Pat dashed around the cook's wagon with Briscoe in furious and unrelenting pursuit. Finally Garrett paused long enough to grab the Winchester. Turning, he fired, and the heavy slug sent Briscoe sprawling into the campfire. Everyone rushed to drag the boy from the burning embers, but he soon died.[15]

On the same day Skelton Glenn returned from Camp Reynolds, but Garrett was not there to meet him. Appalled by the results of his own fury and frightened by the consequences that his act would surely bring, he had saddled a horse and ridden wildly onto the plains, circling the countryside for hours, pushing himself to the point of exhaustion. Throughout that day and night a cold wind nipped him. On the following morning, haggard, shivering, and very repentant, Garrett went back and explained to Glenn what had happened. Glenn suggested that Pat ride to Fort Griffin and surrender to the authorities. He agreed and left immediately. A few days later he returned, saying that the officials had declined to prosecute.

Within two months of Briscoe's death Duke had sold out to his partners, who continued to shoot their way through the dwindling herds. Meanwhile the Plains Indians were watching with dismay and desperation. A few scattered bands were still dodging the sol-

15 Robert N. Mullin, "Pat Garrett, Two Forgotten Killings," *Password*, Vol. X, No. 2 (Summer, 1965), 57–63; "John Meadows Recalls His Association with Pat Garrett," *Alamogordo News*, March 8, 1936 (in this article Meadows mistakenly refers to Skelton Glenn as Briscoe); *Willis Skelton Glenn v. The United States and the Comanche Indians*, National Archives, Washington, D.C. (there are scattered references throughout the trial records to the killing of Briscoe); Glenn manuscript, University of Texas at El Paso Archives. Glenn also wrote a ninety-two-page typescript, more a tirade than a historical evaluation, about Garrett on the buffalo range. The manuscript is now in the possession of J. Evetts Haley, Canyon, Texas.

diers and avoiding the reservations, subsisting largely on buffalo meat. Even this was now being denied them, for the animals were becoming scarcer by the month.

Faced with three choices—starve, surrender, or fight—they chose the last course. Nigger Horse, an obscure Comanche leader, swept across the prairie with approximately fifty warriors. Glenn called the resulting series of clashes the "Hunters War." On February 1, 1877, Nigger Horse's braves struck the Garrett-Glenn camp and destroyed eight hundred hides, burning and gouging holes in them, and stole the horses. None of the hunters were present during the raid, but when Glenn saw what had happened, he vowed vengeance. Garrett was more patient. He cautioned that the Comanches were simply a raiding party, that they would soon sweep their way out of the country, and that it was too late to do anything about the damage.

Glenn was undeterred, and he found forty-eight other hunters who agreed with him. Except for a few men like Garrett, the hunters rendezvoused at the six small huts which made up Camp Reynolds.[16] Loading themselves into a few squeaking wagons and carrying plenty of whisky, they tracked their prey to the entrance of Yellow House Canyon (the site of present-day Lubbock). There a totally inept battle was fought; though only one man was wounded, the whites were completely routed and chased back to Camp Reynolds. The Hunters War was over.[17]

Garrett and Glenn picked up their buffalo business again, but on May 1 disaster struck once more. Another Comanche band attacked their camp, one participant being Herman Lehman, a "white Indian" who had been captured by the Apaches in Mason County, Texas, and traded to the Comanches. Lehman was available a few years later to testify for Glenn when the old buffalo hunter filed a suit against the United States government: "Well, a party of Indians, about forty, headed by a chief whose name I do not remember, started . . . across the plains and struck the buffalo camps. Then we saw some horses . . . and we run down through them. Two men came running toward us shooting at the same time. One of them shot my horse from under me."[18]

[16] Camp Reynolds has also been called Reynolds City and Rath City.
[17] Glenn manuscript, University of Texas at El Paso Archives; John R. Cook, *The Border and the Buffalo*, 260–346. Glenn's and Cook's accounts substantially agree.
[18] *Willis Skelton Glenn* v. *The United States Government*, National Archives, Washington, D.C., testimony of Herman Lehman, April 28, 1903, Comanche County, Okla.

He was describing Skelton Glenn and a skinner known only as Dofflin. When the horsemen first bore down upon them, the two men were unconcerned, thinking that the riders were friendly Tonkawa Indians from Fort Griffin. When they realized what was happening, Glenn grabbed a rifle and fired into the mass. An Indian pony reared, throwing its rider, who seemed to be uncommonly white. At the same instant Glenn was wounded in the leg and he sagged to the earth in pain. Dofflin came rushing by, grabbed him under the arms, and dragged him away from the melee of screaming, rearing horses. An hour later, from behind a knoll, Glenn watched as the buffalo hides were scattered, hacked, and burned.

Pat Garrett was out hunting and thus not involved in the action. A passing hunter told him the news, and he went immediately to Fort Griffin, believing that if Glenn was still alive he would go there. After finding each other, the partners returned to camp and searched for salvageable items. Only a few flint hides[19] that the Comanches had overlooked lay scattered about in the heavy grass. They were piled in wagons, hauled to Fort Griffin, and sold for less than one dollar each. This money was just enough for the two men to buy round-trip tickets to St. Louis, where Garrett gambled away what little he had left.

Pat was realistic about the Indian attack. Buffalo hunting had always been a chancy business, and he and Glenn had lost. He merely shrugged his shoulders and put the incident out of his mind. Glenn preferred to brood, however, and each time he thought about the raid his losses grew heavier. To anticipate the story, in 1892 he filed an Indian-depredation claim against the United States government, charging that the Comanches had violated a peace treaty by attacking his camp. He demanded nearly fifteen thousand dollars in compensation.[20]

He asked Garrett to testify, not realizing just how devastating Pat's testimony would be. Taking the stand in 1899, twenty-two years after the events in question, Pat practically demolished Glenn's claim, stating that their camp had been truly raided but that the total value of materials destroyed had been less than one thousand dollars. Until that time Garrett had been a fine and de-

[19] A flint hide was one that had not been properly cured, and consequently had become hard like flint.

[20] *Willis Skelton Glenn* v. *The United States Government*, National Archives, Washington, D.C.

pendable fellow as far as Glenn was concerned. The old buffalo hunter now turned on Pat, realizing that Garrett's testimony would become the linchpin of the government's defense.

The case dragged on, for Glenn could do little to dispute Garrett's testimony. In 1912, four years after Garrett's death, Glenn testified a little more fully, his strategy being a personal attack upon Garrett's integrity and character. Glenn swore that Garrett had not been his partner during the attack, that Pat had sold out and vanished from the plains after Briscoe's death, and that he had personally expelled Garrett because others in the camp were afraid of being murdered in their sleep.[21]

Glenn's fury carried over into his memoirs, which he wrote in 1910, a remarkable and informative set of manuscripts documenting his life and career during the Civil War and later on the buffalo range. The writings are little known and largely unpublished but are basically accurate and of great historical value. An exception is the ninety-two-page outline describing Pat Garrett.[22]

Regardless how Glenn hated his former friend, he could not erase or explain away one notable point: Garrett had no reason to be untruthful. He had not gained or lost anything in the matter. This fact left Glenn only one alternative: he had to prove Garrett a pathological liar.

Glenn found plenty of people willing to vilify Garrett, all of them claiming to be former "intimate acquaintances." The testimony of one J. W. Dobbs is a good example of the slander that the dead Garrett could not refute. Dobbs testified twice for Glenn, the first time in 1903 when he referred to Garrett as a gentleman whose reputation was above reproach, and the second time in 1909, after Garrett's death, when he said that Garrett's reputation was bad.[23] J. W.'s brother, G. H. "Kid" Dobbs,[24] testified that he had been a Texas Ranger under Garrett and that Pat's character had not been good. Charles B. Thompson,[25] farmer and cattleman; J. S. Thurman,[26] liveryman; and Bert Judia,[27] rancher, all swore that Pat's

[21] *Ibid.*, testimony in Roswell, N. Mex., August 24, 1912.

[22] Manuscript in possession of J. Evetts Haley, Canyon, Texas.

[23] Testimony of J. W. Dobbs, Comanche County, Okla., April 28, 1903, September 8, 1909, *Willis Skelton Glenn* v. *The United States Government*, National Archives, Washington, D.C.

[24] *Ibid.*, Cheyenne, Okla., September 8, 1909.

[25] *Ibid.*

[26] *Ibid.*

[27] *Ibid.*, Roswell, N. Mex., August 24, 1912.

Pat Garrett as he appeared on the buffalo range in the 1870's. Courtesy
C. M. Ismert.

Lincoln, New Mexico, about 1881. Courtesy Fulton Collection, University of Arizona Library Archives.

Pat Garrett and his second wife, Apolinaria Gutiérrez, January 14, 1880. Photograph taken at Anton Chico, New Mexico, on the Garretts' wedding day. Courtesy Pauline Garrett.

John Tunstall, whose death triggered the Lincoln County War. Courtesy Robert N. Mullin.

Alexander McSween. Courtesy Fulton Collection, University of Arizona Library Archives.

Susan McSween as a young woman —possibly in Lincoln County, New Mexico, in the 1880's, when her husband, Alexander McSween, was alive. Courtesy Fulton Collection, University of Arizona Library Archives.

Susan McSween, cattle queen of New Mexico, in the 1920's. Courtesy Zimmerman Library Archives, University of New Mexico.

Lew Wallace as governor of New Mexico Territory. Courtesy Lew Wallace Collection, William Henry Smith Memorial Library, Indianapolis.

Thomas P. Catron, New Mexico's most powerful political figure in territorial days, about 1900. Courtesy Collections in the Museum of New Mexico.

The personnel of the House of Murphy, for several years post traders at Fort Stanton. Seated, left to right: Colonel Emil Fritz and Major L. G. Murphy. Standing, left to right: J. J. Dolan and an unidentified clerk. In the summer of 1873 the firm moved to Lincoln, New Mexico, and erected a large building, which after the dissolution of the firm became the Lincoln County Courthouse. The building was recently restored by the Museum of New Mexico. Courtesy Fulton Collection, University of Arizona Library Archives.

ABOVE, LEFT: John Chisum. Courtesy Fulton Collection, University of Arizona Library Archives. ABOVE, RIGHT: Peter Chisum, John Chisum's brother. BELOW: James Chisum, John Chisum's brother. Both photographs courtesy Zimmerman Library Archives, University of New Mexico.

Billy the Kid. Courtesy Division of Manuscripts, University of Oklahoma Library.

Tom O'Folliard, slain by Pat Garrett in the ambush at Fort Sumner. Courtesy University of Texas at El Paso Archives.

Mrs. Charles Bowdre. Courtesy Fulton Collection, University of Arizona Library Archives.

Dick Brewer, slain by Buckshot Roberts in the Blazer's Mill fight. Courtesy Fulton Collection, University of Arizona Library Archives.

ABOVE: Front view of the Lincoln County Courthouse, from which Billy the Kid made his sensational escape on April 28, 1881. BELOW: Side view of the Lincoln County Courthouse, showing the upstairs right-hand window from which Billy the Kid fired the shotgun blast that killed Bob Olinger. Both photographs courtesy Zimmerman Library Archives, University of New Mexico.

John Poe, who helped track down Billy the Kid. Courtesy James Shinkle.

Bob Olinger, slain by Billy the Kid in the Lincoln County jailbreak. Courtesy Fulton Collection, University of Arizona Library Archives.

John Poe and his wife, Sophie. Courtesy Zimmerman Library Archives, University of New Mexico.

Deluvina Maxwell in old age. She was said to have been a girl friend of Billy the Kid. Courtesy Zimmerman Library Archives, University of New Mexico.

capacity for truth was questionable. Commodor Burge,[28] a laborer, said that Garrett once refused to pay him for work; therefore, Garrett's honesty was questionable. Ed O'Beirne,[29] coproprietor of a Fort Griffin dancehall, and his brother Harry[30] also blackened Garrett's reputation for truthfulness.

Yet not one of these "witnesses" for Glenn offered any firsthand information about Garrett's alleged lack of integrity. Several supported their allegations of "bad character" by citing the Briscoe killing, but none had been an eyewitness. Their knowledge was entirely hearsay, and few could recall much of that. Almost to a man they expressed something akin to shock at the idea that Garrett gambled, was often profane in speech, and frequently consorted with saloon owners and prostitutes. A courtroom observer might have thought that all the witnesses had led very sheltered lives.

Although Garrett's habit of hanging around with shady characters was frequently alluded to, only the name of Tom Powers, owner of the El Paso Coney Island Saloon, was mentioned. And while several witnesses spoke of Pat's heavy drinking, not one claimed to have seen him drunk.

Part of the testimony noted that Garrett was slow about paying his obligations, but Pat had never owed money to any of these witnesses—except perhaps to Burge. Nearly all of them regarded him as having a "bad reputation as a man-hunter" without explaining what this phrase was supposed to mean. The government had a logical interpretation, of course. It pointed out that several of Glenn's witnesses had experienced the law's breath on the backs of their sun-blistered necks.

One of the most damaging charges was that Garrett was an "infidel" who doubted the existence of God. In those days an agnostic was akin to an atheist, and rare was the person who bothered to define the difference. If any testimony carried weight concerning his truthfulness, it was this charge of paganism.

Generally the government refused to quarrel with the statements of Glenn's witnesses—although many discrepancies were touched upon. The federal attorneys did not dispute that Garrett was a drinker, a gambler, a woman-chaser, an agnostic. Nor did they question that he was slow about paying his debts. They did contend that all

[28] *Ibid.*
[29] *Ibid.*, Gainesville, Texas, April 10, 1892.
[30] *Ibid.*, Denton, Texas, May 17, 1893.

this had nothing to do with his basic honesty. To support their belief in Garrett's fundamental integrity, they called their own witnesses.

Nathan Jaffa, a prominent Roswell merchant and former territorial secretary of New Mexico, testified that Garrett's reputation for truth and veracity was very good.[31] Charles Ballard, a Roswell landowner, former sheriff of Lincoln County, former United States deputy marshal, Spanish-American War hero, and president of the Cattle Sanitary Board of New Mexico, called Garrett a friend whose reputation was unsullied.

Charles A. Kinne, secretary of the El Paso Chamber of Commerce testified that Garrett was truthful, as well as brave and courageous. George Harper, former state and county tax collector for El Paso County, called Pat a man with integrity. Ike Alderete, district clerk for El Paso County, said Garrett's reputation was very good. J. S. Smith, postmaster for El Paso, said that the former lawman's character was "first class." Joshua S. Raynolds, president of the El Paso First National Bank, testified that Garrett was "slow about paying his debts, but he was very honest and honorable." U. S. Stewart, president of the El Paso City National Bank, said that he never heard Pat's integrity doubted. Finally, J. D. Ponder, El Paso County treasurer and the editor of the El Paso *Times*, when asked whether he had ever heard Garrett's "character impeached for truth when put to the test," replied that he "never did."[32]

The case finally headed for judgment. The government awarded Glenn damages of $4,150, of which $830 was set aside for King and King, attorneys for the claimant.

But all of this was to occur in the years after Glenn and Garrett parted company. In November, 1877, after returning from St. Louis, Glenn bought out Garrett and employed his former partner as a hunter, paying him sixty dollars a month. Nick Buck was re-employed, and this arrangement lasted until January, 1878, when, with the buffalo hunted out and fast disappearing, the three men abandoned their wagons, equipment, and most of the supplies near Yellow House and rode away with scarcely a backward glance. By February they were near Fort Sumner, New Mexico.

Less than twenty years before Garrett's arrival this area had been the scene of a brutal, shameful incarceration of thousands of

---

[31] *Ibid.*, Roswell, N. Mex., August 27, 28, 1912.

[32] *Ibid.*, all these last-named witnesses testified in El Paso on August 24, 1911.

Navajos and Mescalero Apaches. The forces at the military post at Fort Sumner had driven these suffering people, like so many cattle, to the Bosque Redondo (Round Thicket) Reservation. This remote Pecos Valley region was selected so that the Indians could not escape. But since the prisoners were hundreds of miles from normal settlements, food and rations had to be freighted in at fantastic prices to feed and clothe both the Indians and the soldiers. Everyone suffered, especially the Indians. In 1868–69 the experiment was abandoned, and in 1871 the buildings were sold to Lucien Maxwell, the New Mexico land baron, who for years ran several thousand head of cattle on the land.[33]

In 1875, Lucien died, and his wife, Luz Beaubien Maxwell, built a thirteen-room adobe house a few miles south of the old fort. Several Spanish-American families followed, and a settlement of adobe-and-straw business houses, a post office, and a Catholic church was established. The pueblo of Fort Sumner came into existence about 1876.[34]

Upon arrival at the old fort, Garrett bought $1.50 worth of flour and bacon, enough to last him and his friends for several meals. As they squatted on their haunches and bolted down their first breakfast, Pat noticed a cattle herd being worked along the Pecos River. "Go up there and get us a job," he told Buck.

Nick did as he was told, but was unsuccessful, and Pat uncoiled from his relaxed position and started upstream. When he caught up with Pedro "Pete" Maxwell, Lucien's son, Pat pleaded that he and his friends needed work, that it meant eating or starving.

"What can you do, Lengthy?" Pete asked.

"Ride anything with hair and rope better than any man you've got here."

"Get into the buckboard," Maxwell said, and Pat obeyed.[35]

Garrett's height caused considerable awe among the predominantly Mexican population. They jokingly nicknamed him Juan Largo (Long John), and Pat thrived on the attention. Women were especially attracted to the dark, thin-lipped stranger with the courtly southern manners. They were infatuated in spite of disquieting rumors that Garrett had previously married near Sweet-

[33] James D. Shinkle, *Fort Sumner and the Bosque Redondo Indian Reservation.*

[34] Owing to several large-scale Pecos River floods, the original Fort Sumner no longer stands. The present town is about a mile or two north of the old location.

[35] Emerson Hough, *The Story of the Outlaw*, 292–96.

water, Texas, and that he had abandoned a wife and family there.[36]

Garrett's marriage or marriages in Fort Sumner are also controversial affairs. He is said to have married Juanita Gutiérrez in 1877, although the exact date is as obscure as the time and circumstances of her death. Allegedly they were married only a matter of weeks or months. She may have died of a miscarriage.[37]

Garrett then married Apolinaria Gutiérrez, presumably his first wife's sister, on January 14, 1880.[38] A very refined lady, the daughter of a well-known New Mexico freighter,[39] she gave Pat several children and stood by him in the turbulent times that were to follow. Theirs was an interesting relationship, a loving but almost formal one by modern standards. Garrett was unfaithful to her on many occasions, incidents of which she must have been aware. Yet she gave no trouble, remained faithful and trusting, and apparently at no time remotely considered the possibility of divorce. Correspondence now in the possession of Jarvis Garrett, the surviving son, indicates that Pat kept Apolinaria in his thoughts and in his confidence. Letters penned to her during his frequent absences were long and affectionate, though he addressed her as "Dear Wife" and closed with a simple "Pat F. Garrett."

Their love affair began more by accident than by design. Pat had gone into the Fort Sumner hog business with Thomas L. "Tip" McKinney, a local cowboy who would eventually join him in the hunt for Billy the Kid and whose grandfather had reportedly signed the Texas Declaration of Independence. One afternoon Garrett carelessly ran into the path of a rampaging sow, which knocked him down, trampled, and almost killed him. Apolinaria nursed him back

---

[36] C. L. Sonnichsen, interviews with author, El Paso, Texas, September 1, 1967, June 23, 1968; Eve Ball to author, May 18, 1967, June 1, 1967; Mrs. Rose White, interview with author, Portales, New Mexico, November 1, 1967. Mrs. Ball claimed that she knew whom Garrett married, but she declined to reveal her source of information because of embarrassment to families involved. Mrs. White was unwilling to discuss the subject.

[37] Jarvis Garrett, son of Pat Garrett, interview with author, Albuquerque, N. Mex., December 14, 1967. Garrett said that his father had married someone in Fort Sumner before marrying his mother, but he was uncertain about details. He denied that his father had married near Sweetwater. There are other stories that Garrett married Juanita Martínez in Fort Sumner. She would have been no relation to his second wife.

[38] Jeff C. Dikes, *Four Sheriffs of Lincoln County*, 8-11; William A. Keleher, *The Fabulous Frontier*, 67–75.

[39] Jarvis Garrett has a document drawn up by Ash Upson in which he filed suit against the United States government for losses suffered by the Gutiérrez freighting business during the New Mexico Glorieta Pass Battle of the Civil War.

to health, and they were married shortly afterward in Anton Chico, New Mexico.[40]

While Pat grew to appreciate Fort Sumner's more sterling qualities, his old partners Skelton Glenn and Nick Buck decided to move on. Garrett bade them farewell and remained to follow his vision, the ambition of becoming an hombre to be reckoned with in New Mexico.

[40] Cliff McKinney, son of Tip McKinney, interview with author, Carlsbad, N. Mex., October 9, 1969; Jarvis Garrett, interview with author, Albuquerque, N. Mex., October 18, 1969.

3.

On the Fringes of War

The Fort Sumner atmosphere and the friendliness of the Mexicans appealed to Pat Garrett. He liked his nickname, Juan Largo, and cheerfully went along with the jests regarding his foot-tapping, hand-clapping, eye-winking joviality during the *bailes*. Before long he moved from the desert ranges to the comforts of town, accepting employment as a bartender in Beaver Smith's saloon.[1] There he had the opportunity to meet and talk to every saddletramp, gunslinger, and cattleman in the territory. From this advantageous position he observed one of the bloodiest struggles for power that ever took place in the American West: the Lincoln County War.

While Garrett's role was at first strictly that of an onlooker, the dispute itself was of great significance in his forthcoming career, since he would eventually track down and kill many of the remaining antagonists. Its aftermath made him famous. It brought him into a first-name contact with presidents, governors, and an assortment of local and national politicians, businessmen, authors, and financiers. It even set the scene for his controversial death nearly thirty years later. Because of this conflict he became the best-known and the most feared and hated southwesterner of his time. A brief look at this conflict is necessary since it made him what he came to be.

The cast of the Lincoln County War reads like a *Who's Who* of western titans. There was Billy the Kid, whose remarkable feats of outlawry made him the hero of the Southwest's most incredible legend; John Chisum, who owned more steers than he could count and grazed them on land that it took days to ride across; Alexander McSween, a lawyer who talked piously of the goodness of God but

---

[1] New Mexico Governor Miguel Otero said that Garrett and Pete Maxwell had a dispute and that that was why Garrett moved into town. The governor did not explain what happened. Miguel Otero, *The Real Billy the Kid*, 92.

42

dreamed of riches and power; and McSween's red-haired wife, Susan, who dominated her husband while luring and sometimes dragging (according to local gossip) lonely cowboys into her bedroom.[2] There were Major Lawrence G. Murphy, a discharged military man whose lust for liquor brought about his death before the war he helped instigate came to a close; and John Tunstall, a wealthy English adventurer who has been touted as a "good guy" who finished first and retired to the cemetery but who in reality was a scheming, conniving individual who overmatched himself.[3] Finally there was Lew Wallace, the mediocre former Civil War general who wrote *Ben Hur* while living in the Governor's Palace in Santa Fe and never quite understood or really cared about the drama going on practically beneath his ornate Spanish windows.

Several competent historians have turned their attention to the Lincoln County War, and their conclusions have been largely factual and reliable.[4] But most writers have dramatized the conflict,

[2] In this age of debunking it is interesting that the reputation and character of Mrs. Susan McSween has never been subjected to any serious scrutiny. Historians have tended to treat her kindly, perhaps because she lived a long life and could be a dangerous adversary for those who provoked her anger. Colonel N. A. M. Dudley, commander at Fort Stanton, was the most vociferous concerning her amorous affairs, although it must be remembered that he and Mrs. McSween were bitter enemies and that Dudley tended to vilify practically everyone who opposed him. He wrote eight affidavits attacking Mrs. McSween, and she took him to court on the matter, charging that his statements that she was "a woman of bad character and reputation, a prostitute" brought her "into public scandal and disgrace." She apparently dropped the charges before the case went to court, although there is no evidence that Dudley ever publicly recanted. See N. A. M. Dudley to Actg. Asst. Adj. General, November 8, 9, 1878: 1405 AGO, 1878, National Archives, Washington, D.C.; Civil Case 176, Carrizozo, Lincoln County, N. Mex.; Philip J. Rasch, "The Trials of Lieutenant-Colonel Dudley," *English Westerners Brand Book*, Vol. VII, No. 2 (January, 1965).

Pinkerton detective J. C. Fraser also heard tales of Mrs. McSween's errant sexual activities: "She is said to have handled her virtue in a rather reckless manner [during] former days, but of late she joined the church." Pinkerton Reports, March 10, 1896, C. L. Sonnichsen Papers, University of Texas at El Paso Archives.

Mrs. McSween's bedroom antics still provide grist for the local gossip mills when people gather in Lincoln County. However, while it is not difficult to find those who will talk "off the record," no one will allow himself to be quoted directly.

[3] Frederick W. Nolan, *The Life and Death of John Henry Tunstall*; Philip J. Rasch, "Prelude to War: The Murder of John Henry Tunstall," *English Westerners Brand Book*, Vol. XII, No. 2 (January, 1970), 1–10.

[4] See Maurice Garland Fulton, *History of the Lincoln County War* (ed. by R. N. Mullin); and William A. Keleher, *Violence in Lincoln County*. Philip J. Rasch, Lincoln County authority, has written many articles about the struggle. Most of his publications have appeared in various *Brand Books*, notably those of the English Westerners, the Los Angeles Corral, the Tucson Corral, the Denver Corral, the Potomac Corral, and the New York Westerners.

writing interesting tales but missing the fundamental truths: that the blood-spattered conflict was basically an economic one, that both sides suffered injustices and were the victims of atrocities, and that neither faction held a monopoly on goodness or evil any more than on courage.

In the late 1870's, Lincoln County, New Mexico, was a wild and bloody land. About the size of Ohio, sparsely populated with whites, it had been the ancestral home of fierce Apaches, Comanches, Kiowas, and several smaller tribes. Dwelling and trading among them were the Comancheros, wild and brutal men of Anglo, Mexican, and Indian blood.[5] Today the descendants of the Indians still populate the broad, sweeping plains, the sand hills, the rocky mesas, the dry arroyos, and the wooded mountains and flowing streams of southeastern New Mexico.

During the middle 1860's, John Chisum, a man of average height, dark hair and mustache, whose outstanding physical characteristics were his two protruding ears, rode into New Mexico from Texas. He built a ranch at Bosque Grande and later at South Spring near the Pecos River. Soon he dominated the entire region, and his Jinglebob brand expanded until he owned nearly every steer up and down the length of the valley. The small ranchers feared his economic might, and some of them united under the leadership of Major Lawrence G. Murphy, a former army officer who had been post trader at Fort Stanton until the commanding officer removed him for dishonest dealings. Undaunted, Murphy moved to Lincoln, the county seat, and established the House of Murphy, a store and saloon. Soon he had a monopoly on Fort Stanton's beef and flour, though most of the meat was stolen and the flour was black and of exceptionally poor quality. As his business grew, he took in three partners: James Dolan, John Riley, and Emil Fritz. Together these men formed a political alliance with Thomas B. Catron, the corrupt head of the powerful "Santa Fe Ring."[6] Their aim was to destroy John Chisum and thus eliminate a beef-selling competitor.

First, however, the House of Murphy had to destroy another opponent, John Henry Tunstall, a wealthy young, slightly built Englishman, prone to bilious attacks and frequent headaches, who was moving in on the Murphy empire. With strong verbal support

[5] Charles L. Kenner, *A History of New Mexican–Plains Indian Relations.*
[6] This alliance was apparently verbal. If any records existed concerning their transactions, they have long since disappeared. Few historians doubt that there was a partnership of some sort.

from Alexander McSween and John Chisum, he opened a mercantile store and bank in Lincoln, thus crowding the Murphy faction toward the wall.

Trouble did not break out until Emil Fritz, Murphy's tubercular partner, died intestate in Germany, leaving only a ten thousand-dollar life-insurance policy. The House of Murphy hired McSween to protect its interests and dicker with the insurance company. McSween took the case. In August, 1877, he reported that he had collected over seven thousand dollars, and that the balance had disappeared into the coffers of a New York law firm which he had hired to assist him. The Murphy partners were suspicious but would have accepted the settlement if McSween had turned over the remaining money. The attorney refused, however, claiming that not all possible heirs had been heard from. Thus he gave credence to rumors that he had already spent all or part of the insurance money and had had to create a cover story. On Christmas Eve, 1877, he was charged with embezzlement and taken to Mesilla by Deputy Sheriff A. P. Barrier. Bond was set at eight thousand dollars.

Jimmy Dolan, who controlled Sheriff William Brady by purchasing his scrip,[7] sent the lawman to the Tunstall ranch with orders to foreclose on the cattle, claiming that the steers actually belonged to McSween. Tunstall refused to turn over the animals, and the sheriff, confused and uncertain, agreed to meet the Englishman in Lincoln and discuss the matter further.

On February 18, 1878, John Tunstall left for town. Riding with him, though strung out along the trail, were Dick Brewer, a husky, intelligent farmer who worked as Tunstall's foreman; John Middleton, a desperate-looking but actually mild-mannered cowboy; and a youngster usually referred to as Billy, or simply as the Kid. Although Billy the Kid is the focal point around which most accounts of the Lincoln County War generally revolve, at this time he bore little resemblance to the mythical figure he was later to become. He was as nondescript as he looked: a ragged, gaunt, obscure boy with a heavy revolver sagging on his narrow hips.

When the group reached a wooded canyon near Ruidoso, a flock of wild turkeys exploded through the underbrush. Brewer and

---

[7] The territory had no money in its treasury and so could not pay its officials in cash but instead used scrip, or warrants. These were often sold or discounted to businessmen, and naturally anyone giving full value would rate considerable gratitude.

45

another man galloped through the dry leaves in an attempt to shoot their evening meal. This left Tunstall alone, although about five hundred yards behind loped Middleton and the Kid. In the excitement no one noticed a group of riders charging over the hill, headed by Jesse Evans, leader of a murderous group of Pecos Valley gunmen known variously as the "Seven Rivers Men," the "Banditti," or simply "the Boys." The House of Murphy had employed them to do a job, and Brady had deputized them.

The Kid and Middleton yelled for Tunstall to run, but the Englishman refused. Perhaps it was already too late, or perhaps he did not expect to be harmed. He cantered straight toward the riders, and as he reined up a rifle bullet seared through his chest. As he pitched onto the ground, Jesse Evans reputedly shot him through the back of the head and then killed his horse. The survivors hurried to McSween and described what had happened. They also organized themselves into a group, named themselves the "Regulators," and were duly deputized by Lincoln Justice of the Peace John B. Wilson, who also swore out warrants for the members of Brady's posse. Lincoln County was now in possession of two groups of law officers, each vowing with grim determination to destroy the other.

In early March the Regulators flushed Frank Baker and William "Buck" Morton from a cow camp near the Pecos River. The two men had been members of the posse that had killed Tunstall, and they surrendered upon the guarantee of a fair trial. Their "fair trial" took place about five miles below Aqua Negra Spring, where the death sentence was pronounced and carried out. The exact details remain a mystery. Officially the Regulators claimed that the men were killed while "trying to escape," but other versions indicate that they were positioned near a grassy bank and executed.

The Regulators kept their initiative and marked as next on their list the name of Sheriff William Brady, a ruddy-cheeked Irishman who always walked ramrod-straight. On April 1, Brady and deputies George Hindman, Billy Mathews, John Long, and George W. "Dad" Peppin were lazily strolling down Lincoln's wide, dusty main street toward the Murphy store. They paid no attention to the adobe fence butting against the former Tunstall store. At the wagon entrance sagged a heavy wooden gate, behind which crouched six men, hats pulled tightly across their foreheads, eyes staring through the cracks in the wood. The gunmen had slipped into town during the night and slept in the Tunstall building. Their names are not definitely known, although Billy the Kid was one of them.

The sheriff's party had no warning. Brady did not notice that the corral gate vanished in a cloud of gray gunsmoke; he died instantly. Hindman, shot once, staggered several steps, fell, and writhed in the dust. He moaned and gasped for water, and then he too was dead. Long received a slight wound, but managed to jump to safety—as did the other officials. The assassins escaped.

The killings stunned all of New Mexico, and their effects were felt everywhere. Alexander McSween and Dick Brewer had no advance knowledge of the political assassinations and would not have permitted them had they known. They had no particular sympathy for the dead men, but they foresaw the devastating effect upon public opinion. However, they were too deeply involved now to back out; any hope of negotiation had passed. The struggle had to continue.

On April 4 the Regulators paused at Blazer's Mill on the pine-covered south slope of Sierra Blanca near the Río Tularosa. Dick Brewer, who was somewhat vain about his curly blond hair, spoke briefly to his hungry men and allowed them to enter Mrs. Frederick Godfroy's dining room. The gunmen were later identified as Billy the Kid, John Middleton, Charles Bowdre, and George and Frank Coe. There may have been others. As the ravenous men gulped their food, rattling plates and occasionally reaching for biscuits, no one realized that within moments the quiet valley would explode in one of the West's epic gun battles.

Andrew L. Roberts, one of Tunstall's slayers, veteran of many fights, a scrawny fellow with a crippled arm and a body so full of lead that he was known as "Buckshot," came jolting up toward the mill on a mule. As he approached, he saw guns stacked alongside the dining-room wall. It was too late to run. He pulled his rifle and slid painfully to the ground. Brewer detailed Frank Coe to talk the old fellow into surrendering. As the discussions dragged on and Buckshot steadily refused to turn over his weapon, Brewer sent George Coe, Middleton, and Bowdre to make the arrest. Bowdre walked toward the man and shouted, "Roberts, throw up your hands!"

Buckshot screamed a defiant "No!" and scrambled to his feet as Bowdre shot him in the stomach. The slug's force knocked him backward, but he managed to commence firing his own rifle. The first shot cut Bowdre's gunbelt. Another bullet shattered George

Coe's right hand, severing his trigger finger. A wild slug grazed the arm of Billy the Kid. Buckshot retreated to a nearby room, wrestled a mattress from a bed, threw it across the doorway, and lay down on it with his rifle barrel pointed toward his surprised attackers.

Dick Brewer dashed down the hill and across the road and ducked behind a pile of pine logs. He hoped to get a clear shot, but the second time he rose to look around, Roberts blew off the top of his curly head. That was enough for the Regulators. They hastily rode away, leaving Brewer's body behind. On the following day Roberts also died; both he and Brewer were interred side by side on the lonely mountainside.[8]

After Brewer's death leadership of the Regulators fluctuated among Frank McNabb, Josiah "Doc" Scurlock, Charlie Bowdre, George Coe, and an obscure gunman whom some historians have called William Bonney. All these men had played prominent roles in the Blazer's Mill encounter, but the one best remembered today is Bonney, otherwise known as Billy the Kid. No one knows exactly when or where the Kid was born, although an 1880 Fort Sumner census taker recorded his age as twenty-five and his birthplace as Missouri. Billy gave his occupation as one who "works with cattle."[9]

The Kid's real name was not William Bonney (or Boney). This was an alias, probably taken from the name of a relative. His given name was Henry McCarty. His mother was named Catherine and his brother was named Joe.[10] Mrs. McCarty was a widow who

[8] Paul A. Blazer (as told to Eve Ball), "The Fight At Blazer's Mill," *Arizona and the West*, Vol. VI, No. 3 (Autumn, 1964), 203–10.

[9] Pat Garrett wrote that the Kid was born "in the city of New York, November 23d, 1859," but no scholar seriously believes this. See Pat F. Garrett, *The Authentic Life of Billy the Kid* (biographical foreword by Jarvis P. Garrett), 7 (hereafter cited as *Life*). A few authors have quoted an alleged "birth notice" as it supposedly appeared in a New York newspaper, but no one has yet produced it. Various scholars have listed his birthplace as Indiana, Illinois, Kansas, New Mexico, and even Ireland, but no one has produced any solid evidence, and there is no valid reason to reject the census taker's report. It is true that the Kid could have lied; but why should he? It is also true that someone else might have given the census taker erroneous information; but would not a friend of those days have been more likely to be correct than a speculator, no matter how good his intentions, a hundred years later? It has been argued that the William Bonney mentioned in the census may not have been Billy the Kid, but with Charley Bowdre and his wife on the line above Billy, it is too much of a coincidence to be seriously disputed.

[10] All the several fine publications on the early life of Billy the Kid agree that McCarty was his real name. See Robert N. Mullin, *The Boyhood of Billy the Kid*; W. E. Coop, *Billy the Kid: The Trail of a Kansas Legend*; Robert N. Mullin and Philip J. Rasch, "New Light on the Legend of Billy the Kid," *New Mexico Folklore*

moved from Indiana to Wichita, Kansas, in 1870 and then on to Santa Fe, New Mexico, where she married William H. Antrim in 1873. In September, 1874, she died at Silver City, New Mexico, and the family separated. In 1875, Billy committed his first known crime in Grant County, where he was arrested for stealing laundry from a Chinese.[11] In August, 1877, at Camp Grant, Arizona, where he was known as Kid Antrim, he killed Frank P. "Windy" Cahill, a husky civilian blacksmith, in a dispute stemming from an ordinary exchange of insults. Cahill made the deathbed statement that he had called Antrim a "pimp," and "he called me 'a sonofabitch.'" They wrestled. Young Henry was thrown to the ground and pinned. He pulled Cahill's gun and shot the older and heavier man through the stomach.

Antrim broke out of the post stockade a few days later and in October made his way to the Heiskell Jones Ranch, near Seven Rivers, Lincoln County, New Mexico. In this sparsely settled land he became familiarly known to the Mexicans as Billito. He brought no special reputation as a gunfighter and for the next few years stood in everyone's shadow. The slightly built, five-foot seven-inch youth with scrubby blond hair who habitually whistled "Silver Threads Among the Gold" through crooked front teeth obviously did not attract much early attention. The Kid spent his boundless energies making love to the young dark-eyed señoritas. Tales still circulate that he fathered two girls by different mothers, both children dying of diphtheria while still in infancy. There is also mention of a son who grew to manhood.[12]

Record, Vol. VII (1952–53), 1–5; Philip J. Rasch and Robert N. Mullin, "Dim Trails: The Pursuit of the McCarty Family," New Mexico Folklore Record, Vol. VIII (1954), 6–11; Philip J. Rasch, "A Man Called Antrim," Los Angeles Westerners Brand Book, Vol. VI (1956), 48–54.

[11] Grant County (New Mexico) Herald, September 26, 1875.

[12] When Walter Noble Burns was collecting information for his Saga of Billy the Kid, he visited Lincoln County in search of source material and was fortunate in talking to many of the war's survivors. His personal correspondence states that the Kid definitely had progeny and that the old-timers knew who they were and who the mothers were. Burns wanted to publish his findings, but was overruled by his publisher—evidently on the grounds of a possible civil suit. See Walter Noble Burns to Judge William H. Burges, June 3, 1926, and Burns to James East, June 3, 1926, C. L. Sonnichsen Papers, University of Texas at El Paso Archives. See also undated note from R. N. Mullin to Maurice G. Fulton, Fulton Papers, University of Arizona, for mention of two children whom the Kid fathered. Eve Ball (interview with author, Ruidoso, New Mexico, June 22, 1968) remarked about these children and said that Billy the Kid's son had died in Lincoln County within recent years. To protect him and his family, she would not disclose his name.

Even the Kid's shooting abilities do not seem to have been unusual. Popular accounts say that he slew twenty-one men[13] during his brief lifetime, but a more realistic figure would show a tally of fewer than six.[14] Many killings, such as that of Sheriff William Brady, were the result of the combined efforts of several gang members and not those of a single person.

On April 9, 1878, the Kid and his followers were elated to learn that the Lincoln County commissioners had replaced Sheriff William Brady with John N. Copeland, a supporter of the McSween faction. However, their good fortune did not last long. On June 1, Governor Samuel B. Axtell removed Copeland from office on the grounds (obviously a subterfuge) that the sheriff had not filed bond within the prescribed time limit. In Copeland's place the governor appointed George "Dad" Peppin, Brady's former deputy and an avowed foe of the Regulators.

On Sunday, July 14, 1878, Peppin received his first hard test while half of his deputies were scouring the countryside looking for the Regulators. McSween swept into town, leading fifty or sixty of his partisans. Incredibly, although McSween outgunned Peppin almost three to one, his forces did not attempt to overwhelm the sheriff but instead spent their time barricading windows and punching gunports in the mud walls of three buildings, one of them the McSween home. By the time McSween had decided to fight, the sheriff's posse had returned, and the odds shifted back.

During the following two days of sporadic fighting, only a horse and a mule were hit. On the third day a deputy, sniping from the mountainside, was wounded; he died a month later. On the fourth day the fighting most of which had taken the form of long-range insults, subsided again. Finally the Fort Stanton commander, Colonel N. A. M. Dudley, broke the deadlock. He led his forces into town with a Gatling gun and a mountain howitzer. When they saw the blue coats and heard the squeak of wagons hauling the heavy weapons, two-thirds of McSween's forces deserted across the Río Bonito, leaving McSween and about fourteen fighting men bottled up in McSween's house.

On July 19, after five days of seige, the house was fired, and the flames slowly spread through the building, feeding on flooring,

---

[13] For a brief account of most of these versions see Ramon F. Adams, *A Fitting Death for Billy the Kid.*

[14] It can only be positively proved that Billy the Kid killed four men: Frank Cahill, Joe Grant, J. W. Bell, and Bob Olinger.

rafters, and door frames. The roasting, panting men inside slowly retreated from one room to another, determined to survive until nightfall, when an escape could be attempted. Susan McSween gathered up her skirts and ran to ask Colonel Dudley to protect the men inside the burning building. He ignored her, and she returned to the inferno.

Inside the building Billy the Kid had taken complete charge, for Alexander McSween lay on the verge of mental and physical collapse. Billy diagrammed the escape try, explaining that some of the men would likely get shot, but, if "we run fast and shoot fast, we can hold off Peppin's crowd so that they can't do us much damage."[15]

About nine o'clock that night Harvey Morris, a young fellow who read law in McSween's office, dashed from the burning building. He ran several feet and was shot dead. Next came the Kid and Jim French. Both vanished into the brush and the friendly darkness along the Río Bonito. McSween and the others lost their nerve and asked Robert Beckwith, a Peppin deputy, to accept their surrender. As he stepped forward, fresh shooting mysteriously broke out. Seconds later, Beckwith, McSween, and two of his supporters lay dead. The Lincoln County War had ended with dramatic suddenness. What remained was simply to round up the fugitives.

The five-day Lincoln County battle proved to be too much for President Rutherford B. Hayes. He removed Governor Axtell from office and on September 30, 1878, appointed Lew Wallace, a tall, slender, weather-beaten former Civil War general to govern the territory. On November 13, Wallace, unable to make up his mind about who the injured parties were, issued an amnesty proclamation to everyone who was a bonafide New Mexico resident. The proclamation was generally accepted. Factional bitterness remained, however, and in February, 1879, Billy the Kid met with Jesse Evans and others at Lincoln to discuss and resolve differences. They finally agreed on a truce. As they were leaving the meeting house, they met Huston A. Chapman, a one-armed Las Vegas, New Mexico, attorney hired by Mrs. McSween to prosecute Colonel Dudley and Sheriff Peppin for arson and murder committed during the five-day battle in Lincoln. While Billy the Kid slipped away, Jesse Evans and James Dolan shot Chapman dead in the street, poured whisky on his clothes, and set his body on fire.

A week later Governor Wallace arrived in Lincoln to find out

[15] Fulton, *History of Lincoln County*, 267.

why no arrests had been made. Colonel Dudley was suspended from his command at Fort Stanton, and Captain Henry Carroll was put in charge. The new commander promptly rounded up Evans and an accomplice named Bill Campbell and locked them in the post guardhouse.

The governor's fury motivated the Kid to write that he had been an eyewitness but not a participant in the Chapman slaying. Wallace, answering, suggested a secret meeting in the home of John B. Wilson in Lincoln on March 17. Billy honored the appointment and arrived after dark at nine o'clock. After a long discussion Billy agreed to testify in open court about what he knew. In return he would receive a governmental pardon.

Billy surrendered himself on March 21, but neither Campbell nor Evans was around to hear his testimony. They had escaped from jail two days earlier and fled to Texas.[16] On April 14 the Kid testified before the grand jury in regard to the Chapman murder and other matters. James Dolan was indicted for murder, although he secured a change of venue to Socorro County and never went to prison. Colonel Dudley and Sheriff Peppin were indicted for arson. Billy's testimony helped bring about all these charges, but he did not like the questions that prosecuting attorney William R. Rynerson asked. Obviously Rynerson wanted the Kid indicted for the murders of Sheriff William Brady and Deputy George Hindman. When Billy heard no reassuring words from the governor, and especially when Rynerson asked for and obtained a change of venue to Doña Ana County, he suspected a doublecross. One evening he simply walked away from the jail and never returned. Sheriff Peppin did not offer to pursue him. The recent events in Lincoln County had apparently shattered his nerve and he began to spend most of his time around Fort Stanton, rarely leaving its confines without a military escort.

On February 1, 1879, George Kimball[17] succeeded Sheriff Peppin, but he too showed little inclination to risk his life chasing outlaws. Law enforcement reached a low ebb in Lincoln County. Cattlemen and businessmen were demanding more protection. On

---

[16] Jesse Evans fled to Fort Davis, Texas, where in 1880 he was captured by the Rangers and charged with robbery. Sentenced to the Texas state prison at Huntsville, he escaped soon afterward and dropped from sight. See Ed Bartholomew, *Jesse Evans: A Texas Hide Burner*; Metz, *John Selman: Texas Gunfighter*, 96–120.

[17] There is considerable confusion about the correct spelling of this name. Many historians spell it Kimbrell, but for the purposes of this book the more common spelling, Kimball, will be used.

April 15, 1879, John S. Chisum wrote a letter to Governor Lew Wallace on behalf of Pat Garrett:

Fort Sumner
April 15, 1879

To his Exelency
Gov Lue Wallis
Lincoln, N.M.
Sir:

If 10 good men was stationed at a large Spring 12 miles East of this place, It would prevent Robers from coming in off the plains on to the Pecos and give protection to this place and the Citizens below. Roswell is so far below that the Robers can come in and rob as low down as Bosque Grande a distance of 50 miles and get out unmolested before the Troops can reach them.

If 20 men was stationed at Popes Crossing on the Pecos, it would prevent them from coming up the Pecos, having these two points guarded you then have possession of the two main keys to the Settlements on the Pecos River. Pat Garrett who resides hear would be a very suitable man to take charge of the Squad East of this place if authorized to do so.

I hope Gov you will not think I show any disposition to meddle or dictate. I know the County well, and I am satisfied you are more than anxious to give the Citizens protection and I am equally anxious to see the Robers kept out hence I make these suggestions. Robers cannot very will reach the Pecos by any other rout on the account of water.

I remain yours
Respectfully
JOHN S. CHISUM

During the period of the Lincoln County War, Pat Garrett had lived around Fort Sumner and Roswell, taking no part in the trouble. There seems to be no doubt that he knew Billy the Kid. It has been claimed that Pat Garrett often rode with the Kid and sometimes helped him rustle cattle, but no documentary evidence exists to support such claims. At one time or another in their lives nearly all cowboys corraled steers that did not belong to them, and a few even considered rustling an honorable calling. Some of the big ranchers were equally guilty, branding slicks (unbranded cattle) and even operating "maverick factories," where their irons burned into the hides of newborn calves from cows belonging to someone else's outfit. That Garrett may have once "thrown a wide loop" and engaged in these nefarious practices was looked upon as no great sin, and the lawmen elected by the cattlemen had to be familiar with the tactics, habits, and hiding places of rustlers.

At the base of both outlawry and law and order lay the common enticement of hard money. Just as rustlers stole cattle for cash, sheriffs rode after the rustlers for the same reason. Most of the sheriffs also had appointments as United States deputy marshals, and in addition to their salaries and fees were heavily subsidized by the cattlemen. Besides, a good sheriff might become famous and thus put himself in line for a better-paying political job. In any event, it was the ambitious and determined individual who took a sheriff's job and managed to survive. For a gunman, Pat Garrett was destined to live a long life.

Though it may seem so in retrospect, not all the violence of the time was caused by the factions of the Lincoln County War. Not to be forgotten is the fact that roads between settlements were unsafe for travel because of Indian uprisings—caused principally by Mescalero Apache renegades breaking away from the Fort Stanton reservation and by Comanches striking in small raiding parties from the east across the plains. It was the job of the lawmen to put down these raids.

As the Lincoln County War began, a handful of Comanches stole a herd of horses from a ranch near Roswell, New Mexico. Pat Garrett and others organized a posse and pursued the marauders several miles northeast of town. When the Indians realized that escape was impossible while driving so many animals, they stabbed twenty-seven horses in the neck, killing fourteen. Then, traveling lighter and faster, they watered briefly at Mescalero Springs and disappeared.

Since the posse did not carry sufficient food or water for a long chase, most of them turned back, all except Garrett and a few of the hardiest riders. Grimly they stuck to the dim trail. A week later they wearily rode into Roswell toting a large sack of moccasins and leading a very footsore string of horses.[18] Few men asked any questions, but everyone knew that on the back trail of these riders lay a lot of dead Indians.

Pat Garrett was living at Fort Sumner, in San Miguel County, during this time. News of his bravery and perseverance so impressed the Roswellians that John Chisum and Captain Joseph C. Lea, the latter a prominent local resident who commanded uni-

[18] Georgia B. Redfield interview with C. D. Bonney, *El Paso Times*, November 27, 1949.

versal respect in Lincoln County, approached Pat Garrett and in-
duced him to move to Roswell in time to qualify for the election
and oppose George Kimball in the race for the sheriff's office.[19] As
the November 2, 1880, elections approached, the Democratic party
in Lincoln held a convention. Battling for the sheriff's nomination
were the incumbent, George Kimball, and Pat Garrett. Kimball, a
perpetual office seeker who had held every available position from
justice of the peace to United States deputy marshal, entered as a
strong favorite—and he was a Republican.

In those times it was not unusual for a popular Republican or
Democrat to seek nomination from the opposite party, particularly
in one-party states or counties such as Lincoln, which was almost
solidly Democratic.[20] Since Kimball drew massive support from the
small Anglo ranchers and the Mexican-Americans, some Democrats
had no objection to putting him on the ticket.

Pat Garrett was a Democrat too, and his support came from
John Chisum, a powerful clique of Pecos Valley cattlemen, and
the successors to the House of Murphy. Joseph A. LaRue, a prestigious storekeeper in Lincoln who made most of his money grub-
staking penniless miners, early seized control of the party machin-
ery and became the convention chairman. From his position of
power on the podium he hammered down the Kimball backers and
gave strong support to Garrett.[21]

With LaRue dominating convention procedure, Will Dowlin, for
a while post trader at Fort Stanton and later manager of the one-
time Dolan store in Lincoln, and James J. Dolan made vigorous
speeches for Pat Garrett. David M. Easton, a resident of the South
Fork (Mescalero Reservation) area who two years later would become a political opponent of Pat Garrett, battered Kimball's supporters aside, grabbed the speaker's stand, and in an hour-long
harangue damned Kimball as soft on local badmen. Gradually the
majority of the convention delegates swung toward Garrett, who
heard himself touted in lavish terms as a law-and-order candidate.
The speakers depicted him as a relentless manhunter who would
either run the outlaws out of the county or bury them beneath its
rocky soil. The voting was close, wild, and tumultuous, but the outcome was Garrett's nomination as sheriff.

At election time, with Kimball running as an Independent or a

[19] George Curry, *An Autobiography*, 40–41.
[20] Robert N. Mullin to author, July 26, 1969.
[21] *Rio Grande Republican*, September 2, September 16, 1882.

Republican (the records are very sparse), the candidates set out to woo the most ignored of all citizens, the Mexican-Americans. Many of them could remember when they were part of old Mexico and owned New Mexico Territory. They were a political force to be reckoned with when their votes were needed during an election—and were forgotten immediately afterward.

Although both Kimball and Garrett claimed a share of the Mexican vote because of their Mexican wives, Pat Garrett enlisted few supporters because of his association with the rich cattlemen. In particular the Mexicans hated John Chisum, the largest landowner in New Mexico. Even Chisum did not know how much property he had, because he could enlarge it any time the notion struck him merely by sending out his cowboys to take possession.

John Chisum mistreated squatters caught on his little-used and frequently unoccupied land, and he severely punished men caught stealing his cattle. To the Mexicans, whose economic condition had reduced them to second-class citizens, unproductive land and uneaten beef, taken from a man who possessed so much and used by people who had so little, did not justify any retaliatory actions. They naturally looked with suspicion upon a potential sheriff so closely allied with the big cattleman, and Pat Garrett was so closely tied in with Chisum that he could have easily worn the jinglebob ear-notch brand.

The election controversy became the talk of the county and attracted attention from all over the territory. One afternoon George Curry, a future governor of New Mexico but then manager of Lincoln County's Brock Ranch, noticed a gunman ride into camp. The youth dismounted and, upon being invited, ate chuck with the cowhands. Curry noticed that the boy did not introduce himself, but paid little attention since silence about one's past was respected. As the stranger mounted to leave, he spoke of plans to spend the night dancing at Las Tablas, a sheep-herding community. Curry was immediately interested, for he had plans to go there the next day to campaign for Garrett's election.

"Do you know Garrett?" the youth asked.

"No, I don't, but from what I hear, he is a splendid man. He'll carry this precinct. I have a gallon of whisky on hand, and I think that will help. . . ."

The rider merely waved his hand and disappeared in the direction of Las Tablas. With the early sunrise he returned to eat a breakfast of flapjacks and to bid his final *adios*. As he started to go, he grinned and said, "You are a good cook and a good fellow, but if you think Pat Garrett is going to carry this precinct for sheriff, you are a damn poor politician."[22] Moments later one of Curry's cowboys nudged him and said that he had been discussing the elections with Billy the Kid.

Curry, worried now that the Kid might exercise some influence with the Las Tablas herders, grabbed a jug of whisky and a can of tobacco and headed for the polling place. All morning he strolled about, cajoling the voters, shaking hands, and telling everyone how Garrett would rid the county of Billy the Kid. So grateful did the Mexican natives seem for his gifts that, as the afternoon passed, Curry grew overoptimistic. Finally he could restrain his enthusiasm no longer and wired Garrett that Las Tablas had supported him almost unanimously. When the votes were counted, however, the tally was thirty-nine for Kimball and only one for Garrett.

Fortunately for Garrett, the Las Tablas votes were not representative of the county. A final tally showed 179 votes for Kimball and 320 for Pat Garrett.[23] Kimball capitulated graciously, and Lincoln County had a sheriff-elect.

[22] There are two versions of this incident, both of them substantially the same. In George Curry's autobiography he omitted most of the conversation shown here; William A. Keleher supplied the dialogue, which was taken from an interview with Curry. See Curry, *An Autobiography*, 18–19; Keleher, *The Fabulous Frontier*, 72–73.

[23] Lincoln County Commissioners Record Book (unnumbered and unlettered), November 2, 1880, p. 66.

4.

The Treasury Department Steps In

The ambitious Pat Garrett was no idle dreamer. Before he could bring Billy the Kid to heel, there had to be plenty of hard work. Now that the elections were over he could get started. Although Pat's term of office did not officially begin until January 1, 1881, the incumbent, George Kimball, under pressure from the cattlemen, appointed him deputy for the months of November and December, 1880.

The United States Treasury Department in Washington, D.C., also took a hard look at the Kid's activities. In October, 1880, Azariah F. Wild, a secret-service agent, paid thirty-six dollars for a private conveyance from Santa Fe to Fort Stanton, a distance of 160 miles, and shelled out a dollar more for the nine-mile stage ride to Lincoln.[1] There Wild examined a counterfeit hundred-dollar bill passed upon none other than James J. Dolan by Billie Wilson, a young fellow who has sometimes been confused with Billy the Kid. Soon other illegal money began turning up, all of it curiously full of pinholes. The Treasury agent named the distributors as Wilson, W. W. West, Sam Dedrick, and Tom Cooper, the last three being outlaws of little notoriety or significance. Their names rarely appear in Lincoln County War histories, but because of them and Wilson the federal government became indirectly involved in the chase of Billy the Kid. It would be fair to say that had it not been for this counterfeiting the incidents involving Pat Garrett and Billy might have taken other twists.

According to Wild, the distributors were merely "shoving the queer." He did not know where the counterfeit money was manu-

---

[1] Wild's reports, voluminous, perceptive, but often inaccurate, have lain undisturbed in the National Archives since being placed there with other government records. They add a new dimension to the hunt for Billy the Kid and are used here for the first time.

factured but thought it was well made, in spite of the poor quality of the paper. New to New Mexico's corrupt politics, Wild thought that the solution to the counterfeiting was a simple one: ask United States Marshal John Sherman, Jr., to make arrests. After all, the crooks were known. But when Wild approached the marshal, named names, and requested warrants, Sherman declined with the statement, "I prefer not to do so."[2]

Although the marshal's reply stunned the secret-service man (and Wild never forgave him for it), Wild soon realized why Sherman hesitated to move. The outlaws had terrorized the inhabitants of southeastern New Mexico. A few Lincoln County historians have lost sight of this fact, one explanation being that most authorities take an apologetic attitude toward the Kid. They have tended to ignore the fact that the highways of Lincoln County were unsafe for travel because the Kid or his comrades were moving across the hills, pillaging and spoiling. The writers have rarely commented on the fear that prevented officials from performing their duties—the fear of murder. The reason so little is known about the true situation is that it detracts from the popular image of Billy the Kid. Special Agent Wild called the situation exactly as he saw it. He not only considered the Kid and Billie Wilson ordinary cutthroats but also considered the public officials fawning weaklings. And he saw this fear extending all the way to Santa Fe.

Since United States marshals and deputy marshals were too frightened to help him, Wild purchased eleven dollars' worth of miners' clothes and slipped quietly into Lincoln for some under-cover work. Gradually he compiled a list of brave citizens willing to risk death if it would hasten the day of law and order. Among them were Benjamin Ellis, George Kimball, John Hurley, Captain J. C. Lea, Frank Stewart, and Pat Garrett. Using this group as a lever, he wrote Sherman saying that these men would do the work if Sherman would simply sign United States deputy marshal commissions for all of them. Sherman happily complied, sending everything the Treasury man asked for, except that he mistakenly dispatched two commissions for Hurley and none for Garrett. Wild rectified this error by scratching Hurley's name from one of the papers and substituting Garrett's.[3]

Then Wild planned a three-pronged attack upon the outlaws and

[2] Wild to Brooks, October 2, 1880, National Archives, Washington, D.C. Wild's reports are full of derogatory statements about John Sherman, Jr.
[3] *Ibid.*, January 2, 1881.

counterfeiters. Kimball and Hurley were to flush the bandits from White Oaks and drive them west. Stewart would block their entry into Texas. With Garrett and himself charging in from the south and two other posses held in reserve to block any unforeseen escape routes, Wild felt certain that all the outlaws would soon be dead or captured.[4]

The elaborate plan might have worked except that the gunmen robbed the United States mail and read some of Wild's confidential reports. This caused him to cancel everything and to guard his own life a little more closely, since his undercover activities were now surely known. According to Wild's reports, Billy the Kid, Billie Wilson, and hordes of other gunmen whom Wild lumped together as "the rustlers" were prowling the remote roads of Lincoln County. Citizens rarely moved any distance except in armed groups of six or more, and Wild himself now rarely traveled without an escort.

Soon, however, unwilling to be bottled up by outlaws whom he was supposed to be capturing, he concocted another plan. He wrote Captain J. C. Lea in Roswell, explaining that he desired some "discreet and reliable person" to work undercover at Fort Sumner and report on the gang's activities. For this dangerous task the government was prepared to pay two dollars a day plus expenses. The agent would have to furnish his own saddle horse.

On November 20, 1880, Deputy Garrett rode in from Roswell with Barney Mason, claiming that both he and Lea would swear to Mason's "honesty and fidelity."[5] Garrett described Mason as an experienced stockman who had been employed for the last several years by Pete Maxwell in Fort Sumner and said that the young cowboy would make an excellent undercover man.

Barney Mason told how he had recently wandered into the West and Dedrick corral at White Oaks. Stomping around in several inches of icy slush and horse manure were Billy the Kid, Billie Wilson, and Dave Rudabaugh, the latter having a price on his shaggy head for the brutal slaying on April 30, 1880, of a jailor in Las Vegas

---

[4] *Ibid.*, November 10, 1880.

[5] *Ibid.*, November 20, 1880. Very little is known about Mason's life and career. He and Garrett knew each other at Fort Sumner and in fact were each other's best man at a double wedding. In the early days of Garrett's pursuit of Billy the Kid, Mason was Garrett's constant companion. However, their relationship cooled quickly thereafter for reasons which have never been stated. Probably Garrett tired of Mason's lies, cold-bloodedness, small-time criminal activities, and general lack of dependability. Mason is reported to have died when the roof of an adobe house caved in on him.

while liberating a friend and convicted murderer, John J. Webb. The outlaws had no reason to be suspicious of Mason. Though a friend of Garrett, his back trail had as many buried criminal acts as their own.

Mason also told of a recent meeting between himself and Daniel Dedrick, a Bosque Grande resident and a brother of Sam Dedrick. Daniel had recently escaped from a Fort Smith, Arkansas, jail, where he had been serving time for stealing horses from the Indian reservation.[6]

A man named Duncan had recently arrived from New York carrying so much counterfeit money that the outlaws had trouble getting rid of it. Taking Mason into their confidence, they had suggested that he take a trip to the Río Grande country around El Paso and use the counterfeit money to purchase thirty thousand dollars' worth of Mexican cattle. Delivery would be made to Daniel Dedrick at Bosque Grande.[7]

Wild had no way of knowing that Mason's word was unreliable. He happily wrote this man's name on the government payroll as an informer. He also reimbursed Benjamin Ellis for Garrett's and Mason's hotel and stable bills, the amount coming to eight dollars for supper, breakfast, horse feed, and lodging.[8]

Agent Wild sent Mason back to Bosque Grande to gather more information on the gang's activities. When Mason had not returned by November 26, Wild became concerned and noted that a posse from Roswell wanted to search for him but could not ride because all the available horses had distemper.

On November 29 informer Mason returned and said that counterfeiters W. W. West and Daniel Dedrick had decided against the purchase of any Río Grande cattle at that time. The thieves were worried about the excitement all over the county. Deputy Sheriff Garrett was expected to strike immediately against Billy the Kid. Also on the same day[9] a posse guided by Pat Garrett, United States Deputy Marshal Robert Olinger, Barney Mason, and Azariah F. Wild left Roswell at night and charged up the Pecos River toward Bosque Grande. They hoped to capture the counterfeiters and perhaps Billy the Kid too.

The posse, consisting of twenty men, had barely left the Roswell

---

[6] *Ibid.*, November 27, 1880.
[7] *Ibid.*, November 20–21, 1880.
[8] *Ibid.*
[9] Wild's dates generally differ from Pat Garrett's by a few days to a week.

lamplights before they stumbled over Joseph Cook, a Texas outlaw, in possession of two stolen horses. Although Cook's reputation was that of a loner, he had often been seen in the company of Billie Wilson and Billy the Kid. Cook was chained and returned to Roswell with Wild and two deputies. Pat Garrett and several others continued on.

With Garrett and his posse gone, the jittery Roswell citizens heard rumors that the hills were swarming with outlaws seeking an opportunity to burn the town and free Cook. As the days went by, the talk grew more exaggerated until finally everyone was certain that an attack was imminent. The citizens gathered in the Roswell postoffice to make their last stand, but after spending several hours there with nothing happening, they all sheepishly went home.[10]

In the meantime Pat Garrett was keeping his eye on the prime objective, the capture or killing of Wilson and the Kid. At daybreak on November 30 he and his posse stormed the Dedrick ranch at Bosque Grande—and discovered that nearly everyone had left. They did capture John J. Webb, the Las Vegas murderer, and George Davis, a horse thief. The captives' wrists were ironed, and they were thrust roughly onto horses and made to ride along with the posse toward Fort Sumner, where it was hoped that the Kid's gang might be.

When the deputies rode cautiously into town, expecting a stiff fight, they learned that the outlaws, moving leisurely ahead and unaware of pursuit, had vanished in the direction of Yearby's Ranch at Las Cañaditas, about twenty miles northeast of Sumner.

Garrett detailed four of his possemen to guard the prisoners while he and the others pressed on. He and his men expected a hard fight at the ranch and probably would have got it had they not accidentally stumbled on Tom O'Folliard about eight miles from Yearby's Ranch. O'Folliard was a perfect follower for the Kid. A good-natured, rollicking fellow with reddish-blond hair and an oversize nose, he could be counted on to follow instructions. He had no designs on leadership and was completely loyal.

Since Garrett knew that Tom was riding to join the Kid at Yearby's Ranch, Pat sought to cut him off by riding across some rough mountain passes. The strategy failed. Arroyos were overgrown with mesquite and cactus and littered with loose rock. When Garrett's

[10] Wild to Brooks, November 29, December 2, 1880, National Archives, Washington, D.C.

posse, scratched, bleeding, and exhausted, again pulled onto the road within a few hundred yards of O'Folliard, their horses were too tired to close the distance quickly. O'Folliard gradually pulled away, occasionally turning to fire his Winchester so that his pursuers would keep a respectful distance. Garrett's men returned the fire, but everyone was too weary to shoot with any accuracy.

When the saddle-sore possemen closed in on Yearby's Ranch, they were not sure what to expect. No one had been seen leaving, and it was possible that the bandits might be holed up there and ready to fight. Some precious moments were lost in debate before the men cautiously approached the house and kicked the door open. Inside was Charlie Bowdre's chubby twenty-five-year-old Mexican wife and another woman. Disgusted, Garrett turned the women loose. The only prisoners taken were a pair of mules that had been stolen from a stage station and four horses that had been taken from a rancher.[11]

On December 5, after the posse returned to Fort Sumner, Garrett telegraphed Wild that some of his horses were suffering from distemper and asked for more men and fresh animals, since he did not have "force enough to guard his prisoners and stock, and make the arrests he had in view."[12] Wild wired back that he would send Deputy Marshal John Hurley and Sheriff George Kimball to reinforce Garrett.

Unwilling to waste any more time, Pat Garrett gathered his weary men together once again, ordered them into the saddle, and rode away toward Los Portales, about fifty miles southeast of Fort Sumner. This ride was as futile as the earlier ones. Billy the Kid had simply disappeared, and there was little left to do except go back to Fort Sumner.

About twelve miles east of Fort Sumner the posse stopped at the Wilcox Ranch for supper. There Garrett received a message that the dark-haired, mustached Charles Bowdre wanted to parley. Pat suggested a fork-of-the-road meeting about two miles from Sumner. Both men kept the appointment, and Garrett handed Bowdre a letter from Captain Lea promising leniency to any of the Kid's men who defected and turned to honest ranching. Bowdre was not convinced of the letter's sincerity, but he did promise as a good-will gesture to scale down his association with the Kid and perhaps halt it altogether if Lea would give more assurances. With these words

11 Garrett, *Life*, 91–94.
12 Wild to Brooks, December 5, 1880, National Archives, Washington, D.C.

the two men parted, each little realizing that within days they would meet again, with dramatic consequences.

Returning to Fort Sumner, Garrett found no reinforcements. He wired Don Desiderio Romero, the San Miguel County sheriff, reporting that he had Webb and Davis in custody and requesting Romero to meet him somewhere along the Las Vegas road. At the same time Pat dismissed his posse, except for Barney Mason. He rented a buggy to transport his prisoners.

When Romero received the wire, he deputized Francisco Romero (no relation) and four assistants, a Dutchman named Baker, Vidal Ortiz, Doroteo Sandoval, and Martin Vigil. The deputies went to Puerto de Luna, about forty-five miles northwest of Fort Sumner but found that Garrett had not yet arrived. During the delay the Las Vegas possemen refreshed themselves with a few drinks, and, after boasting about their fearlessness they picked up several equally drunken volunteers and hustled out to meet Garrett. Pat first saw them from his carriage. According to his account, the relief came charging down upon him "like a whirlwind of lunatics —their steeds prancing and curveting—with loud boasts and swaggering airs."[13]

Garrett choked back his anger. When he reached Puerto de Luna, he turned his prisoners over to Romero, obtaining a receipt for them, and strolled over to Alejandro Grezelachowski's store to wash two weeks of gritty sand and dust out of his mouth. Webb and Davis, who had been dragged all over the country, protesting every foot of the way, were taken directly to the blacksmith's shop, where fetters and manacles of a stouter quality were fastened to their wrists and ankles.

While Pat Garrett and Barney Mason relaxed in the store, trouble approached from the volunteer Mexican-American deputies who had not yet sobered. One of these men, Juanito Maes,[14] staggered up to Garrett, described himself luridly as a thief, a desperado, and a murderer and inquired if Pat wanted to accept his surrender. The sheriff merely stared at him for a long moment and finally shook his head and said that he did not know him, had no warrant for his arrest, and did not want him.

When this irritation failed to disturb the lawman, a local badman named Mariano Leiva entered the store and snarled that no

---

[13] Garrett, *Life*, 94.

[14] The *Santa Fe Weekly New Mexican*, December 20, 1880, reported that the name was not Juanito Maes but Juan Silva.

gringo dared arrest him. Garrett did not speak but merely turned his head away, rubbing his black mustache. Finally Leiva stomped outside, where he harangued the crowd, saying, "By God, even that damned Pat Garrett can't take me!" When Leiva turned around to point his finger at the sheriff, who he thought was still inside, his head rocked to the jolting slap of Pat Garrett's hand, and he was knocked off the porch into the sand. Humiliated, the Mexican gunman reached for his pistol, and although he beat Garrett to the draw, his shot went wild. At almost the same instant Garrett's .45 roared, but he too was hasty, and the slug merely kicked up dust at the rowdy's feet. Pat then fired a second time with more finesse. The bullet shattered Leiva's left shoulder blade.

Leiva was helped on his horse and led away, while Garrett, wary of the threatening faces around him, backed into the store and picked up his Winchester. Moments later Deputy Romero staggered inside and told Pat that he was under arrest for shooting Mariano. Garrett brushed Romero aside, telling him that he was going to keep his arms and defend himself. Barney Mason said that he felt the same way. Picking up his own rifle and glancing down the barrel, now pointed at Romero's round, protruding stomach, Mason cracked, "Shall I cut the sonofabitch in two, Pat?" Suddenly interested in staying in one piece, Romero retreated. On the following day Pat agreed to submit himself to a justice of the peace, who released him.[15] Leiva was later tried for attempted murder, found guilty, and fined eighty dollars.[16]

Although Garrett had immediate plans for returning to Lincoln County, John Webb begged for his protection on the trip to Las Vegas. Pat agreed, knowing that the man had little chance of reaching town alive if he did not tag along. When they were just a few miles from Las Vegas, another group of "possemen" came riding drunkenly out to meet them, bragging about how they would soon capture Billy the Kid. Some of them even wanted to arrest Barney Mason, who in their drink-fogged minds was associated with the Kid's gang.

While the party continued to drink, Garrett seized the opportunity to escape and rode into town alone. He wrote later that he

[15] In an undated letter to Colonel Maurice Fulton (Fulton Papers, University of Arizona), Deputy Romero denied that his men had been drinking or that they had charged about Garrett's buggy. He claimed that Garrett was drunk in Grezelachowski's store and surrendered his weapons upon being asked.

[16] *Las Vegas Daily Optic*, August 19, 1881.

Pat Garrett

"was ashamed to be seen with the noisy, gabbling, boasting, sense-less, undignified mob, whose deportment would have disgusted the Kid and his band of thieves."[17]

[17] Garrett, *Life*, 96.

5.

Gun Battle Before Christmas

While Sheriff-elect and Deputy United States Marshal Pat Garrett involved himself in chasing shadows and fighting with Deputy Francisco Romero's men, Billy the Kid and several gunmen were, according to Azariah F. Wild, holed up at the Greathouse Ranch with some stolen horses. The ranch and a small trading post, both owned by "Whiskey Jim" Greathouse and Fred W. Kuch, lay along the main road about forty miles north of White Oaks, near the south slope of the Gallinas Mountains. Wild described Greathouse as a "hard character," a receiver of "stolen stock," and "a pal of Wilson and company."[1] Wild claimed that Kuch had been "connected with several post office transactions of a very doubtful character" and was "smuggling goods in from Mexico and other foreign countries."[2]

Treasury Agent Wild also noted that on Saturday, November 20, 1880, seven of the Kid's men rode into White Oaks, nudged their ponies in between the ramshackle, false-fronted, wood-and-adobe buildings and burglarized two stores. As they left, they were detected by several alert, although somewhat inebriated, citizens, and a short battle followed. No one was injured, but a large bundle of blankets, rifles, overcoats, and other provisions disappeared into the darkness with the outlaws.

It took two days for the residents of White Oaks to work up enough nerve to pursue the bandits. On Monday a deputy sheriff led a small (and very timid) posse to the Greathouse Ranch and tried unsuccessfully to arrest everyone. Billy the Kid's entrenched forces greatly outnumbered the lawmen, and so after firing a few "respectful" shots at the heavy walls, the posse retreated. With them they dragged some captured camping equipment that the out-

[1] For a short biography of Greathouse's career see W. H. Hutchinson and Robert N. Mullin, *Whiskey Jim and a Kid Named Billie.*
[2] Wild to Brooks, November 22, 1880, National Archives, Washington, D.C.,

67

laws had already abandoned. Surprisingly, they also brought in two prisoners (most likely taken while sleeping), one of whom was Moses Dedrick, a brother of the Dedrick boys who were passing counterfeit money.[3]

When the news of this "pitched battle" (as some called it) reached the military post at Fort Stanton, the army was disturbed enough to dispatch a Lieutenant Clark with twelve soldiers to meet the military paymaster before he reached the Greathouse Ranch. The army did not wish to interfere in civilian affairs, but it was feared that a sizable payroll might prove too much of a temptation for the outlaws. These suspicions may or may not have been justified, but no robbery was attempted. Clark met the paymaster, escorted him safely through the Greathouse Ranch area, and wrote a report on or about November 28 stating that when he left Billy the Kid and seventeen men were still there.[4]

On November 30, 1880, in bitter-cold weather that knifed through all but the heaviest buffalo coats, an incessant snow fell from the dark cumulus fractus clouds hanging over the Jicarilla Mountains. Below this range lay White Oaks, and on this particular night Billy the Kid, Dave Rudabaugh, and Billie Wilson lashed their horses over the frozen mud lane that served as the main street of the town and fired several shots at Deputy James Redman (or Woodland?), who evidently was doing little more than making an appearance on the street. Perhaps the gunmen thought that Redman had led the posse that chased them to the Greathouse Ranch. The assassination attempt failed. At daybreak James Carlyle, a White Oaks deputized blacksmith who possessed a plentiful supply of grit and courage, rounded up twelve men and tracked the gunmen back to the Greathouse hideout.

The manhunters paused in the deep twilight and heavy snow. Through the icy mist billowing from the flaring nostrils of the horses they observed fresh tracks leading straight into the Greathouse house. Silently the possemen fanned out, covering the exits and ducking behind what scrubby bits of shelter they could find. When they were satisfactorily deployed, Carlyle cupped his hands over his mouth and called for those inside to come out and surrender.

Slowly the heavy door cracked open. Framed against the room's

---

[3] *Ibid.*, November 22, 1880.

[4] *Ibid.*, November 28, 1880. Clark and Wild are obviously in error here. The Kid at no time had more than half a dozen men with him.

firelight Carlyle saw a dark, bearded face peering out. Then the door and the bolt slammed at almost the same instant, and the lamplight inside dimmed. Obviously the gunmen did not intend to surrender. They could out wait the posse.

"Whiskey Jim" (sometimes called "Arkansas Jack") Greathouse especially dreaded a protracted siege. Years before it would not have bothered him, for he was used to violence and had graduated from the buffalo flint-hide business at Fort Griffin in the early 1870's. Among his exploits he had ridden with Skelton Glenn, Pat Garrett's old buffalo-hunting partner, and the drunken group of hunters who planned to harass the wayward Comanches at Yellow House (Lubbock, Texas) in 1877, but were thoroughly beaten. In partnership with Fred Kuch he had opened Greathouse's Tavern and trading post along the White Oaks–Las Vegas road near present-day Corona, New Mexico. Although contemporary news stories refer to him as running a respectable "store and camp house for travelers,"[5] he was wary of having the authorities nose too deeply into his activities, for Greathouse traded primarily in cheap whisky, his customers were generally lawbreakers, and often the horses hobbled in his back corrals were stolen.

Whiskey Jim suggested that he offer himself as a hostage to the posse while Deputy Carlyle came inside to negotiate the terms of surrender. The outlaws agreed, and Greathouse stepped outside.

The parley began as full darkness dropped over the scene. The Kid told Carlyle that there would be no surrender, and the word was passed on to the men outside. About midnight a note was handed to the outlaws warning them that if Carlyle was not returned within five minutes the posse would kill Jim Greathouse. Shortly afterward someone outside the house fired a shot.

An instant crash of glass, a scattering of curses, and a roar of gunfire followed the explosion. Deputy James Carlyle, evidently thinking that Jim Greathouse had been gunned down by the posse, jumped through the window in an attempt to save his life. He fell in the snow and struggled to his feet, lurching forward with awkward steps as he sought to recover his balance. He did not get far. Gunshots cut him down. Doubt exists whether the Kid's gang murdered him or the posse mistakenly shot him, thinking he was one of the outlaws.

The possemen gaped in stunned unbelief as Carlyle stiffened in

---

[5] Hutchinson and Mullin, *Whiskey Jim*, 15.

the snow. What courage and aggression they possessed seemed to die with him. They barely looked up, and certainly no one raised his rifle as Billy the Kid's men stampeded through the doorway, mounted their horses, and escaped. So paralyzed were the possemen that when they did move they silently returned to White Oaks, not even pausing to pick up Carlyle's body, lying twisted on the ground. Two days later the Greathouse Ranch underwent a mysterious fire in which every building burned completely.

Within a day or two Deputy United States Marshal John Hurley and Sheriff George Kimball were again in pursuit of the gunmen, although they were no more aggressive than the White Oaks posse. On December 4, Hurley reported to Agent Wild that they had lost the trail and were returning to Lincoln.

Once back at headquarters the marshal and the sheriff's posse slept soundly. Wild learned on December 7 that Billy the Kid and his outlaw gang had visited a brothel in Lincoln, romped for several hours, and scampered away before their presence became known.[6]

James Carlyle's death had repercussions for Billy the Kid. The deputy was a popular and respected man, and the citizens were outraged by his senseless murder. On December 12, 1880, Billy once again wrote Governor Lew Wallace, this time vigorously denying that he or any of his men had slain Carlyle. The Kid swore that when the unexpected gunshot occurred outside the tavern, Carlyle jumped through the window and met death from the rifles of his own men.

Billy next took a written poke at Pat Garrett, whom he knew to be in the field against him:

> During my absence Deputy Sheriff Garrett . . . went to Mr. Yearby's ranch and took a pair of mules of mine which I had left with Mr. Bowdre who is in charge of Mr. Yearby's cattle. He [Garrett] claimed that they were stolen . . . and he had a right to confiscate any outlaw's property.[7]

The Kid's letter rambled on as he further protested his innocence, claiming that he made his living at Fort Sumner. What he neglected to mention was that on the previous July 10 he had shot and killed a man named Joe Grant during a saloon brawl in Fort Sumner. Billy even reached out to touch those whom he blamed for his misfortunes:

[6] Wild to Brooks, December 7, 8, 1880, National Archives, Washington, D.C.
[7] Bonney to Governor Lew Wallace, December 12, 1880, Lew Wallace Collection, William Henry Smith Library, Indiana Historical Society, Indianapolis.

John S. Chisum is the man who got me into trouble . . . and is now doing all he can against me. There is no doubt but what there is a great deal of stealing going on in the Territory . . . but so far as my being at the head of a band there is nothing to it.[8]

All these assertions did Billy no good. General Wallace read the note with an unsympathetic eye. The governor was fed up to his elegantly bearded chin with the bucktoothed outlaw who just a few months earlier had first accepted and then walked away from the governor's promise of immunity from prosecution. On December 15, 1880, Wallace published a note of his own, which appeared in the New Mexico newspapers:

$500 REWARD

NOTICE IS HEREBY GIVEN THAT FIVE HUNDRED DOLLARS REWARD WILL BE PAID FOR THE DELIVERY OF BONNEY ALIAS "THE KID" TO THE SHERIFF OF LINCOLN COUNTY.

LEW WALLACE
GOVERNOR OF NEW MEXICO

One group chasing the Kid was led by Charles Siringo, who was working as a cowboy at the LX Ranch in the Texas Panhandle in late 1880. "Outlaw Bill" Moore, his boss, ordered him to take five of the toughest hands into New Mexico and pursue Billy the Kid, thus shutting off the horse raids that the Kid had been making into Texas. Siringo chose Big-Foot Wallace (Frank Clifford), Jim East, Cal Polk, Lon Chambers, and Lee Hall. At Tascosa, Texas, Siringo was joined by Bob Roberson, "Poker Tom" Emory, Luis "The Animal" Bozeman, and three others from the nearby Littlefield Ranch.[9]

Upon entering New Mexico, Siringo sent his boys on to Anton Chico, while he headed for the monte tables in Las Vegas. There he lost all his money and had to purchase supplies on credit. When he obtained enough equipment to move, he rejoined his men and went into winter quarters at White Oaks.[10]

In the meantime Garrett had learned that Frank Stewart, one of Wild's United States deputy marshals and a representative of the Canadian River cattle owners in Texas, had left Las Vegas with ten men on December 10 and was actively searching for the

[8] *Ibid.*
[9] Philip J. Rasch, "The Hunting of Billy the Kid," *English Westerners Brand Book,* Vol. XI, No. 2 (January, 1969), 1–10. This Big-Foot Wallace is not the man of Texas fame.
[10] Charles A. Siringo, *Riata and Spurs,* 75–91.

Kid. Garrett sent Barney Mason to intercept Stewart and return him to Las Vegas. Mason did so, but Stewart did not bring his men back with him. He sent them on to White Oaks.

In Las Vegas it was agreed that the three posses should combine under the leadership of Pat Garrett, and he and Frank Stewart took the remainder of their men to White Oaks for discussions with Charles Siringo. Gathering all the men for a conference, Garrett and Stewart warned them bluntly that they could expect heavy fighting once Billy the Kid and his followers were cornered. Then Garrett chose the few men he wanted to accompany him: Frank Stewart, Lon Chambers, Lee Hall, Jim East, Tom Emory, Luis Bozeman, and Bob Williams. The others, including Charles Siringo and Big-Foot Wallace, decided to remain in White Oaks and sample the meager delights there. At least there would be no cold camps every night.

The crew was tough, as harsh and brutal as the bitter cold of the December morning, when, snaking single file out of the White Oaks country, they made a forced march northeast for a nearly one-hundred-mile ride to Puerto de Luna. Sheriff Pat Garrett noted that his reception in the village was more cordial than when he last visited it, but his attempts to pick up additional deputies among the able-bodied residents were only partly successful. Juan and José Roibal joined him, as did a clerk named Charles Rudolph and George Wilson, a cattleman. Pat's mind harked back bitterly to only a few days before, when all the townspeople boasted of how they would capture Billy the Kid. Now, aside from the four men, none of the remaining braggarts could be persuaded to go along.

While Garrett and his men relaxed in the local tavern, José Roibal was sent ahead to Fort Sumner with instructions to see what he could find out about the Kid's activities. Roibal did his job well, moseying around the settlement, brushing against Mexican cowboys and businessmen, seeking, looking, pretending to be a sheepherder rounding up strays. In this small settlement it was not hard to locate Billy and his followers, notably Tom O'Folliard, Charles Bowdre, Dave Rudabaugh, Billie Wilson, and a small-time badman named Tom Pickett. Finding Anglos in this part of the country was easy since there were so few of them.

A little past midnight on December 18, Garrett listened to Roibal's report and then rode to the edge of Fort Sumner. Stationing his men on the outskirts, he and Barney Mason slipped quietly into town and began searching to see whether the Kid was about.

First he checked Smith's corral, where the gang's mounts should have been hobbled. But no outlaw's horses were quartered there. Nudging Smith and bringing the sleeping man to his feet with a start, Garrett learned that the gunmen had left the night before. Disappointed, he called in the rest of his posse, and everyone bedded down in the corral.

At sunrise Garrett cautioned his men to remain hidden while he and Mason continued their reconnoitering. Making no effort to conceal his identity, Garrett hoped that any information spreading to the Kid would mention that only he and another deputy were in town.

As the morning passed, Pat noticed that a Mexican named Juan Gallegos seemed to be watching him. So he placed Juan under arrest and sweated out of him the confession that Billy was at the Thomas W. Wilcox ranch twelve miles east of town and that he knew Garrett was looking for him. Juan was being paid by the Kid to watch the sheriff's activities and report what he did and when he left.

Juan Gallegos was so badly scared by the sheriff's threats that Pat decided he could use the Mexican as a double agent. Cornering another Mexican named José Valdéz, Garrett forced him to write a letter to the Kid saying that the sheriff's posse had left for Roswell and the danger had passed. On another piece of paper Garrett wrote a note for Wilcox, reporting that he and the posse were in Fort Sumner on the Kid's trail and asking his cooperation. Both messages were given to Juan with the stipulation that since he could not read he had best not get them mixed up.

The plan worked perfectly. Garrett claimed that the outlaws shouted and hollered with joy, laughing at how they intended to "give them [Garrett's men] a fair fight, set them afoot, and drive them down the Pecos."[11] Garrett figured that if the Kid now believed it safe he would ride into Sumner that night to celebrate. He reasoned that the logical first stopping place would be the dilapidated old adobe hospital on the east boundary of the plaza, where Bowdre's wife lived. The building sprawled on a direct line of travel for the outlaws when they came into town, and they would be eager to see her and get a firsthand account of Garrett's recent activities.

On the night of the nineteenth Pat quietly took over the build-

[11] Garrett, *Life*, 104–105, 110–11.

ing, stationing his posse inside, except for Lon Chambers and Lee Hall, whom he assigned to guard the horses. As he positioned his men, he noticed several Mexicans lolling about the plaza, an unusual gathering place in the bitter weather. He reasoned that they might try to warn the Kid as he rode into town, and so a couple of deputies were sent to round up the Mexicans, place them under temporary arrest, and lock them in a vacant hospital room. Then a blanket was spread over a bed, and the possemen settled down to pass the time with a few hands of poker.

It was about eight o'clock when Lon Chambers sprang excitedly into the room, exclaiming, "Someone's coming!" Garrett had not expected the Kid for at least two hours; he grabbed his rifle and stepped toward the door. "No one but the men we want are riding this time of night."

The snow had stopped falling and the moonlight reflecting off the frozen crust lit up the plaza, creating a brilliant contrast of brightness and heavy shadows. The darkness of the hospital building provided excellent protection for Pat Garrett and his posse. Pat, standing behind a porch post and further obscured by a dangling harness, was well concealed. Beside him in the shadows stood Lon Chambers. Barney Mason and some of the others had slipped away from the building to cut off any retreat.

Into this trap, pacing slowly, strung out, hunched against the cold, rode Billy the Kid and his party. The Kid, however, possessed a crafty intuition that rivaled Garrett's. When he was almost to the plaza, he seemed to sense the chill of death waiting to settle upon him. On impulse he turned his horse, rode to the rear of his party, and asked Billie Wilson for a chew of tobacco. The plug saved his life.

The Kid's switch in position left O'Folliard and Pickett leading the way, and they rode up to the hospital building without even lifting their eyes. O'Folliard's horse paused and stuck its head under the porch roof, a rifle barrel's length away from the waiting sheriff.

"Halt!" yelled Garrett. Tom O'Folliard made a grab for his pistol just as Pat and Chambers fired. Garrett's bullet ripped through his chest, and O'Folliard screamed in pain. Pat meant to deal as harshly with Pickett, but a flash from Chamber's rifle blinded him, and the slug went wild. The gunmen fled, leaving only O'Folliard's blood darkening the snow.

O'Folliard painfully wrestled his plunging mount under control after the horse had run about 150 yards down the road. Slowly he turned back toward the posse, pleading, "Don't shoot, Garrett. I'm killed."

Pat ordered O'Folliard to surrender and throw up his hands. Unable to do so, the outlaw hung over the saddlehorn and sat unmoving, moaning, as the men in the posse approached him cautiously and eased the 175-pound man down. He was carried inside and laid on a hospital cot, where his wound was diagnosed as fatal. "Take your medicine, old boy!" Barney Mason said unsympathetically, leaning over him. "Take your medicine."

Pat Garrett was more compassionate. When O'Folliard struggled to rise, he gasped and looked pleadingly toward Garrett. "Oh, my God, is it possible that I must die?"

"Tom, your time is short," Garrett replied softly.

"The sooner the better. I will be out of pain."[12] In less than forty-five minutes, his eyes had closed for the last time.

12 *Ibid.,* 107.

6.

Shootout at Stinking Springs

As the Kid and his men thundered away from the Fort Sumner ambush, Dave Rudabaugh's horse took a bullet. Faltering and gushing blood, the wounded animal managed to race several miles before toppling over dead. Rudabaugh, feeling the horse losing stride, grabbed his saddlebags and hit the frozen ground on his feet. Several jumps later he had straddled Wilson's horse and was clinging to Billie when the frightened outlaws again reached the Thomas Wilcox Ranch. This time there was no banter. They kicked open the door and began rummaging around the house, grabbing food from the shelves and supplies from the drawers.

Some of the gunmen wanted to leave the Wilcox Ranch before Garrett trapped them. Others, noting by the low, snow-filled clouds that a fresh storm was blowing in, believed that the sheriff's posse would stay in Fort Sumner until the weather mellowed.

The Kid himself settled the squabble by deciding that Garrett would probably sit tight through the night. The question was, what would he do tomorrow? Pursue them once more or return to Roswell?

Since the answer was critical the Kid looked about him for another spy and settled upon Emanuel Brazil, a partner of Tom Wilcox. Brazil was told to ride into Fort Sumner to watch Garrett and then return to the ranch and report on his activities.

What Billy did not know was that Brazil had read the letter Garrett had sent to Wilcox, and his sympathies lay not with the outlaws but with the lawmen. Instead of observing Pat from a distance, Brazil approached him, reported what was happening at his ranch, and sought Garrett's assistance. Pat told Brazil to return to the ranch and stay there if the Kid was still around but to report back to him immediately if the outlaws had left.

At midnight on December 20, Brazil returned to Fort Sumner.

Icicles clung to his beard and eyebrows. As he sat on the hospital-building floor, pulling off his boots and poking his feet close to the fire, grimacing from the thawing-out pains in his toes, he told Garrett that the outlaws had gone. He did not know where.

Early the next morning Garrett's men circled the ranch, picked up the trail in the snow, and once again started their stalking. Across the plains the tracks led due east toward Arroyo Taiban, about twenty-five miles from Fort Sumner and three miles from the Wilcox Ranch.

The well-marked trail stretched in a straight line, and Pat had no trouble judging the outlaws' destination to be an abandoned rock house at Stinking Springs, an overnight way station for cattle drivers and sheep herders. The hunted men had now blundered twice in two days. First they had allowed Sheriff-elect Garrett to slip into their home base at Fort Sumner, set up an ambush, and drive them from the community. Second, they had underestimated Garrett's intelligence and tenacity. They either forgot that he was as familiar with the country as they or reasoned that in the bitter weather he would give up the chase and go home.

Late at night, when the posse was half a mile from the way station, Garrett assembled his men for a conference. He stated with confidence that the outlaws were trapped, asked everyone to be especially quiet, and led them to within four hundred yards of the building. Then he split the posse and sent Stewart with half the men to cover one side while he took the others and crept up a dry arroyo almost to the very doorstep of the house.

The reins of three horses were tied to projecting rafters outside the building, which meant to Garrett that two other animals had to be inside. A close look showed him that the front door was missing, and Pat saw his chance to slip unnoticed into the interior. Hastily sending a messenger to Stewart, the lawman proposed that they slide into the house, cover everyone with their guns, and hold the fugitives until daylight. Stewart did not favor the plan. He wanted to wait until the bright light of day to take the outlaws.

There was little to do except spread their blankets in the snow and shiver until morning—or until movement from inside the house triggered the start of action. As the men lay huddled in their heavy coats, the plan that Garrett explained to them was simple: kill Billy the Kid.

To the deputies riding with Garrett the plan was both rational and practical. While the Kid was alive, there was no telling how long a fight or siege would last—and no telling how many posse-men might be killed.

Pat Garrett was the only man who could positively identify the Kid. The members of his posse were primarily Texans who had never seen the young outlaw. Pat knew that in the uncertain light of dawn, with the gunmen inside the house heavily bundled against the cold, he might not be able to make a positive identification. He explained that Billy would probably be recognizable only by his peculiar headpiece, a broad-brimmed sombrero with a bright Irish-green hatband. Garrett whispered that when he saw someone wearing such a hat, he would raise his rifle. That would be the signal for the possemen to commence shooting.

With daylight the sounds of activity within the rock house indicated that the outlaws were stirring, making preparations to leave. A gunman, the collar of his coat pulled tightly about his head, stepped gingerly through the empty doorway, a nosebag for his horse dangling from his hand. Pat raised his weapon, set his finger on the trigger, and glanced down the sights. Everyone else did the same. The sombrero looked familiar.

The possemen's guns roared, but following the flash of powder Pat could see that they had mistakenly fired on the wrong man. Instead of the Kid the slugs had ripped through the body of Charlie Bowdre, the thirty-two-year-old former Mississippian[1] whom Garrett had urged to surrender a short time ago when they had met at the fork of the road. Charlie screamed, staggered backward, and disappeared into the building.

Seconds later Billie Wilson called to the posse that Bowdre was dying and wanted to surrender. Garrett shouted back in agreement, but, as Bowdre tottered out, the Kid caught hold of him, pushed Charlie's revolver into his hand, and muttered, "They've murdered you Charlie, but you can get revenge. Kill some of the sonsofbitches before you die."

Appearing to be a man near death, Bowdre lurched across the hard-crusted snow, his pistol clutched in his hand, though obviously not intending to use it. Tottering straight toward Garrett, his face sagging in pain, he motioned once toward the house, then, trying to swallow the blood that gushed from his mouth and down across his dark beard, he said, "I wish—I wish—I wish—." Then he whispered, "I'm dying," and pitched into Garrett's arms.[2]

[1] 1880 census, Fort Sumner, New Mexico. Bowdre listed his birthplace as either Mississippi or Tennessee. Apparently Charlie did not know where he was born.

Pat laid Bowdre gently aside. He deeply regretted this killing. Charlie had seemed to be the only gang member capable of better things. Garrett remembered that Bowdre had seriously considered quitting the rustling business and settling down to a life of ranching. Their conversation had taken place only days ago at the fork of the road near Fort Sumner. Now Charlie was dead.

From the interior of the house someone had taken hold of a horse's halter and was trying to pull the animal inside. Garrett waited until the horse clopped into the doorway and then sent a rifle bullet crashing into its heart, killing the animal and effectively blocking the entrance. Now, taking even more careful aim, he shot through the tethered ropes of the other animals. Panicking, they sprang away.

The siege at the rock house wore on while Garrett taunted the outlaws. "How're you doing?" he called in to them.

"Pretty well," the Kid cheerfully replied, "but we have no wood to get breakfast."

"Come on out and get some," Pat replied. "Be a little sociable."

"Can't do it, Pat. Business is too confining. No time to run around."

"Didn't you fellows forget part of your program yesterday?"[3] Garrett asked, referring to the threat that the outlaws intended setting the men of the posse afoot and driving them down the Pecos.

This time there was no reply.

The day slowly passed, with intermittent conversations between the two camps. Finally they ceased altogether as the thoughts of both the hunters and the hunted turned to food. Pat had the advantage. He took half his men and rode back to the Wilcox Ranch for a late breakfast, later returning and sending the remainder of the posse back to eat. It was arranged to send supplies directly to the posse at the siege site for the afternoon meal.

For the Kid and his trapped men it was a desperate day. Since they obviously could not flee, they released the horses that were inside the house, and the animals carefully picked their way across the dead horse in the doorway. Hastening the outlaws' planning was the maddening odor of fresh-cooked beef that wafted in through the door and windows. Within minutes after the aroma had floated around the room, Dave Rudabaugh was delegated

[2] Garrett, *Life*, 111.
[3] *Ibid.*, 111–14.

by Billy to shove a dirty handkerchief through an open window and offer to discuss surrender terms.

Garrett ordered him outside, and the outlaw stepped through the doorway yelling that all of them would lay down their arms if Garrett would guarantee their lives. Pat agreed to this condition, and soon the fugitives came straggling out. They were fed a warm meal before the trip back to Fort Sumner.

The procession was a sad sight. Everyone hunkered against the wind, the prisoners slouching forward across the backs of their horses. Only Charles Bowdre did not curse the cold. His body bounced and jolted inside a wagon as it creaked along over the rough roads. When they reached the village, Pat gathered the corpse into his arms and carried it to Charlie's sobbing wife. As he stretched out his former enemy on the bed, he gently told Mrs. Bowdre to purchase her husband a suit of burying clothes and send the bill to him.

At Fort Sumner the prisoners were taken to the blacksmith shop, where the ropes around their hands and ankles were removed and replaced with handcuffs and leg irons. From across the plaza a knot of citizens quietly watched the proceedings.

That afternoon Mrs. Pete Maxwell sent an old Navajo woman to Garrett asking that she and her daughter Paulita be allowed to say good-by to Billy. The lawman grudgingly consented. Pete Maxwell, after all, had once done him a favor by giving him employment. Within minutes the Kid, shackled to Dave Rudabaugh and guarded by deputies James East and Lee Hall, shuffled in lockstep up the porch to the Maxwell home. Mother Maxwell pleaded with the guards to unlock the irons fettering Billy so that he might be allowed to enter a private room for an affectionate farewell with Paulita. East wrote later that, although "all the world loves a lover," he did not think it wise to allow such a meeting, and permission was refused.[4]

After Billy and Rudabaugh were led back to join the other outlaws, and after Pat decided that everyone had rested long enough, the posse and the captives set out on the overland trek to Las Vegas and the railhead. The posse, now consisting of Pat Garrett, Barney

[4] James East to Judge William H. Burges, May 20, 1926, copy of letter in possession of C. L. Sonnichsen. East said that Lee Hall was not the Captain Lee Hall of the Texas Rangers. His true name was Lee Hall Smith, and he was raised in Coldwell County, Texas. He was killed in the summer of 1881 when a horse fell on him.

Mason, Lee Hall, Frank Stewart, James East, and Poker Tom, reached Puerto de Luna in the early afternoon of Christmas day. There is no record of any particular celebration. After the midday meal the captives were loaded into a wagon, and on the following afternoon they entered Las Vegas from the southeast. The prisoners sat inside the mule-drawn wagon, the Kid and Dave Rudabaugh chained together. With his slouch hat pulled well down over his eyes, Rudabaugh looked neither left nor right, and only the fierce scowl on his dark-bearded face indicated that he was aware of the screams around him. The townspeople had long memories; they would not soon forget the jailor killed by Rudabaugh in the Webb prison break of April 2, 1880. They were now demanding that the outlaw pay for that murder with his life.

Sheriff Pat Garrett led the posse and the prisoners straight into the mob. Riding a tough little cow pony, his stirruped boots dangling less than two feet off the ground, Pat never slackened his pace. Only once did he glance around, and that was to motion the wagon teamster to move the vehicle sharply along. Within a couple of minutes the prisoners were being unloaded at the jail.

7.

A Prisoner Delivered

The capture of Billy the Kid was so newsworthy that the *Las Vegas Gazette* dispatched a reporter (probably the editor himself) to interview Billy. The conversation was published on December 28, 1880.

"You appear to take it easy," the reporter said.

"Yes, what's the use of looking on the gloomy side of everything? The laugh's on me this time." Then pausing for a second, he spoke again. "Is the jail in Santa Fe any better? This is a terrible place to put a fellow in."

When informed that the capital's accommodations were no more sanitary or comfortable, Billy shrugged his thin shoulders and said that he would simply have to put up with it.

"There was a big crowd gazing at me [yesterday], wasn't there? Well, perhaps some of them will think me half a man now. Everyone [thought] I was some kind of animal."

The reporter agreed that Billy did indeed look human, although he seemed no more than a mere boy. Scribbling quickly, the reporter's sharp eye darted back and forth between his writing pad and the subject's smiling face. He jotted down what was probably the Kid's first reliable description:

> He is about five feet eight inches tall, slightly built and lithe, weighing about 140; a frank and open countenance, looking like a school boy, with the traditional silky fuzz on his upper lip, clear blue eyes with a "roughish snap" about them, light hair and complexion. He is quite a handsome looking fellow, the only imperfection being two prominent front teeth, slightly protruding like a squirrel's teeth, and he has agreeable and winning ways.

As the Kid stood there, shivering and kicking the toes of his boots into the stone floor to drive out the numbness, the reporter turned his attention to Dave Rudabaugh. He wrote that it was readily apparent that Rudabaugh had made no recent raids on any clothing stores. Actually, Dave Rudabaugh had two reputations. The first was for uncleanliness. The few friends that he managed to acquire said that he had taken his last bath at a very early age while making a Kansas cattle drive. From that time forward he would not even drink water but stuck strictly to whisky, tequila, and sotol, depending on which part of the country he happened to be in. His other reputation stemmed from his callousness; the values of love, mercy, compassion, understanding, he had never heard of—and would have laughed at if he had. If ever Billy the Kid was afraid of any man, it had to be Dave Rudabaugh.

Because cattle driving proved so arduous, Rudabaugh dropped that occupation for the more dangerous but immensely more profitable work of removing gold from stagecoaches. From that he graduated to robbing Kansas trains and soon had none other than the indomitable lawman Wyatt Earp on his trail. However, it was Marshal Bat Masterson who brought Rudabaugh in, and he did it by offering the gunman a deal. If Rudabaugh would inform on his associates, he could go free while his partners went to prison. Rudabaugh grinned and agreed.[1]

It was this act that brought Rudabaugh to Las Vegas, New Mexico, hoping that he had outrun any vengeful comrades from Kansas. Eventually he joined up with Billy the Kid, a not-too-brilliant course of action which brought him into conflict with the New Mexico authorities and his present predicament in the Las Vegas jail.

As the *Gazette* continued with the interviews, Pat Garrett was dismissing his posse, except for Frank Stewart and Barney Mason. He explained to the men that the chase and the capture of the outlaws had been completed, and that all that remained was to load the prisoners on a train and deliver them to John Sherman, Jr., the alcoholic United States marshal at Santa Fe.

When they were ready, Garrett and Stewart went to pick up the prisoners. An argument followed with the authorities concerning who had official jurisdiction. Pat finally agreed to relinquish his claim on Tom Pickett, stating that he held no warrant for Pickett and would not have arrested him if he had not been holed up in the way station with the Kid.

After the dispute was settled, the jailer disappeared into the

---

[1] Bill McGaw, "Dave Rudabaugh—Las Vegas Badman Loses Head in Parral," *Southwesterner*, Vol. II, No. 2 (August, 1962), 1–2.

back, and Garrett heard the sound of muttered curses and the clanking of chains. The Kid and Billie Wilson were shoved into the front office. A paper slid across the rough wooden desk, and the jailer motioned to Garrett to sign it and accept the two men.

Pat paused, shook his head, and angrily demanded that Dave Rudabaugh be turned over to him also. Another furious argument followed. Garrett shouted that he held office as a deputy United States marshal and as such held prior claim to any lawbreaker with federal charges pending against him. Garrett pointed out that Rudabaugh had confessed to a stage and train robbery in 1879, when some mail sacks were opened and rifled. This act made Rudabaugh a government prisoner and meant that he would have to stand trial in Santa Fe before facing murder charges in Las Vegas.

Garrett's forcefulness carried the day, and he hustled his prisoners toward the train. On the way he recruited Las Vegas mail carrier Mike Cosgrove to assist and stand guard if necessary. No doubt Garrett now regretted releasing his posse, for he and the outlaws had to outface a threatening crowd before he managed to gather everyone in a private railroad car.

The train eased forward, its whistle screaming, cinders showering down. Suddenly several well-armed citizens clambered aboard, stepped through the oil slicks, and ordered the engineer to put on the brakes. Garrett knew what was happening when the engine jolted to a halt. The townspeople wanted to keep Dave Rudabaugh with them long enough to exact quick justice for the prison-break killing.

"Don't you think we should make a fight of it?" Garrett asked Stewart.

"Of course."

"Let's make it a good one," Pat growled.[2]

Garrett sent Stewart to cover one end of the car while he long-legged it to the other. Just as he stepped out onto the grated iron platform, he met Deputy Sheriff Desiderio Romero climbing up. Behind him scurried five more men, each grabbing at the railing to pull himself forward.

Romero paused when he saw the sheriff's grim face. Turning, he tried to take courage from the confused mass of shoving, shouting people behind him.

"Let's go right in and take him [Rudabaugh] out of there," he yelled.

[2] Garrett, *Life*, 116.

Pat Garrett drew his pistol. Romero wavered. Continuing to press the initiative, Garrett ordered Romero and his men off the train and later scornfully noted that "they slid to the ground like a covey of hardback turtles off the banks of the Pecos."[3]

As the beleaguered lawman turned back inside the car, he saw that Rudabaugh was jumping nervously about, fearful that the defense line might be breached and that he would yet strangle at the end of a noose. Pat pushed him into a seat. He promised that if it came to a gun battle he would furnish him and the other prisoners with firearms and give them a fighting chance for their lives.

Unexpected help arrived. J. F. Morley, another deputy United States marshal, offered his assistance, and Garrett hurried him to the offices of A. F. Robinson, chief engineer for the Santa Fe Railroad, to demand that he furnish a crew brave enough to move the train out.

In his office Chief Engineer Robinson puffed on a cigar as he looked out his second-story window at the angry crowd below. He did not like the ominous situation. Rifles were already poking across a pile of crossties lying beside the tracks. Turning from Deputy Morley and exhaling a cloud of blue smoke across the room, he muttered that the government could have all the locomotives in Las Vegas, but they would have to run the trains themselves.

Hitching up his gunbelt, a determined Morley stomped outside. He elbowed his way through the shouting mob, climbed aboard the locomotive, guessed at which levers to pull, and smiled triumphantly as the train lurched forward. Not a shot was fired, and Las Vegas soon disappeared behind them.[4]

Both prisoners and guards became jovial as the train chugged across the countryside. During the midday meal, as the train moved along the top of the Glorieta Mountains, Billy the Kid humorously demonstrated how far he could bite into a piece of pie. He stuck out his protruding squirrel's teeth, dug in, hung on, and finally extracted a mouthful that amazed friend and enemy alike.[5]

The train arrived safely in Santa Fe. When the prisoners were turned over to Deputy United States Marshal Charles Conklin, the entire Territory began cheering for Pat Garrett and his weary

[3] *Ibid.*
[4] J. F. Morley to James H. East, November 29, 1922, James H. East Papers, University of Texas at Austin Archives.
[5] *Ibid.*

allies. On December 28 the *Santa Fe New Mexican* printed an editorial exclaiming that "every law-abiding man will be delighted to hear that they [the outlaws] were landed safely in . . . jail. For this . . . Sheriff Pat Garrett and his posse of brave men are to be thanked."

The lanky lawman appreciated the applause, of course, but he still regretted the accidental killing of Charles Bowdre during the rock house gun battle. Soon he felt even worse. On the day after Pat's arrival in Santa Fe he learned that Acting Governor W. G. Ritch had received a letter from Bowdre. Evidently Charlie had been thinking about Garrett's amnesty offer and had proposed to surrender if the indictments against him for the murder of Buckshot Roberts were dropped. The *New Mexican* dryly commented on December 29 that the authorities probably would not have complied with the request anyway, but, at any rate, "Charlie is now where no indictments will reach him."

Indictments did plague the rest of the gang, however, and Billy the Kid was so worried that he made plans to leave jail by the "back door." Using spoons, forks, boards, and bedsprings, he and the others started digging. The sheriff heard about it and bribed another prisoner to spy on them. On March 1, 1881, word came that a breakout was imminent. The cell was searched and a tunnel located under a mattress. Stones and earth filled the bed ticking.

Dave Rudabaugh, in particular, was dejected. He had the most to gain from an escape. In January, Judge Bradford Prince had sentenced him to ninety-nine years for robbing the United States mail, and now he was scheduled to face murder charges in Las Vegas. The authorities realized, however, that he could not obtain a fair trial in that community, and so his case was transferred back to Santa Fe County, where Judge Prince once again pronounced sentence—this time to hang.

Rudabaugh was taken to Las Vegas to await execution, but there was to be no hanging. On December 3, 1881, this durable badman tunneled through the walls and escaped. Reportedly he fled to Parral, Mexico, where he terrorized the town so thoroughly that the natives finally rebelled, shot him, hacked off his head, and paraded it around the pueblo on a broomstick.

As for Billy the Kid, when he attempted to escape from his cell, all he got for his efforts was a term in solitary confinement. He was put in a stone vault, described by one newspaper as a place "where even the light of day is denied admittance and only when some of the jailors or officers enter can he be seen at all."

But Billy was just as interested in walking out of jail a free man as he was in escaping, and when he could he used the mail. On January 1, 1881, he wrote Governor Wallace saying that he would like to see him if the governor could spare the time. The governor had none to spare. On March 2, the Kid wrote again:

Dear Sir:
   I wish you would come down to the jail and see me. It will be in your interest to come and see me. I have some letters which date back two years, and there are parties very anxious to get them; but I will not dispose of them until I see you. That is, if you will come immediately.
                                                    Yours respect,
                                                    WM. H. BONNEY

The Kid was sure that the governor would respond to this implied blackmail. Wallace ignored him. On March 4 a more urgent letter found its way into Governor Wallace's mailbox: "I have done everything I promised you I would and you have done nothing that you promised me. I expect to see you sometime today."

On March 28, 1881, the Kid was transferred from Santa Fe to Mesilla, Doña Ana County, New Mexico, to stand trial on several counts of murder. The day before he left, Billy scribbled one last note to Governor Wallace: "For the last time I ask. Will you keep your promise? Send answer by bearer."[6] And still the governor remained silent.

A Mesilla dwelling was converted into a courthouse. On April 6, Judge Warren Bristol, in his black robes, entered the small room and sat behind a splintered desk near the rear wall. A spring breeze whispered through an open window. Across from the judge, silent and handcuffed, squirmed a brooding Billy the Kid. A couple of rough wooden benches provided seats for the spectators who came to watch the show and stare at the slim, light-haired boy they had heard so much about. On one side of the room sat a jury composed entirely of Mexican-Americans. Although the Kid's strength stemmed from a sympathetic and friendly native population, there was a depressingly grim look about the twelve jurymen that day. In truth, the territory would not have permitted an all-Mexican jury to be chosen unless it was fairly certain which way the final judgment would go.

[6] All the notes from Billy the Kid to Lew Wallace are preserved in the Lew Wallace Collection.

Two federal indictments hung over the Kid. One was for the slaying of Buckshot Roberts, the other for the almost-forgotten slaying of Morris J. Berstein, a clerk on the Mescalero Apache Indian Reservation. Like the killing of Roberts, the death of Berstein had come about through a gang action over two years before, on August 5, 1878. The prosecution admittedly had a weak case on both counts against the Kid, and so they dropped charges rather than risk an acquittal. It was far easier to get a conviction by transferring the Kid to the territorial court (same building, same judge, same jury) and try him for the slaying of Sheriff William Brady. Although his death was a gang killing similar to the murders of Roberts and Berstein, the evidence of Billy's participation was much stronger. In addition, the killing had been so cowardly that even the Kid's most ardent supporters had trouble justifying his actions.

Almost as controversial and interesting as the Kid himself was his lawyer, Albert Jennings Fountain, who had been appointed to defend him. This was a man whose stormy life would involve him in a political power struggle destined to destroy him. His mysterious death in the White Sands gypsum desert in the not-distant future would cast a dark and long shadow across the trail of Sheriff Pat Garrett.

Defense counsel Fountain announced on April 8 that the defendant was ready for trial. Two days later it was all over but the hanging. Judge Bristol had permitted a choice of only two verdicts: murder in the first degree (for which the punishment was death) or acquittal.

Judge Bristol wrote a remarkable charge to the jury, instructing them that "there is no evidence before you showing that the killing of Brady is murder in any other degree than the first." The judge's charge appalled Fountain, who insisted that a second set of instructions be given which would soften the harsh wording of the first. His efforts were successful, but his pleas came to nothing. The jury found the Kid guilty as charged, and Bristol gave him an opportunity to speak before sentence was passed. The record states that the Kid remained silent.

On April 15 the judge ordered that the prisoner be delivered to the custody of Lincoln County Sheriff Pat Garrett and that on Friday, May 13, 1881, William Bonny, alias the Kid, alias William Antrim, "be hanged by the neck until his body be dead."[7]

[7] Case No. 532, *Territory v. William Bonny,* District Court, 3d Judicial District, Doña Ana County.

The Kid Escapes

By the end of 1880, Pat Garrett's reputation as an outlaw hunter had made him the best-known and most popular man in New Mexico. On December 20 the *Las Vegas Daily Optic* happily opined that Garrett should be "retained as deputy sheriff of Lincoln for 250 years, and at the expiration of that time his lease on life should be extended."

Yet no matter how much Garrett thrived on praise, it did not pay his expenses. It still took money to feed and clothe his family, it took money to pay his deputies and informants, it took money to buy drinks for his sycophants (of which there were no small number), and it took money to support Garrett's poker-playing habits (he usually lost).

The popular lawman looked forward to collecting the five hundred-dollar reward that rested on the scruffy blond head of Billy the Kid. In this respect Garrett's feelings about money were no different from those of other lawmen. He considered a bounty on outlaws a "fringe benefit," as everyone else did. Even the prestigious Texas Rangers were quick to pocket any rewards, and their correspondence with headquarters reveals that considerable attention was given to the amount of silver someone's body might be worth—and if an outlaw was worth more dead than alive, then that was the way they usually delivered him. City marshals also stayed particularly alert for men with prices on their heads. Dallas Stoudenmire, who tamed El Paso—and lost his life in the process—is an excellent example of an officer who played all the percentages.

Collecting the reward was not always as simple as counting the money afterward. Often it was easier to catch an outlaw than to get paid for him. First an officer had to locate the criminal. Then he either had to shoot him or put him in irons. But to collect the reward a bounty hunter had to deal with an individual more crafty than the criminal—the politician. The politicians were too smart to use a gun; they used the law instead and found loopholes to avoid paying the advertised reward.

But since Governor Wallace himself had posted the reward for the capture of Billy the Kid, Pat Garrett expected to be paid promptly. He had done his part. That the Southwest's most noted and dangerous criminal now languished in jail and was soon to drop through a trap door should have reminded the governor of his part of the bargain. As it happened, Wallace had other things on his mind. He had just published *Ben Hur*, and the first five thousand copies were almost sold out. The governor-author had no time to make good on his promise to pay reward money to diligent, hard-working sheriffs. He was back East counting his own money.

Both Pat Garrett and Frank Stewart laid their claims before Acting Governor Ritch, who ignored them, saying that technically he had no authority to draw warrants on the treasury. He also questioned the legality of the claims, saying that the reward had been posted for the "capture and delivery of the Kid to the sheriff of Lincoln County." Since Pat would not legally be sheriff until January 1, and since he had not delivered Billy to George Kimball, Ritch said that the terms of the offer had not been strictly complied with.

Ritch's arbitrary decision stunned not only Garrett but several newspapers as well, especially the *Santa Fe New Mexican*. It commented angrily that "the reward of $500 was very small in the first place and should be promptly and cheerfully paid over to the men who had done New Mexico such a great service."[1] The newspaper further argued that Garrett was in effect the sheriff, and that thus the prisoner had been legally in his hands.

In the uproar that followed, individual citizens, appalled by the territory's lack of fiscal integrity, began making contributions. Marcus Brunswick, of Las Vegas, and W. T. Thornton personally paid the five hundred dollars to Garrett and took an assignment on the claim. In addition, five other citizens sent a hundred dollars apiece, three people made fifty-dollar donations, four gave twenty-five dollars, and twelve mailed in lesser amounts of money. With all this cash in his pocket, plus the four dollars daily per diem and the six and one-half cents per mile that the county paid,[2] Garrett

[1] *Santa Fe New Mexican*, December 30, 1880.

[2] Territorial Auditor Papers, Sheriff's account, 1881–97, State Records Center and Archives, Santa Fe, New Mexico. The per diem and mileage records cited in

became a comparatively well-to-do man around Lincoln. He purchased a small ranch near Eagle Creek and a hotel in town.[3]

While Garrett looked for places to spend his money, a procession of heavily armed men were preparing to deliver the Kid to him for execution. Leaving Mesilla with the prisoner were Deputy United States Marshal Robert Olinger and Deputy Sheriff Dave Woods. With them rode an armed escort consisting of Tom Williams, Billy Mathews, John Kinney, D. M. Reade, and W. A. Lockhart.

The Kid hobbled out of the Mesilla jail, describing it as the "worst place he had ever struck," and managed a grin for editor Simeon Newman of the *Semi-Weekly*. Newman noted that the youthful killer's attitude was "quite cheerful" and that "he wanted to stay with the boys until their whiskey gave out."

Taking choppy steps toward the horse-drawn ambulance, the Kid lifted his chains and climbed inside. He watched gloomily as they fastened him to the back seat. Up front, Lockhart lashed the four horses through the heavy sand and across the wide arroyos. Flanking the sides and rear rode Woods, Williams, and Reade.

If Billy bothered to consider the irony of his situation, he did not indicate it. He was to be hanged as a convicted lawbreaker. Yet beside him sat John Kinney, one of the worst cattle rustlers and killers in the Territory, and squatting on the opposite end of the seat was Billy Mathews, a deputy in the posse that murdered Tunstall (although Mathews may not have had anything to do with the actual slaying). Hunkered on the seat facing him grinned Bob Olinger, a locally well-known manslayer who liked to flex his muscles and stroke his double-barreled shotgun. Several times along the trip, Olinger patted his weapon and asked Billy whether he would like to make a run for it.

The posse had a threefold purpose. The first was to prevent the Kid from breaking free; the second was to make sure that no rescue was attempted; and the third was to guard against assassination. In everyone's mind echoed Newman's grim warning: "We expect every day to hear of Bonney's escape."

The procession arrived in Lincoln without incident, and the

---

the text were not for the chase and capture of Billy the Kid but for lesser-known criminals. However, since the dates are but six months apart, it is assumed that Garrett collected at the same rate for both incidents.

[3] Deed Records, Book C, p. 281, August 12, 1881, Lincoln County Clerk's office, Carrizozo, New Mexico.

prisoner was transferred to the second floor of the vacant Murphy-Dolan store. The stairs terminated in a hallway across which the Kid was led through the sheriff's office and into what, by some accounts, had been Murphy's former bedroom on the northeast corner. A large window carved out of the adobe wall faced the main street, and another window looked out into the yard. Until the day of his execution, this would be the Kid's home. There were no bars across the windows or doors, and except for the chains fastened to the floor the room did not resemble a jail.

Across the hall from the sheriff's office and alongside the staircase was the housekeeper's former bedroom, now used as a jail for ordinary prisoners. There were no bars in the window there either. The prisoners' chains were anchored near the open fireplace, where the men alternately froze and roasted throughout the cold nights. On the other side of the stairs was the former bedroom of James Dolan and John Riley. It now served as an armory where the guns were locked up.

With the Kid chained to the hardwood floor, Pat Garrett dismissed all the possemen except for Bob Olinger, whom Garrett wanted to remain as guard for the last few weeks of the prisoner's life. Pat knew of the controversy surrounding Olinger, who was tall and muscular, part Cherokee Indian but with reddish-blond hair and who liked to be called "Pecos Bob." Some men feared him, saying he was a bully and a brute; others were more tolerant, crediting him with bravery. He was a man who did his duty, even though sometimes blood was unnecessarily spilled in the process. Olinger's principal champion felt that the deputy may have "hurrahed" the Kid at times, but "it was not his character to be fiendish or taunting."[4]

Nevertheless, Garrett selected Olinger to guard the Kid simply because Garrett knew of the hate existing between them. They had fought on different sides during the Lincoln County War, and Bob Beckwith, a close friend of Olinger's, had died at the very end of the fighting as he stepped forward to accept McSween's surrender. Olinger blamed Billy in part for Beckwith's death. Deputy Sheriff James Carlyle was also a close friend of Olinger's, and Billy the Kid was deeply implicated in his killing at the Greathouse Ranch. Now that Bob Olinger had his chance, he is said to have frequently

[4] Maurice G. Fulton to Walter Noble Burns, December 14, 1927, Fulton Papers, University of Arizona Archives, Tucson. It is well to remember that Fulton spoke kindly of nearly everyone.

taunted the Kid unmercifully, daring him to run and implying that on hanging day it would be Pecos Bob Olinger who would flip open the trapdoor.

Also assigned to watch over the Kid was Deputy Sheriff J. W. Bell, who had a reputation for being a sensitive, quiet individual. Unlike Olinger, he carried only a holstered six-shooter.

On the morning of April 28, Olinger drew guard duty. Sitting on a bench in front of the Kid, the deputy broke open his breech-loading shotgun and dropped a slug containing eighteen grains of buckshot into each barrel. Looking straight at Billy with a grin and a chuckle, he said, "The man that gets one of these loads will feel it."[5]

At noon Olinger was relieved by Bell, and Bob placed his shotgun in the sheriff's office without bothering to lock it up in the armory. From the office he strolled across the street to Wortley's Restaurant.

As the dull thump of Olinger's boots died away, the prisoner asked Bell for permission to use the outside toilet. According to the most reliable reports, once inside the privy he found a pistol hidden there earlier by a confederate. Hiding the gun inside his shirt, the Kid bounded up the stairs. As Bell reached the top, the Kid either ordered him to surrender or struck him over the head with the handcuffs and pistol, depending upon which account one prefers to accept. Bell turned and reeled backward down the stairs, followed by two quick shots. Both bullets missed, but one slug ricocheted off the wall and drove through Bell's body. The deputy managed to stagger into the yard, where he died in the arms of caretaker Godfrey Gauss.

The Kid hobbled across the hardwood floor to the sheriff's office, where he grabbed Bob Olinger's still-loaded shotgun. Then he shuffled to the window overlooking the yard and a portion of the street and smiled as he saw Olinger come dashing out of the restaurant. As the marshal entered the yard, Gauss raced around the building shouting, "The Kid has killed Bell!"

Glancing up, Olinger saw the shotgun barrels pointed at him. "Yes, and he's killed me too."[6] The weapon roared, and Pecos Bob took eighteen buckshot in the chest. He died instantly.

Billy jumped to the hallway and crossed outside to the second-story porch, where he fired another load of shot into Olinger"s body. Then he broke the shotgun across the banister and threw it at

[5] Garrett, *Life*, 121.
[6] *Ibid.*

his enemy. "Take it, damn you!" he snarled. "You won't follow me any more with that gun."[7]

The Kid now yelled for Godfrey Gauss to remove his shackles, and the frightened caretaker tossed him a small prospector's pick. Although Billy hacked at the chains for almost an hour, he could free only one leg. Finally he tied the loose shackle to his belt, limped outside, and called for a horse. When he passed Bell's body, he muttered, "I'm sorry I had to kill him, but I couldn't help it." As for Deputy Olinger, the Kid felt less charitable. Giving his limp body the tip of his boot, Billy said, "You are not going to round me up again."

In spite of his dangling shackles and the excitement of the last hour, Billy the Kid paused long enough to shake hands with some awed Lincoln citizens. Then he climbed on a horse and galloped away.

[7] *Ibid.*

9

The Kid Dies

Sheriff Pat Garrett was in White Oaks collecting taxes and talk-ing with Deputy John W. Poe when the staggering news arrived that Billy the Kid had slain both his guards and escaped. Garrett had warned Bell and Olinger that the Kid "was daring and un-scrupulous, and that he would sacrifice the lives of a hundred men who stood between him and liberty . . . with as little compunction as he would kill a coyote."[1]

In disgust Pat rode back across the high plains to Lincoln and led several posses in a futile search of the green, brush-covered countryside. Saddle-weary cowboys even jogged as far east as the Staked Plains, but not a trace of the Kid could be found. Nearly everyone believed that Billy had fled to Mexico.

The next few months were difficult ones for Garrett. Only a few weeks earlier he had been praised as a hero. Now, through no fault of his own, the bright glory of his achievement had begun to dark-en. People began to act as if the Kid had never been captured. Billy's incredible luck and feats of nerve, recounted with gusto by the excited citizenry, seemed awesome, even supernatural. Without saying it aloud, folks figured that Sheriff Pat Garrett had been fortunate once—but that he would never be able to outsmart and corner the Kid again. They also censured Garrett for his "seem-ing unconcern and inactivity."[2] Pat defended himself by admitting that he spent a great deal of time on his ranch instead of seeking out the Kid's trail but claimed that he was "constantly but quietly at work, seeking sure information and maturing my plans for action."

The manhunter's confidence began to wane, however. Those who hesitated to assist him quickly drew his resentment. Because

[1] Garrett, *Life*, 123.
[2] *Ibid.*, 125.

Garrett represented the New Mexico power structure, many of the Mexicans generally sided with the Kid and would not turn against him, and others would not move out of fear. As for the Anglos, most of the small ranchers, themselves being squeezed by the power structure, plus the Anglo residents of the small communities, disliked, even despised, the sheriff because of his sarcasm and high-handedness. Some ranchers considered him to be a tool of John Chisum. One visitor muttered that "Pat Garrett rustled as many cattle as Billy ever did. Now he's doin' Chisum's dirty work."[3] By June 1, Pat was threatening to resign unless the citizens showed "more readiness to support him in the execution of his arduous duties."[4]

Actually assistance had arrived from the Canadian River Cattle Association in the Texas Panhandle, an organization guided by Charles Goodnight. For years these cattlemen had battled the New Mexico rustlers, and Billy the Kid had been an especially sharp thorn in their boots. Seeing that Lincoln County finally had a sheriff who meant to enforce the law, and knowing that he could get little assistance from the local ranchers, the association passed the hat and called for help from John W. Poe, the replacement of Frank Stewart. The financial board, presided over by Oliver Goodnight, instructed Poe to draw upon the association for whatever funds he needed.[5]

The stocky, muscular Poe, his black mustache drooping toward his chin, had recently been deputy sheriff of Wheeler County, Texas, and still held a commission as a deputy United States marshal. Poe's record as a lawman was basically good. He brought his man in alive when possible and generally was a fair and honest administrator. For this reason he would like to have forgotten that dark night in June, 1878, at Albany, Texas, when, as a deputy sheriff, he had been ostensibly guarding the jail. Inside, chained to the floor, lay former sheriff John Larn. Larn and a nefarious sidekick named John Selman—who would go on to fame in El Paso many years later by killing John Wesley Hardin—had used the law to rustle cattle and occasionally exterminate an enemy. These two men also headed up the local vigilantes (of which John Poe was a member), but the nightriders finally turned against Larn, captured him, and

---

[3] Ball, *Ma'am Jones of the Pecos*, 178.
[4] Cimarron *News and Press*, May 26, 1881.
[5] Oliver Goodnight to Maurice G. Fulton, May 29, 1927, Fulton Papers, University of Arizona Archives, Tucson.

locked him in his own jail. While Poe stood guard, several masked men reportedly seized his arms, pinned him down, clumped inside the wooden prison, and shot Larn dead.[6]

John Poe set up headquarters in White Oaks, where he and Pat Garrett met for the first time in March, 1881. While the Kid was languishing in the Mesilla jail Poe's job was to help wipe out the rest of the cattle-rustling operation. To do this, he asked Garrett to commission him as a special deputy, and Pat did so, since the Texas cattlemen were paying the bills. When the Kid escaped from the Lincoln jail on April 28, Garrett ordered Poe to seek out the Kid's whereabouts and submit a report.

In the meantime another reward notice bearing the New Mexico governor's signature was published on April 30, 1881:

BILLY THE KID

$500 Reward

I will pay $500 to any person or persons who capture William Bonny, Alias the Kid, and deliver him to any sheriff of New Mexico. Satisfactory proofs of identity will be required.

Several intriguing questions lie buried in the governor's seemingly routine offer. Did he mean to pay the reward personally, or did he intend to draft a warrant out of treasury funds? Governor Wallace's poster also said that the prisoner had to be "delivered" to a sheriff, but what if the sheriff himself made the capture? The ambiguous wording would soon cause Garrett considerable trouble. And what of the previous reward notice? Since it had not been paid, was this latest offer simply a restatement of the first? (It would seem so since there is no written evidence, other than the newspaper mention, of the second reward offer.) What would constitute "satisfactory proofs of identity"? And, finally, the notice omitted the usual phrase "dead or alive." This omission could be interpreted as stipulating that the Kid must be kicking when brought in.

Whatever the case, the reward was offered, but none of the local figures seemed eager to collect it. Law officers still believed that the Kid had fled to Mexico, and while they continued to keep their ears to the ground, no one really expected to hear any hoofbeats.

In this atmosphere of public opinion the Kid, incredibly enough, returned to Fort Sumner and hid out right under the noses of those

---

[6] Metz, *John Selman*, 88–89.

who never expected him to be there. Such an arrangement, with the Mexicans covering up for him, might have gone on indefinitely had not Billy paid too much attention to pretty Paulita Maxwell. The love affair so disturbed her brother Pete that he finally notified the authorities. A trusted vaquero slipped into White Oaks and gave the news to John Poe, who in turn relayed the message to Pat Garrett. The sheriff thought the entire yarn unbelievable, and only after the strongest urgings by Poe did he agree to check it out. Then, because of the possibility of retaliation falling upon Maxwell's head, both men concocted the story that Poe had learned of the Kid's whereabouts through a conversation he had overheard in White Oaks.[7]

Even though skeptical, Garrett holstered his favorite weapon, a .44–40 Frontier Colt with a seven and one-half inch barrel and plain wooden grips. It was the revolver, along with the model 1873 lever-action Winchester carbine, that he had taken from Billie Wilson following the Stinking Springs battle. This weapon would not only shortly kill the Kid but it in 1933 became the subject of an interesting lawsuit filed on behalf of Garrett's descendants, who were seeking (successfully, it turned out) its return from the display rack of the El Paso Coney Island Saloon.[8]

Garrett and Poe rode first to Roswell where they recruited Thomas L. "Tip" McKinney, who thought the tale a little far-fetched too. But he had little else to do, so he pulled his short frame into the saddle and tagged along for the eighty-mile trip.

On the night of July 10, the three men rode out of Roswell and on the evening of the 13th, camped in the sand hills five or six miles

[7] Most of this information came from Cliff McKinney (son of Tip McKinney), interview with author, Carlsbad, N. Mex., October 9, 1969. See also John W. Poe, *The Death of Billy the Kid*, 16–18; Garrett, *Life*, 126.

[8] The revolver and rifle were manufactured in 1880, and so were practically new when Garrett obtained them. Both weapons used the same ammunition. (James Gillett, a former Texas Ranger to whom Garrett once showed the revolver, later identified the pistol and remarked in passing that the .44–40's had an unfortunate tendency for the cartridge to expand and jam the cylinder when fired in a revolver, and for this reason the Rangers had stopped using them.) Around 1904, Garrett either lent or sold the rifle and pistol, and a gold-plated .45 which had been given him by the Customs Service employees to Tom Powers, proprietor of the El Paso Coney Island Saloon. The weapons were subsequently displayed, along with many other guns, such as those belonging to John Wesley Hardin and Dallas Stoudenmire. The pistol which killed the Kid is now in the possession of Jarvis Garrett, the rifle and gold-plated revolver are in other private hands. See James B. Gillett to *El Paso Herald-Post* January 27, 1933, and *El Paso Times*, January 23, 24, 25, 26, 1933; Tom Powers Probate Record, Number 6049, El Paso.

from Fort Sumner. On the following morning John Poe agreed to drift into town alone and make some discreet inquiries. He was completely unknown there.

Arriving at mid-morning, he mingled with the hundred or so citizens who populated the town, all but a half-dozen or so of Mexican descent. An Anglo in town always gave rise to suspicions, and the townspeople gave him little assistance and frequently answered his questions with suspicious inquiries of their own.

Garrett heard Poe's story of the day's events and, despite Poe's suspicion of the townspeople's reticence, was more convinced than ever of the futility of the trip. Still, he had come this far. He thought he might as well spend a little more time and watch the home of Celsa Gutiérrez, the Kid's girl friend, who lived with her husband in a portion of the former post quartermaster's store.

A peach orchard near the Gutiérrez house gave good cover for such a surveillance. It also provided cover for clandestine romancing, for, as the lawmen stole into the grove, they overheard voices speaking softly in Spanish. Minutes later a man wearing a broad-brimmed hat, a vest, and shirtsleeves, rose from the ground, sauntered toward a fence, vaulted it, and disappeared. The night was too dark and the figure was too far away to be recognized. It was not until afterward that Garrett learned that he had been watching Billy the Kid.

The posse crept as close to the Gutiérrez home as they dared. At the nearby García house, revelers at a *baile* stomped and catcalled to the fiddler's music and got in the way of the grim-faced possemen who were watching Celsa Gutiérrez' residence. The posse decided to stay clear of the confusion until the dance ended.

Near midnight Garrett and his two deputies circled toward the Maxwell home, a rectangular one-story adobe dwelling, formerly an officer's quarters when a military garrison had lived there. A wooden porch wrapped around three sides of the house.

Garrett crept across the south porch toward Pete Maxwell's room, where the door stood open against the hot weather. The two deputies waited silently outside, McKinney slouching against a weather-beaten picket fence and Poe squatting on the splintery porch edge.

Pat slipped to the edge of the dark doorway of Pete Maxwell's bedroom and, after pausing to adjust his eyes to the blackness, moved cautiously inside toward the sleeping figure whose bed lay against the outside wall, directly to his right. The rangy lawman sat down on the edge of the bed and gently shook Pete's shoulder.

While these events were unfolding, Billy the Kid was enjoying his last hours alive. Like almost everyone else in Fort Sumner, he laughed, clapped his hard, curiously small hands, and danced in the García home. At eleven he reluctantly left to return to a sheep-herder's camp on the outskirts of town, where he had been hiding since his escape from Lincoln. But as he reined up, he had re-newed thoughts about his girl friend, Celsa, and decided to go back to see her. Whether or not Zaval Gutiérrez knew about these atten-tions to his wife—or whether he even cared—is not recorded. What is known is that for the charms of Celsa Gutiérrez the Kid rode back to Fort Sumner to his doom.

After spending a few minutes with his girl, the Kid wandered off to the nearby home of a friend, Bob Campbell, where he re-moved his vest and shoes and then relaxed in the comfort of an old chair. As he sat there, he spoke of being hungry. Campbell tossed him a carving knife and mentioned a fresh quarter of beef hanging on the north porch of the Maxwell home. Sliding from the chair, the Kid did not bother to pull on his boots but yawned, fin-gered the knife, and moseyed from the house.

The brisk night air perked Billy up. He moved along the fence at a rapid pace as he approached the Maxwell house. Deputy Poe first noticed him when he was forty or fifty yards away, moving briskly and fastening his trousers as he stepped closer.

The deputies paid little attention. Neither of them knew Billy by sight and thought him to be a friend of Maxwell's, or possibly even Maxwell himself. They sat motionless in their positions—Poe partly concealed by a post—and allowed the Kid almost to trip over them.

Surprised by the two men and uncertain of their identity, the Kid jerked his six-shooter, a self-cocking, caliber .41, and mistaking the shadowy figures for Mexican idlers, called out, "Quien es? Quien es?" He became fully alert when McKinney stood up, accidentally caught his spur in a loose board, and nearly toppled over. As Mc-Kinney struggled to right himself, Billy noticed that he carried side arms.

Inside the building Pat Garrett was questioning Pete Maxwell. They talked in low tones, but the conversation suddenly froze when they recognized the Kid's startled voice outside. Billy leaped across

100

LEFT TO RIGHT: Pat Garrett, James Brent, and John Poe, about 1884.
Courtesy Robert N. Mullin.

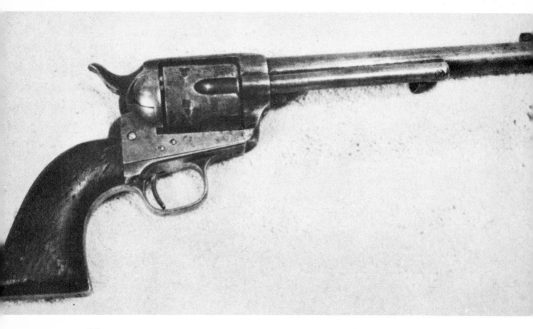

The weapon Garrett used to kill Billy the Kid at Fort Sumner, New Mexico. It had been taken by Garrett from Billie Wilson after the Stinking Springs shootout. It is a single-action .44–40 Colt, serial No. 55093. Courtesy Jarvis Garrett.

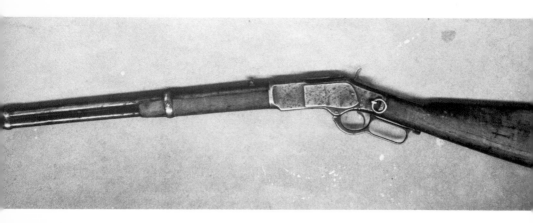

The rifle taken by Pat Garrett from Billie Wilson in the Stinking Springs gunfight and kept by Garrett. It is a Winchester 73 carbine, .44–40, serial No. 47629. Courtesy Bob McNellis, El Paso.

Pat Garrett, 1881. Courtesy Western History Collections (Rose Collection), University of Oklahoma Library.

Pat Garrett, about 1890. Courtesy Special Collections, University of Arizona Library.

Pat Garrett's home in Roswell, New Mexico, 1898. Photograph taken in 1940's. Courtesy James Shinkle.

Ash Upson, the true author of Garrett's *The Authentic Life of Billy the Kid* and probably the best
friend Pat ever had. Courtesy Fulton Collection,
University of Arizona Library Archives.

Herbert J. Hagerman, governor of New Mexico
Territory. Courtesy Collections in the Museum of
New Mexico.

James East, a New Mexico sheriff who rode with Pat Garrett during the hunt for Billy the Kid. Courtesy University of Texas at El Paso Archives.

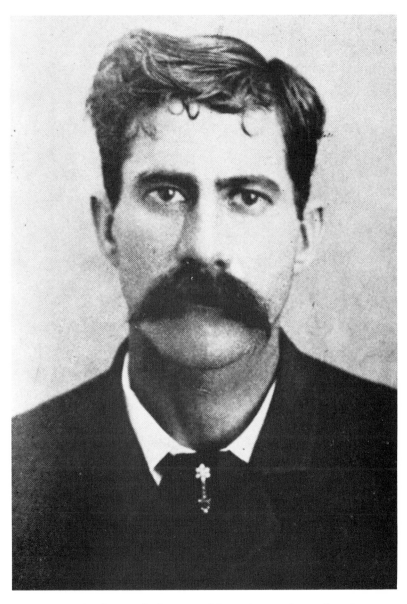

Pat Garrett (a disputed photograph), perhaps taken when he was a
Texas Ranger. From John L. McCarty, *Maverick Town: The Story of
Old Tascosa*. Reproduced by permission.

This photograph was taken in the 1880's, probably in Tascosa, Texas, when Garrett commanded the Ranger company. Standing, left to right: W. S. Mabry, Frank James, C. B. Bivian, I. P. Ryland. Seated, left to right: James East, James McMasters, and Pat Garrett. From John L. McCarty, *Maverick Town: The Story of Old Tascosa*. Reproduced by permission.

J. C. Lea, industrialist, capitalist, and railroad magnate. He lived in
Roswell, New Mexico, in the late 1800's. Courtesy Fulton Collection,
University of Arizona Library Archives.

Pat Garrett, photograph probably taken in Uvalde, Texas, about 1895. Courtesy Robert N. Mullin.

Colonel Albert Jennings Fountain. Courtesy William H. Keleher.

Albert B. Fall in his Spanish-American War uniform. Courtesy Mrs. C. C. Chase.

Pat Garrett as sheriff of Doña Ana County, New Mexico, 1898.
Courtesy University of Texas at El Paso Archives.

William T. "Poker Bill" Thornton, governor of New Mexico Territory, about 1894. Courtesy Collections in the Museum of New Mexico.

the porch and backed into the blackness of the bedroom. "Pete, who are those fellows outside?" he asked.

Garrett's pistol and holster had slipped around to his back as he slouched on the edge of the bed. While he reached for his weapon, the Kid noticed Maxwell's companion for the first time but did not recognize him because of the darkness and because Garrett's height did not betray him while sitting down.

Billy stepped to the bedside and laid his left hand on the covers. "Pete, quien es?" he asked again. As Garrett moved, the Kid jumped backward to the center of the room, hesitating, pistol at full cock and leveled, yet not wanting to mistakenly kill a friend. He whispered twice more, "Quien es? Quien es?"

Pat did not bother to answer. His pistol swung free, and he fired twice. The first bullet tore into the Kid's body near his heart, and the young gunman died almost instantly. The second slug thundered into the wall. Before the echo of the gunshots drifted away, Garrett stormed outside, almost knocking Deputy Poe down in his hurry. "That was the Kid in there, and I think I got him!" he yelled.

Poe yelled back: "Pat, the Kid wouldn't come to this place! You shot the wrong man!"

For a second Garrett paused, shaken. Then he shook his head. "I'm sure it was him; I know his voice too well to be mistaken."[9]

Just then Pete Maxwell charged outside, dragging his bedclothes behind him. Confused and excited, John Poe cocked his revolver and would have shot the frightened Maxwell, but Garrett hastily knocked his six-shooter aside, shouting, "Don't kill Maxwell!"

Maxwell was not the only jittery man on the porch. Garrett and his deputies huddled, trying to decide whether the Kid was dead. No one was willing to try the simple expedient of re-entering the room to see whether a corpse lay on the floor. John Poe later spoke of hearing a death rattle very distinctly. Maxwell agreed that he had heard it too. He lit a candle, holding it up to the window to peer inside.[10] He waved the tiny light around while Pat Garrett and the others stood back in the darkness and finally got a glimpse of the Kid lying on his back, staring upward, a butcher knife in one hand and a pistol in the other.

Billy the Kid was dead. But his legend was about to come alive.

[9] Garrett, *Life*, 130; Poe, *The Death of Billy the Kid*, 37–38.
[10] J. Evetts Haley, interview with Deluvina Maxwell, Fort Sumner, New Mexico, June 24, 1927, on file at the Panhandle Plains Museum, Canyon, Texas.

10.

An Empty Grave?

Early the next morning the Kid's body, the wound covered with a borrowed, outsized white shirt, lay stretched out on a bench while a coffin was knocked together from scrap lumber. The barren and ugly caliche earth of the Fort Sumner military cemetery swallowed up the body, the grave supposedly lying between those of the Kid's two comrades-in-arms, Charles Bowdre and Tom O'Folliard. Until that moment the funeral was a quiet and decorous affair attended by Garrett and his deputies and by nearly all the sympathetic Mexican-American population of the village.

The staid affair erupted suddenly in an outburst by Deluvina Maxwell, a former Navajo slave who now worked for Maxwell and had adopted his name. The emotional woman's eyes were heavy and red; tears had etched deep lines down her high-boned face. She burst through the crowd to confront Pat Garrett. "You piss-pot! You sonofabitch!"she screamed. She would have clawed the sheriff's face had not the mourners held her back.[1]

Garrett was not particularly surprised by her outburst. Accusations and recriminations, like poor pay, went with the job. But, as usual, his stony face did not reflect any emotion. He stared impassively at her.

Pat might not have stayed so impassive had he known that almost ninety years after the Kid's death Billy's restless ghost would be refusing to stay underground. Almost from the moment that Garrett's pistol cracked in Pete Maxwell's bedroom and Billy toppled to the floor, controversy has surrounded the killing.

A good place to begin a discussion of this intriguing event might

[1] Most printed accounts have Deluvina Maxwell screaming at Garrett on the night Billy was killed. By her own account, however, she did not go near the death scene that night. See Deluvina Maxwell, interview with J. Evetts Haley, Fort Sumner, June 24, 1927, interview on file at Panhandle Plains Museum, Canyon, Texas.

be at the alleged gravesite of the young gunman. Originally the plot was marked by a small wooden headboard or cross. Gradually with the years the marker wore away or blew down in the sweeping winds or vanished in one of the Pecos River floods that frequently surged over the graveyard and obliterated most of its identifying marks. Since many soldiers were also buried there, almost all the corpses were disinterred—identified or not—when the army finally removed the bodies to the Santa Fe National Cemetery.

Years after the killing historians and a scattering of veterans who survived the Lincoln County War became interested in preserving the Kid's grave. After all the elapsed time, however, and after so many changes had occurred in the graveyard, how or if they selected the right site is a matter for conjecture.

In 1926 a then little-known writer named Walter Noble Burns published his most enduring work, *The Saga of Billy the Kid*. Although Burns did some research in Lincoln County (he visited the area and interviewed many people), his decision to make Billy the Kid the protagonist was based not on the facts but on the dramatics of the situation. Burns occasionally shifted the events to fit the character he created. His sales justified his assessment of his reader. Overnight *The Saga* became a bestseller, and an obscure young outlaw, Billy the Kid, became an established southwestern figure.

The book's success brought a host of imitators, nearly all of them following Burns's general format. The result was an impact upon the economy of Fort Sumner. Finally this badman really was worth more dead than alive, and the Fort Sumner Chamber of Commerce decided to do what any public-spirited community would do: they made a tourist attraction out of the Kid's grave.

Today where muleskinners once cursed and sweated their way across the country, tourists in air-conditioned cars make a quick turn off Highway 60 and drive right up to the grave. Loading their cameras, they snap pictures of the plot and stone, all the while feeling certain that the caliche they stand upon is indeed historic ground. What the tourist sees, of course, is just a concrete tombstone with the names Charles Bowdre, Tom O'Folliard, and Billy the Kid chiseled into it, plus a concrete slab over the graves, all three plots surrounded by a high, heavy wire fence. Underneath that concrete and dirt may lie the remains of a soldier or perhaps some unknown moldering corpse or—perhaps—Billy the Kid. Or there may be nothing. Nobody really knows, and it is not likely that anyone is going to find out.

Then there is the possibility that the real Billy the Kid might never have been buried in the Fort Sumner cemetery. There is enough evidence, indeed, to make one wonder whether Garrett actually killed him at all.

The generally accepted coroner's report[2] of the time describes first the events leading up to the slaying and then concludes:

> We the jury unanimously find that William Bonney was killed by a shot in the left breast, in the region of the heart, fired from a pistol in the hand of Patrick F. Garrett, and our verdict is that the act of the said Garrett was justifiable homicide, and we are unanimous in the opinion that the gratitude of the whole community is due the said Garrett for his act and that he deserves to be rewarded.
>
> M. Rudulph, President
Anton Sabedra
Pedro Anto Lucero
Jose X Silba
Sabal X Gutierrez
Lorenzo X Jaramillo

All of which information I bring to your notice.

Alejandro Segura, Justice of the Peace

What happened to this document—the original of which was written in Spanish—signed with an X by three of the jury members, and, according to Garrett, deposited with the district attorney of the first judicial district in Las Vegas, New Mexico?[3] No one knows. According to José E. Armijo, district attorney for that county in 1951, the statement "is not now, and never has been, among the records of this office."[4] Thus, as the matter now stands, Billy the Kid is not legally dead.

It might be argued that New Mexico kept poor records in those frontier days and that the inquest paper could have been mislaid or accidentally destroyed. Such a possibility is not questioned. That the document has not yet turned up does not necessarily mean that it will not do so in the future.

Other strange circumstances surround this particular document. A. P. Anaya, a former member of the New Mexico legislature, wrote George Fitzpatrick, editor of the *New Mexico Magazine*,

---

[2] The original document does not exist. The Lincoln County Museum, Lincoln, New Mexico, has a photostat (which is claimed to be from the original), and this statement was taken from that photostat.

[3] This statement was part of Pat Garrett's official report, July 15, 1881, and forwarded from Fort Sumner to Acting-Governor W. G. Ritch in Santa Fe.

[4] C. L. Sonnichsen and William Morrison, *Alias Billy the Kid*, 109–10.

that he and "a friend were called as members of the coroner's jury the night the Kid was killed and that this jury wrote out a verdict stating simply that the Kid had come to his death as a result of a wound from a gun in the hands of Pat Garrett, officer." Anaya further claimed that "this verdict was lost and that Garrett had Manuel Abreu write a more flowery one for filing." New signatures other than Anaya's and his friends' appear on the semiofficial verdict. "Milnor Rudulph, who signed as 'presidente' of the jury, was not an original member of the jury who viewed the body."[5]

But whether or not he actually had a coroner's report to give to the district attorney, Sheriff Pat Garrett, his shoulders beginning to stoop from the pressures of his office, contacted Charles Green, editor of the *Santa Fe New Mexican* and a significant member of the "Santa Fe Ring." He was asked by Garrett to file an application on July 20, 1881, with Acting Governor Ritch. Pat claimed the five hundred-dollar reward that Governor Wallace had offered on December 13, 1880, for the capture of Billy the Kid.

It was not to be so easy. Acting Governor Ritch became even more fidgety about the reward money than he was when it was first juggled about after the Kid's capture at Stinking Springs. He made the extraordinary statement that the reward "was a personal offer of Governor Lew Wallace" and that it was not intended to "bind the Territory." The acting governor even swore that "there is no record whatever, either in his office or at the Secretary's office, of there having been a reward offered . . . nor was there any record on file in said offices of a corresponding reward in any form."[6] These incredible allegations were simply not true. As Secretary of New

[5] George Fitzpatrick to C. L. Sonnichsen, January 19, 1952, Sonnichsen Papers, University of Texas at El Paso Archives.

[6] Sonnichsen and Morrison, *Alias Billy the Kid*, 115; see also Governor Lionel A. Sheldon to Honorable S. Baca, President of the Council, February 14, 1882, New Mexico State Archives, Santa Fe. Sheldon wrote that he favored paying Garrett the reward, although technically he could not comply with the terms because "when Garrett met the 'Kid' in Maxwell's room, it was very certain that one or the other would be killed. It was not a reward [whereby] the payment depended upon a conviction. The Kid had [already] been convicted, and was under sentence to be hanged. Garrett was in pursuit with an intention to capture if it could be done reasonably, but under the circumstances of their meeting, capture was out of the question. [Therefore] it will not do to be technical in this case because men will not be so likely to take risks and perform services for the protection of society against bad men if capricious objections are imposed to avoid the discharge of public observations. The case under discussion is too notorious and too memorable to be made a precedent for the refusal to pay for services performed substantially in compliance with the promise of high authority."

Mexico, Ritch actually countersigned the reward offer and attached the territory's great seal. Why Ritch should refuse to honor this legitimate request is a question to ponder. His reluctance to pay off might indicate a suspicion that the claim was not legitimate. Did he harbor suspicions about an alleged coroner's inquest that he had never seen? Did he have good reason to doubt its authenticity?

Even if there had never been a coroner's report, it does not necessarily mean that the Kid was not dead. Nor does the fact that Ritch's refusal to pay the reward mean that the acting governor had serious doubts about the death. The reluctance could have been a political matter, and politics in New Mexico Territory ranged from partially to absolutely corrupt.

More questions were found noticeably unanswered almost before the dirt hardened over the Kid's alleged gravesite. Stories quickly began circulating that he was still alive. People claimed to have seen and talked to him in Mexico, in South America, in all parts of western America, and even in Canada. Many of these stories have been preserved in taped and written interviews. Although they have generally been given little credit by scholars, no researcher can work on Lincoln County history without running into them time after time.

Let us examine the liveliest, the most interesting, and the best-documented account of how Billy the Kid escaped Pat Garrett's bullets and lived to brag another day. The story came from the lips of O. L. "Brushy Bill" Roberts, who claimed to be Billy the Kid himself.

It began in 1948, when William V. Morrison, a reputable attorney working as an investigator for a legal firm, handled a case for a man named Joe Hines, a survivor of the Lincoln County War then living in Florida. During their discussions Billy the Kid's name frequently came up. Hines stated flatly that Garrett did not kill the Kid in Fort Sumner or anywhere else. He swore that the Kid was alive, living in Hamilton, Texas, and that he called himself Brushy Bill Roberts.

Morrison looked up Brushy Bill, a man claiming to be ninety years old, who stood five feet eight inches tall and weighed 165 pounds. He had blue-gray eyes, large ears, and (very unusual) hands nearly as small as his wrists. His body bore the ragged scars of twenty-six bullets and knife wounds. Here obviously stood an hombre who had lived an active and dangerous life on the early frontier.

A puzzling fact about Roberts was that, though nearly illiterate, he knew as much about the Lincoln County War as most experts. Although many books were in print concerning the war, most of them made little pretense at scholarship. Factual accounts of the Lincoln County affair were tucked away in obscure publications and in books from university presses, places far removed from the corner drugstore where Roberts would have purchased any material simple enough for him to read.

Roberts told Morrison how the soldiers fired on the burning Mc-Sween house (a disputed subject among historians). He described the layout of the Lincoln County courthouse in the 1880's, something about which no one today is exactly sure. He mentioned battles that took place, and generally his descriptions closely matched that of the scholars.

Bill Morrison sensed a good story. He approached C. L. Sonnichsen of El Paso on the Brushy Bill research, knowing Sonnichsen to be a well-known and reputable southwestern writer and researcher, a scholar who knew the history of Lincoln County and its troubles and who had enduring friendships with the better-known authorities of that period, such as R. N. Mullin, Colonel Maurice Garland Fulton, Phil Rasch, Will Keleher, and Eve Ball.[7]

Sonnichsen and William V. Morrison collaborated on a biography of Roberts entitled *Alias Billy the Kid*, but their views failed to receive wide acceptance in spite of the fact that this slender volume is one of the best documented pieces of material ever put together on the youthful gunman's career. The authors point out that, if the old man was not Billy the Kid, then who was he? Almost every Anglo-American in Lincoln County at that time has been identified and his wanderings traced. But a man named Roberts? No one ever heard of him.

Roberts' story misfires on several points, however, and Sonnichsen and Morrison do not hesitate to mention these contradictions. In November, 1950, Roberts requested an official pardon before New Mexico's Governor Thomas J. Mabry. Here Brushy Bill missed his chance at belated fame. As Sonnichsen wrote of the occasion:

[7] This statement is not meant to imply that the authorities believed Brushy Bill's story. None of them did.

Roberts couldn't remember Pat Garrett's name. He couldn't remember the places they asked him about. When Will Robinson [one of the many persons allowed to question Roberts] asked him if he killed Bell and Olinger when he escaped from the Lincoln jail, he said he didn't do any shooting—just got on his horse and rode off. He watched the policemen at the door and was upset when the governor pointed out one of the guests as the sheriff of Carlsbad.[8]

Although the old man had discouraging lapses of memory when he sat before the governor and dignitaries, he felt perfectly at ease with Morrison and told his story with considerably more accuracy and detail. His account of the Lincoln County War continued in detail until the very night Garrett was supposed to have shot the Kid.

Roberts claimed that he knew Garrett was in Fort Sumner and consequently decided to lie low until all danger had passed. However, on the night of July 14, 1881, Roberts heard shooting and ran into Pete Maxwell's back yard and started firing at the shadows there. The shadows (Garrett, Poe, and McKinney) shot back, and Roberts lurched across a fence as a bullet tore through his mouth, through his left shoulder, and across the top of his head. He collapsed and stumbled into an adobe house, where a Mexican woman took care of him.

Later Roberts said that he learned that Garrett had killed a man named Billy Barlow and was trying to pass the body off as Billy the Kid. However, since Garrett in his *Authentic Life* and John Poe in his *Death of Billy the Kid* make no mention of this wild shooting, nor are there any newspaper or personal accounts of it elsewhere, the alleged events strains one's credulity.

Such a thing as passing off a phony corpse could be done, of course, since neither John Poe nor Tip McKinney recognized the Kid, and both would be inclined to accept almost any body that Garrett claimed was Billy's. Garrett could thus claim the reward, as well as the honor and prestige that went with killing the Southwest's most noted outlaw.

The fallacy here is that local citizens could not be counted upon to remain silent. Although the Kid was popular in Fort Sumner, the village doubtlessly contained a number of individuals who disliked him. Some local citizens would have remained silent, but a number—probably a large number—would have said to each other and anyone passing through, "Hell, that wasn't the Kid Garrett

[8] Sonnichsen and Morrison, *Alias Billy the Kid*, 9.

shot! It was poor old Billy Barlow." If Garrett had not, in fact, killed the authentic Kid, his secret would not have remained a secret long enough for him to get to Santa Fe.

Also, in order for Garrett to palm off the Barlow body as that of Billy the Kid, there had to be collusion between Garrett and the Kid. Otherwise, how would Garrett know that Billy would not turn up very much alive, and in fact rustling horses, within the next few days or weeks? Such a showing would have ruined Garrett—and Pat was an exceptionally proud man.

Sonnichsen's book makes no mention of any such collusion, although the possibility is frequently hinted at. But if it did happen, the question pops up again. If Garrett got together with the Kid, why not shoot him then and thus settle all future problems?

We can always wonder.

11.

Loose Ends

If Pat Garrett figured that his troubles with Billy the Kid were over once the young gunman lay cradled in the hard caliche soil of the Fort Sumner graveyard, he was mistaken. He did not have regrets or reservations about the slaying, and he was not the type of man to analyze himself or his motives. Nevertheless, few others could dismiss the Kid's memory as easily as he.

Years later, in 1902, while kicking aside dry, sticky tumbleweeds in an effort to precisely locate the Kid's grave for Chicago author Emerson Hough, Garrett tramped around until he finally found the common plot of the Kid, Tom O'Folliard, and Charles Bowdre. Pat remarked that the Kid's wooden headboard was missing. Cowboys who lacked adequate courage to face the gunman in life had months earlier shot it full of holes.

As Hough stood contemplating the dismal salt-grass and mesquite-covered soil, Pat returned to the buckboard. He picked up his canteen, held the container high, and offered a symbolic toast to the three dead outlaws. "Here's to the boys," Pat said quietly. "If there is any other life, I hope they make better use of it than the one I put them out of."[1]

What the Kid and his friends might have been doing with their other lives is not known, but back in 1882, Pat Garrett was certainly having trouble with his earthly one. Rumors circulated that some of the Kid's friends planned vengeance and one of the first of these threats was alleged to have come from Joe Antrim, Billy's older brother who vanished from Silver City, New Mexico, when the two parted company after the death of their mother, Mrs. Catherine McCarty Antrim.

Unlike Billy, Joe was a humorless, colorless individual with tight lips, a rectangular head, large ears, high forehead, and droopy

[1] Hough, *The Story of the Outlaw*, 311–12.

mustache. For a while he lived in Trinidad, Colorado; then he drifted to Denver, where he became a faro dealer, clerk, and non-entity existing near the fringes of the red-light district. He died on November 26, 1930, at seventy-six years of age. No one paused to mourn his passing, and no one asked for his remains. His body wound up on a marble dissecting slab at the Colorado Medical School.[2]

Somehow Garrett learned that Antrim was looking for him, and they met in August, 1882, in the Armijo Hotel lobby at Trinidad. After several hours of quiet, uninterrupted conversation, the two rose and shook hands. Both made statements to the press that they had discussed the killing of Billy the Kid. Antrim remarked that he now better understood the sheriff's difficult position—that Garrett had merely carried out a disagreeable duty that demanded the Kid's death. Furthermore Antrim disavowed any ill will against the lawman. Then they parted, never to meet again.[3]

Pat Garrett was also still having problems collecting the five hundred-dollar reward resting on Billy the Kid's head. Since Governor Wallace refused to honor his obligation, Pat turned to the New Mexico territorial legislature and asked for justice. He became a lobbyist, buttonholing statesmen and setting up drinks. Finally on February 18, 1882, the state houses acted and paid the full amount. Oddly enough, the official minutes note that the Kid's death occurred "on or about the ninth of August," almost a month after Garrett actually pulled the trigger.[4]

The delay caused Garrett to stumble into an unexpected financial windfall. Many New Mexicans were so disappointed by the territory's lack of fiscal integrity that they mailed him more than $1,150 in private, individual contributions.[5] D. M. Easton, an early Garrett supporter for sheriff, and James J. Dolan of the defunct House of Murphy were instrumental in raising the money. Most of the cash, however, did little more than pay Garrett's liquor and gambling bills as he lounged about the territorial capital.

In the meantime he was taking cognizance that hack writers from all over the United States were busily writing bloodthirsty tales of the American West and that easterners were purchasing and

2 Bill McGaw, "Even the Reporter Who Interviewed Joe Antrim Didn't Suspect the Truth," *Southwesterner*, Vol. II, No. 2 (August, 1962), 8–9.

3 *Albuquerque Review*, August 8, 1882.

4 Territorial Auditor Papers, Sheriff's accounts, 1881–97, State Records Center and Archives, Santa Fe, N. Mex.

5 *Río Grande Republican*, September 2, 1882.

reading these dime novels at a prodigious rate. Thus Garrett was primed when Charles W. Greene, editor of the *Santa Fe New Mexican,* approached him and inquired why he did not cash in on this profitable market by writing a factual account of Billy the Kid's life and career.

Greene agreed to publish the book if Pat could find someone to write it. So Garrett asked his friend Marshall Ashmun Upson, better known as Ash, to do the job. Ash had joined the Garretts in August, 1881, and had lived with them on a ranch Pat had purchased near Roswell, New Mexico.[6] The garrulous, frequently troublesome, heavy-drinking, stubborn old iconoclast proved to be possibly the best friend that Pat Garrett would ever have. During many of their long conversations the Holy Bible underwent a constant, heavy philosophical sledgehammering. Thus Pat's religious views, still as profoundly agnostic as when he shot buffalo for a living, were heavily reinforced.

Born in Connecticut, Ash was in his early fifties when he met Garrett. A member of that wandering newspaper tribe known as "boomers," he drifted west during the Civil War after working as a reporter for the *New York Tribune.* He established the *Albuquerque Press* in 1867 and then scattered printer's ink in such diverse places as Fort Stanton, Las Vegas, Central City, Elizabethtown, and Mesilla—all in New Mexico. About 1876 he arrived in Roswell and soon found employment as a justice of the peace, postmaster, real-estate agent, and notary public. Newspaper advertising indicates that he gave special attention to "claims against the United States government for depredations by Indians."[7]

The *Las Vegas* (New Mexico) *Gazette* of September 13, 1879, commented that as a justice of the peace Upson had "more country within his jurisdiction than half the district judges in the states." Nevertheless, even with all this responsibility, he frequently used legal license unthinkable to even the most liberal district judge. For instance, Ash held a lifelong suspicion of women, having once been married and divorced. In effect he became a watchdog over bashful cowboys who spent too much time on the range and away from the often deceptive comfort of a woman's touch.

Once, against his better judgment, he married a young cow-

---

[6] Colonel Maurice Garland Fulton to Marshal W. Fishwick, March 29, 1952. Fulton Papers, University of Arizona Archives, Tucson.

[7] *Roswell Record,* March 4 (no year), random newspaper clipping, Fulton Papers, University of Arizona Archives, Tucson.

puncher to a female who, Ash figured, had more miles on her than a covered wagon just arriving from Tennessee. But Ash did as he was asked, matched the couple, and settled back to wait. Sure enough, within weeks the waddy appeared suddenly in Upson's office complaining that the marriage had not worked out, that his wife often refused to jump out of bed before sunup, and, even more outrageous, that she would not assist in rounding up cattle and breaking horses. Obviously the man had sufficient cause to be disappointed, according to Upson's view anyway. Ash therefore told the cowboy: "You don't need a divorce. I sized up that woman the day I was marrying you two people. So I never sent the marriage certificate to Lincoln to be recorded." Upson then pulled open a desk drawer, extracted a somewhat battered certificate, tore it up, and threw the pieces away. "Go back to the ranch and take the saddle and bridle off that woman, and turn her back to grass in Texas where she came from."[8]

Owing to the remoteness of Roswell's justice court, the legal trade often grew slack, so much so that Upson occasionally worked in Captain J. C. Lea's general store. Once he waited upon a lady who, after glancing about to make certain no one could hear, ordered a bottle of Hostetter's Bitters, a popular snake-bite and nervous-stomach remedy of the day that contained a generous alcoholic content.

Upson coughed softly and then muttered that he had recently sold out of the potion, a statement that startled and bewildered Captain Lea, who happened to be passing by as Ash spoke. Lea paused, turned, and commented that he distinctly remembered stocking a considerable supply. An investigation followed, the result being that Ash finally admitted he had consumed every jug in the store.

"How in the hell was I to know," Upson snorted as he quit upon request, "that some damn fool woman would come in here wanting a bottle of bitters."[9]

It is not known how Ash Upson and Pat Garrett met, although they probably knew each other for several years in Roswell. In those days men either liked each other or they did not. Beyond that they did not try to reason out their relationships. Because Garrett and Upson were so outspoken, so crusty, so individualistic—

[8] Keleher, *The Fabulous Frontier*, 146.
[9] *Ibid.*, 147–48.

each possessing weaknesses for fast horses (and sometimes fast women), the cards, and, to a certain extent, the bottle—they blended together like water and good whisky. Garrett gave Upson the benefit of a home and family surroundings. Although he rarely followed the former newspaperman's cantankerous advice, Pat was always there to defend him, pull him out of trouble, or sober him up. Upson in return gave loyalty and understanding. He ignored without hostility Garrett's biting, often surly disposition and made an honest effort to accept the sheriff's complexities without criticism, as others were not prone to do.

Together the two men wrote a book with a jaw-breaking title: *The Authentic Life of Billy, the Kid, the Noted Desperado of the Southwest, Whose Deeds of Daring Have Made His Name a Terror in New Mexico, Arizona, and Northern Mexico.* On the cover is Pat Garrett's name as author, although Ash Upson claimed to have written every word. He hung his prose together in the typical swashbuckling style of the day.

Because Ash claimed to have known Billy the Kid in Silver City and roomed in a house owned by Billy's mother, he supplied many details of the Kid's early career—details now known, for the most part, to be false. Whether or not Upson actually was acquainted with Billy and his mother is questionable. Probably he did, but then there existed no valid reason for paying close attention to the comings and goings of a ragged, obscure boy scurrying about in the muddy streets. And Upson's newspaper training can be blamed for the blatant falsehoods he wrote about Billy. During those times libel was as natural as advertising, and truth became relevant only if an editor went to court. Thus Upson's version of Billy the Kid's early life has been almost completely destroyed by modern historians, and those readers interested in a truly authentic story must consult other, more historically reliable sources.

When the book reaches the point where Pat Garrett enters the narrative, however, he obviously starts to dominate the writing. *The Authentic Life* now becomes basically accurate and finally begins to live up to its long and tedious title. Other sources in regard to the Kid and the Lincoln County War may still need to be consulted, but these references should primarily be for filling out specific details.

The Upson-Garrett handling of Billy the Kid's career treats the young outlaw kindly. Garrett took great pains to defend the Kid's reputation from those who said, now that he lay safely dead, that

Billy "was a coward." "There is not one of these brave-mouth fighters that would have dared to give voice to such lying bravado while the Kid lived; not one of them that were he on their track, would not have set the prairie on fire to get out of his reach."[10]

The biography was a financial flop, and Upson laid the blame squarely on Garrett and Greene. Upson said that Greene lacked the money and distribution facilities to guarantee a nationwide sale. "It has been bungled in the publication," he said. "The Santa Fe publishers took five months to do a month's job and then made a poor one. Pat F. Garrett, who killed the Kid, and whose name appears as author of the work (although I wrote every word of it) as it would make it sell, insisted on taking it to Santa Fe, and was swindled badly in his contract. The publisher does not know how to put a book on the market."[11]

With the volume in print, Pat Garrett decided that he had finally had enough and that he would not be a candidate for sheriff in the 1882 elections. Instead he threw his support to James J. Dolan, whose name, because of its connection with the defunct House of Murphy, received considerable attention.[12] However, for reasons unknown, Dolan's ambition fizzled quickly, and John William Poe, Garrett's companion and deputy during the Billy-the-Kid killing, took his place.

Poe easily won the election and proved to be radically different in temperament, character, and disposition from his predecessor. Although Garrett was tough and canny, his business methods were thoroughly inept. Pat did not like paperwork, facts and figures confused him, and he hated to hang around the office. Poe, on the other hand, was incredibly efficient. His red-wheeled buggy and fast horse soon became well known about the county as he briskly hustled about collecting taxes and familiarizing himself with the voters.

Pat Garrett and John Poe were to remain good friends once the election was over, and Pat, along with Captain Lea, was instrumental in selecting a suitable wife for Lincoln County's new sheriff. The young lady they chose was Sophie Alberding, who went west from Missouri in 1882 to visit with the Leas of Roswell, close family friends.

After Miss Alberding had settled in her new home, Lea and Garrett gently began closing the trap. One evening Captain Lea called

[10] Garrett, *Life*, 138–39.
[11] James D. Shinkle, *Reminiscences of Roswell Pioneers*, 22.
[12] *Río Grande Republican*, June 17, 1882.

her into a private room for a discussion. Upon entering, she noticed that Pat Garrett was sitting with his long legs stretched toward the fire, staring into the embers. Pat did not glance up, and she was forced to concentrate on Lea, whom she found already in the process of pacing about on the rough, hardwood floor.

"Sophie," the captain began, "I just had a letter from John W. Poe, our next sheriff. He's coming to Roswell for a visit and he'll stay with us."

Lea now glanced toward Garrett for assistance, but Pat was busily shifting his attention from the fire to the scuffed stitching on the toes of his boots. Sophie, however, suspected that Garrett was watching her with sidelong glances, although he was studiously contemplating his toes whenever she turned his way.

"You see, Sophie," Lea began again, even more hesitantly, "he'll be one of the really big men of this whole section. Pat and I have decided that you should marry him."

For a long moment the room grew very still. Then Sophie exploded. "Do you think you can dispose of me as if I were one of your prize shorthorns?"

Now Garrett decided to interrupt. "It's like this, Miss Sophie," he stammered. "You're not looking at the proposition in the right way. The Captain only means that we've talked this over and decided that it would be a mighty fine thing for you both if you married John Poe. He's really a wonderful man; I know him well."

Lea then jumped back into the discussion. "We're just trying to help you, Sophie. Pat and I can't see anyone else around here good enough for you. Take Alderberry, for instance. He's a good fellow, but he's got consumption. Dalton's even worse for he likes liquor."[13]

The end result was that Sophie Alberding won her right to select her own husband. A few days later she was introduced to John Poe and lost her heart. They were married soon afterward.

Now that Pat Garrett was no longer shooting gaping holes in the Southwest's most noted outlaws, he turned his attention to territorial politics. The United States Congress had recently ordered New Mexico to reapportion. The territorial legislature should have acted immediately, but it had ignored its obligations and adjourned on March 2, 1882. This left the work to Governor Lionel A. Sheldon (who replaced Lew Wallace in 1881), along with the president of the Territorial Council (similar to a state senate), and the speaker

13 Sophie Poe, *Buckboard Days*, 168–71.

of the House of Representatives. The result was that Pat Garrett became a resident of the Ninth Council District, consisting of Grant, Doña Ana, and Lincoln counties. Two councilmen were to be elected at large.[14]

The *Río Grande Republican* of Doña Ana County quickly announced support for John A. Miller, of Grant County, and David G. Easton, of Lincoln County. Both of these men had been staunch backers of Pat Garrett during his race for sheriff two years before. On August 12, 1882, the *Republican* noted uneasily that Pat Garrett had called for a special convention in Lincoln on the twenty-fourth to nominate a "Peoples Ticket" of officers. The newspaper rumbled that it suspected political treachery but spelled out no specific accusations.

A convention was held in Lincoln on August 22, and party lines were apparently ignored. The *Republican*, giving a slanted version of the affair, noted only that the names D. M. Easton and John A. Miller had been proposed for councilmen. The article was primarily a tirade against a man named Sligh, editor of the *White Oaks Golden Era*. It claimed that Sligh and his "kickers" (of whom Garrett was apparently one) were trying to stampede and capture the organization. What Sligh replied to this accusation is regrettably not known, since there are few extant issues of his newspaper.

Oddly enough, although this particular article did not once mention Garrett, the same issue carried on another page a savage story entitled "Ungrateful Garrett." It noted that the former sheriff had indeed been nominated as a candidate for councilman, apparently on a fusion ticket. Since this pitted Pat squarely against Easton and Miller, two old friends who had earlier supported him for sheriff, his candidacy, according to the *Republican*, marked him as totally lacking in gratitude. The story also called Garrett an "illiterate man" and remarked that "the newspaper notoriety he received from his success in killing Billy the Kid has upset his brain."

On September 16 the *Republican* lashed out once again at Pat Garrett's candidacy, printing a letter signed X, and probably written by the editor himself. The writer claimed that any man serving in the legislature should be educated, and this requirement would thereby eliminate Garrett. He further commented that "the trouble with Garrett is that the praise of the newspapers, together with the toadying flattery of those surrounding him, has made him egotistic to a superlative degree." The writer accused Fountain,

14 "Proclamation," *Río Grande Republican*, April 8, 1882.

of Mesilla, New Mexico, and Captain Lea, of Roswell, of using Garrett's popularity for their own ends. Fountain, the statement claimed, sought to use Garrett's name to bolster his Doña Ana County political fortunes. Lea wanted Garrett in the legislature so that Lincoln County might eventually be split in two and Roswell made the county seat of one half.

The letter concluded by saying that the Fountain-Garrett coalition was indeed a strange one. The latter had obtained his reputation for killing Billy the Kid while the former had obtained his by being the "Kid's apologist and defender," a reference to Fountain's defense of Billy the Kid during the gunman's trial in Mesilla for the killing of Lincoln County Sheriff William Brady.

Pat Garrett finally struck back, using the *Río Grande Republican* as a literary podium. In a long letter penned during the first week or so of September and finally printed on September 23, Garrett freely acknowledged that he appreciated the help of Easton and others when he had run for sheriff. He snapped, however, that simply because these people had once assisted him did not mean that he "had forever forfeited to them his rights as an American citizen." Garrett claimed that he had nothing personally against Easton but was running against him because "he had been caught in the company of X and others of his tribe whom I am proud to oppose."

As for alleged illiteracy, Garrett said, "If this be true, I claim that it is more my misfortune than my fault, and I must say that it does not look very generous for X to blame me for faults over which I have no control."

Garrett continued to hammer away at his detractors. "As to newspaper notoriety that I received for killing the Kid, X says that it has upset my brain and flattery has turned my head and clouded my better judgment. I think I know my mind as well as X does, and if there is a higher court than Judge X's, I beg to leave to appeal his decision."

Some candidates might have forgotten the episode, but Pat Garrett was a proud and bitter man and he expressed determination to track down the actual author of the letter. He suspected Lincoln attorney W. M. Roberts, perhaps because Roberts was one of the few men literate enough to write something of that nature.

Garrett accosted Roberts in Lincoln storekeeper J. A. LaRue's place of business on the morning of September 19. Reports differ about what happened. Only the *Río Grande Republican*'s version is available, and it indicates that there existed several different stories concerning the affair, but the newspaper elaborated only on its own, naturally one favorable to their point of view—which was anti-Garrett.

Using the newspaper version, and trying to sort the logical from the illogical, one concludes that this is roughly what happened: Garrett asked Roberts about the letter's authorship and Roberts vigorously denied any responsibility. Pat nodded and seemed satisfied with the reply. However, the two men strolled out into the street and Garrett began to ask more questions. Evidently he forthrightly accused Roberts of being the writer and was called a "God damned liar."

With this epithet burning his ears and stretching his nerves past what he considered their limit, Pat Garrett jerked his long-barreled Colt .45 and bashed Roberts at least twice across the head, inflicting deep gashes and leaving the lawyer sprawled unconscious in the street.

Surprisingly, no charges were filed against Garrett, and the incident was soon forgotten. Elections were rapidly drawing to a close anyway, and candidates for every kind of office all over the territory were clamoring for their fair share of newspaper space. Everyone screamed accusations at his opponent. One man was accused of grave robbing; another, of stealing and selling the public archives. Thus the politicians lurched down to the finish line.

In a close election Pat Garrett lost by a handful of votes, not too bad a decision considering that he had almost no newspaper support and did not get on the Grant County ballot until the last minute and that the voters in Doña Ana County were not particularly familiar with his record. He did carry Lincoln County, which unfortunately did not have the population of Doña Ana and Grant counties.[15]

The ex-manhunter took his loss without bitterness. The records indicate that he continued occasionally to serve his county as a delegate to Santa Fe for the next few years. In the meantime he considered other fields.

[15] *El Paso* (Texas) *Lone Star*, April 26, May 14, 1884.

12.

The LS Rangers

With no political office now beckoning, Pat Garrett turned his attention to ranching. In early 1884 he reputedly paid five thousand dollars to an English nobleman named Ki Harrison for some rangeland along Lincoln County's Eagle Creek. He registered his brand as PAT. Fifteen years later in Doña Ana County, Garrett would use the O brand. Both brands were registered.

Whether Garrett prospered in the cattle business is debatable. He was unhappy. His restless nature was not adjusted to raising cattle, an occupation he considered dull and monotonous—far different from the excitement of tracking criminals. At this time he was just an out-of-work sheriff, bitter experience having taught him that fame, slow to flower, tended to wither fast. Pat Garrett yearned to return to the outlaw wars. So it was that he watched with considerable interest events shaping up in eastern New Mexico and the Texas Panhandle.

Garrett had long known that big-name gunmen were not unusual in the panhandle region. Billy the Kid had been merely one of many to frequent the cattle, adobe, and scrap-lumber community of Tascosa in Oldham County, Texas. The town experienced a peaceful birth in June, 1877, but lost no time growing up to a reputation for rustling, vice, and violent death. The brothels in Hogtown (Tascosa's south side) were an oasis for sex-starved cowboys. Only in Tascosa could a gunslinger like Billy the Kid be considered a first-class citizen. Townspeople remembered that he minded his manners, drank very little, and was a favorite on the dance floor. Pedro Romero, one of the town's leading residents, had particularly liked the Kid and often sent *baile* invitations to him and his friends. Romero's only stipulation was that his guests come to the party unarmed.

One moonlit evening, while local citizens danced at Pedro Romero's house, the Kid and the town's physician, Dr. Henry F. Hoyt, left the Romero residence on the plaza's east side and strolled across the park to Ira Rinehart's general store. Returning to their host's home, Dr. Hoyt challenged Billy to a footrace. The gunman accepted and started to run.

Adobe homes generally were constructed with a doorstep a foot high to keep out water during a flash flood. As the Kid swept toward the house without slackening speed, he tried to spring inside. His boot heel caught the doorstep and he sailed through the doorway and sprawled on his face at the feet of the merrymakers. Instantly the Kid's four companions jerked their revolvers, cocked, and leveled them. Uncertain of what was taking place, they braced for a fight. Judging by what had happened, their reflexes were remarkable—as remarkable as their ability to hide weapons, for no one suspected them of carrying guns. Pedro Romero was indignant. He ordered them from his home and barred their return.[1]

In the meantime the big ranchers were getting tired of the Kid's rustling activities. They met at Mobeetie, another cattle community not far from Tascosa, in March, 1880, to organize the Panhandle Cattlemen's Association. They chose Frank Stewart and several cowboys to assist Pat Garrett in tracking down Billy the Kid. After the Kid had been captured at Stinking Springs, sentenced to be hanged, and then escaped, the cattlemen selected John Poe to help Garrett. This time the Kid was tracked down permanently.

After Billy's death the Panhandle stockmen turned their attention to local problems. Specifically, they wanted to suppress the growing economic independence of their own cowhands and cut the small ranchers down to size.

As usual with most troubles, both sides shared right and wrong. As the large ranchmen sprawled across the free government land, fencing in the waterholes and posting guards (for whoever controlled a waterhole controlled all the land around it), buying out the Mexicans and small squatters, they began to regard themselves as a privileged class and their cowboy help as little more than "hired men." It is astonishing that big stockmen would risk losing the magnificent loyalty of the cowboy. The cowhand regarded himself as "belonging to the brand," and he rode untiringly from sunup to sundown, usually eating only two meals, herding the owner's cattle. He even fought and occasionally died for his outfit.

[1] Henry F. Hoyt, *A Frontier Doctor*, 92–93.

The cowboy drew twenty-five to thirty dollars a month, often being paid only at roundup time. He was in constant debt to his employer since most personal items were picked up at the ranch-house and a receipt signed for them. To supplement these wages, the cowhand often slapped his own brand on any stray cow without markings and called it a maverick. An east Texas rancher named Samuel A. Maverick had brought the word into common usage. If a wild animal was found in the brush, a cowhand might say, "Here's one for Maverick." Later he might simply ram spurs to his mount and shout, "There goes a maverick." Thousands of these wild cattle roamed over northwest Texas after the Civil War, and any cowboy with enough nerve and talent to rope and drag one out of the thickets claimed the long-horned, short-tempered animal for his own. No one regarded it as rustling, and many cattlemen, large and small, started in this fashion.

A vast difference existed between mavericks and unbranded cattle belonging to someone. Generally an unbranded animal, not a maverick, was defined as one found grazing with "tame steers," or a calf still following its mother about—the mother, of course, being branded. Naturally, honest differences occasionally arose over whether an animal was wild or had simply been missed in the roundup.

Difficulties started when the big cattlemen began (with some justification) to accuse cowboys of branding cattle known not to be mavericks. In order to stop this practice, they ordered a complete halt to all private branding on land controlled by the ranchers. This stopped, or at least slowed down, many of the worst offenders, but it seriously hurt the honest individual who was trying to establish a modest spread for himself. The ruling might have been reasonable had the cattlemen owned the land instead of merely controlling the waterholes. They rarely had any lease rights and would have pulled a six-shooter on any official rash enough to suggest that they pay their rightful and proportionate share of taxes on the property.

If the cattlemen had offered extra compensation to their cowhands to make up for the loss of extra income, the resultant troubles might never have happened. Instead, as the big ranchers tightened their economic grip, the cowboys finally rebelled and demanded more money. In early 1883 an ultimatum, signed by approximately twenty-five cowboys, was circulated throughout the Panhandle:

We, the undersigned cowboys of Canadian River, do by these presents agree to bind ourselves into the following obligations. viz— First, that we will not work for less than $50 a month, and we furthermore agree no one shall work for less than $50 per month.

Second, good cooks shall also receive $50 a month.

Third, anyone running an outfit shall not work for less than $75 a month. Anyone violating the above obligations shall suffer the consequences.[2]

The strike had a quick effect. Two of the Panhandle's largest and most influential ranches tried to compromise. The LIT Ranch offered to pay thirty-five dollars a month to its cowboys and sixty-five dollars a month to its wagon bosses. When the strikers refused, the LS Ranch upped the ante slightly to forty dollars a month, with wagon bosses getting proportionally more, depending upon ability and experience.

The last offer lured Tom Harris, strike leader and LS wagon boss, into negotiations with LS manager J. E. McAllister and part owner W. M. D. Lee. The bargaining discussions were short. The LS sweetened its proposition even more, offering Harris one hundred dollars a month to continue on the job. Lee also agreed to pay fifty dollars a month for each cowboy that Harris would designate as a top hand.

Harris hesitated and then declined. He knew that many of the boys were not worth fifty dollars a month. He also knew that an offer of this kind would split the movement unless everyone received the same money. When Harris refused the offer, McAllister and Lee promptly fired him.

The plight of Harris' men soon became as desperate as his own. Numbering between eighty and one hundred, the strikers drifted into Tascosa while waiting for a solution to their demands. Their recreation site proved unfortunate. Hogtown was too close. With its easy ladies tramping the muddy streets, dressed in everything from slinky bustles to buffalo leggings, with its gambling and drinking halls beckoning, practically all of the strikers quickly went broke. In less than thirty days the strike ended.[3]

With the cowboys hungry and destitute, the large ranchers

[2] The original of this strike manifesto is in the Panhandle Plains Historical Museum, Canyon, Texas.

[3] There are two published accounts of the cowboy strike John L. McCarty, *Maverick Town: The Story of Old Tascosa*; and Dulcie Sullivan, *The LS Brand*.

might have been charitable. Instead, W. M. D. Lee blacklisted the cowboys participating in the strike, and the names were published all over the Panhandle. Even ranchers who needed help turned dazed waddies from their doors. Many top hands left the country. Others, bitter and resentful, drifted into New Mexico and established small spreads of their own—stocking them with steers taken from their former bosses.

Mavericking now became a word for outright rustling. Whereas earlier most cowboys had branded more or less legitimate strays, now they began "creating" the strays. Sometimes they separated the calf from its mother and fenced in the little one until it was weaned. This procedure had disadvantages, however, since a corral could not be built for every calf, and several calves penned together could attract the wrong kind of attention. There were rare instances where brutality was practiced, such as burning a calf's feet to keep it from following its mother, or slitting a calf's tongue so that it could not suck. These acts were infrequent, however. Cowboys were generally proud and gentle men who did not condone cruelty to animals, even though they occasionally practiced it on each other. Sometimes the New Mexico rustlers did not simply take one calf at a time; they rustled whole herds and changed the brands. Gradually the loose-knit organization became known as "the System." A few bitter men, still angry over the treatment accorded them in Texas, referred to themselves as the "Get Even Cattle Company."[4]

Another method by which rustlers acquired Texas cattle and slipped them into New Mexico was to draw up fraudulent bills of sale for nonexistent cattle. Attached to this piece of paper would be a power of attorney authorizing the holder to pick up cattle bearing a specific brand and drive them into New Mexico. If the theft was successful, the rustler made money; and if arrested he promptly pleaded ignorance and showed his bill of sale and power of attorney.[5] The plan was not foolproof, but it was remarkably effective.

The System's troubles came not so much from Texas men as from the Lincoln County stockgrowers. The angry ranchers complained that when the Texas steers stopped to graze in New Mexico the domestic cattle coming along behind usually sickened and died within a month. The dramatic and little-known illness afflicting

---

[4] McCarty, *Maverick Town*, 123.
[5] Keleher, *The Fabulous Frontier*, 81.

the cattle was the Southwest's first bout with the tick, causing what was known as Texas fever.

On November 15, 1884, a special meeting of the Lincoln County Stock Growers Association[6] passed a resolution stating that the large herd of Texas cattle which were being turned loose in eastern New Mexico threatened both the grass and the water and endangered the domestic livestock with Texas fever. Recommendations were that these trespasses be halted and a suitable punishment given to those who ignored the warnings.

A week later territorial Judge Warren Bristol gave the Lincoln County ranchers some relief. Bristol, who won a sliver of fame when he sentenced Billy the Kid to death for Sheriff William Brady's murder, ruled that, even though New Mexico rangelands were public domain, the water holes were not. Where one party owned the water, another party would not turn his stock loose on the land without first acquiring water rights to serve his cattle.[7]

With the New Mexico livestock growers preparing to get tough, Panhandle cattlemen decided to do the same. In the spring or early summer of 1884 the Panhandle men, prodded principally by the owners of the LS Ranch, released Pat Garrett from his restless exile. They asked him to organize a group of rangers to stop the rustling, and he jumped at the opportunity.

Garrett is supposed to have received a commission from Governor John Ireland to organize these men, but there exists no record of such an arrangement. Probably the governor gave his permission either orally or in the form of a private letter, instructing Garrett and the LS Ranch owners to organize their own people and to be responsible for all pay and provisions. However it was accomplished, the organization quickly became known as the Home Rangers, although many of the small nesters and ranchers, seeing the developments as a plot by the big cattlemen to take over the country, sneeringly referred to the outfit as the LS Pat Garrett Rangers.

[6] Stock associations were large and amply financed in early New Mexico. The Northern New Mexico Cattle Growers Association, whose ranges comprised most of Colfax, Mora, and San Miguel counties, embraced 15,000 acres of land and 800,000 cattle. Other associations were the Agua Caliente, with 240,000 cattle and capital of $2,500,000, the Wagon Mound association with 17,500 cattle, and capital twenty times as great as the worth of the livestock, and the Central New Mexico Association, the Doña Ana Association, and the Southwestern Association, having altogether 675,000 cattle and proportionate capital. *Río Grande Republican*, December 13, 1884.

[7] *Ibid.*, November 22, 1884.

Garrett brought only two assistants with him: Barney Mason and a little-known cowboy named George Jones. At the LS Ranch headquarters he recruited Ed King; Charlie Reason, who stayed drunk most of the time; Lon Chambers, who fought alongside Garrett at the dramatic battle at Stinking Springs; and four LS employees, Bill Anderson, John Land, Albert E. Perry, and G. H. "Kid" Dobbs, a former buffalo hunter. Perry claimed to have had experience as a cattle detective, and Pat appointed him first sergeant.

Jim East, the Oldham County sheriff, who also had been a member of Garrett's posse at Stinking Springs, had nervous reservations about the appointments. He believed the rangers to be unpopular, hard-drinking, and vindictive. "I will have nothing to do with these men [whom] the cattlemen have recommended," he said.

Garrett had to accept what manpower was available, however, and the cowboys were the only ones who wanted the job. There were no other takers, even though the pay was sixty dollars a month, about twice what an ordinary cowpuncher was drawing—and ten dollars more than what the strikers had asked. As for Pat, the ranchers promised him a salary of five thousand dollars a year,[8] and J. E. McAllister, the LS Ranch manager, threw in some fringe benefits: he sold Garrett some prize cattle at one-fourth their value and bought them back at market prices when the ranger captain resigned.[9]

With the organizational agreements worked out, the cattlemen persuaded Governor Ireland to issue a proclamation against carrying six-shooters. When the ban on firearms went into effect, the owners of the LS Ranch loaned Oldham County twenty-five thousand dollars to build a rock courthouse and jail in Tascosa, an exceptionally generous and civic-minded act which kept the residents wondering about the motives. An answer came soon. Garrett had refused to make arrests without warrants and other legal papers, and a courthouse was necessary in order to have a grand jury. During the first session the jury handed down 159 bills, most of them for stock theft. These indictments were the legal papers that Garrett and his rangers needed to clear the Panhandle of its undesirable citizens.[10]

[8] G. H. "Kid" Dobbs, testifying in Cheyenne, Okla., September 8, 1909, in behalf of Skelton Glenn, *Willis Skelton Glenn* v. *The United States and the Comanche Indians*, National Archives, Washington, D.C.

[9] Joe H. Smith, Jr., to author, July 4, 1969.

[10] McCarty, *Maverick Town*, 131.

Pat and his men rode the bleak back trails, serving their warrants and making arrests where possible for violations of the six-shooter law. Gradually it became apparent to everyone that the real intent of the warrants and the gun ordinance was not to put men in jail but to scare them out of the country. The practical effect, however, was to force the citizens into taking sides either for or against the rangers. Many of them chose to oppose the LS men, and private wars began springing up between the rangers and some of the cowhands—the former becoming known in their off-duty hours as "barroom gladiators." When the rangers were finally disbanded, old hatreds did not die with them, but simmered in the form of grudges which were settled long after Garrett had left the area.

Garrett's most significant arrests were carried out in February, 1885. He obtained cattle-theft warrants for Charlie Thompson, Bill Gatlin, and Wade Woods. Thompson had been a leader of the cowboy strikers, and the other two were shady characters who used a versatile brand called the Tabletop to change or expand any brand in the Canadian River valley except the XIT. These worthies raised branding to a fine art. After a steer was trussed up by the fire, a running iron blitzed across the old identifying mark; the difference could not be seen unless the animal was killed and skinned and the hide turned inside out so that old and new burns could be compared.

Information had reached Garrett that the three outlaws were holed up in a rock house at Red River Springs on the Canadian River. Taking Sheriff James East, the rangers rode out one night after supper as the countryside lay paralyzed in the grip of a swirling snowstorm. A theory of Garrett's, one that he successfully practiced twice on Billy the Kid, was that a storm offered the best time to hunt a badman. Few but lawmen would travel in such weather.

Kid Dobbs, who knew the country, acted as guide. All night long the silent, bundled rangers, bending into the wind, rode across the plains, pausing stiff and nearly frozen at two o'clock in the morning to feed their horses and bolt down a warm meal at Trujillo. At daybreak they reined up on the ice-clogged banks of the Canadian River. Dobbs cautioned Garrett that once across the next windswept, barren hill the posse would be within sight of the house, but unfortunately the rangers would also be within sight of the outlaws inside.

Pat asked Dobbs how far it would be if they went up the river-bed and approached the rock house from that direction. About two and one-half miles, he was told. "Then put the steel to your horse and lead the way," Garrett commanded.[11]

As they closed in on their quarry, the rangers dismounted, being careful to take positions calculated to choke off any escape. In spite of all precautions, however, they were seen by a cowboy named Bob Bassett, who was gathering an armload of wood. Scattering sticks with every stride, he raced toward the house, yelling that the Pat Garrett Rangers were coming.

Tom Harris, leader of the defunct cowboy strike and the wagon boss who had tried unsuccessfully to negotiate with the LS, stepped outside and angrily asked whether the rangers wanted him. Garrett said that he had come only to arrest Wade Wood, Charlie Thompson, and Billy Gatlin. With this assurance, nine men walked out of the house and said that they wanted no part of a shootout. They told Garrett that Woods was gone but that Thompson and Gatlin were still inside.

Thompson pushed open the door and came out next, but as he stood there talking and shivering in the cold, Pat gave him permission to go back inside for his coat. Once inside, however, Thompson slammed the heavy door and shouted his intention of standing and dying beside Billy Gatlin. Jim East began to plead with Thompson, urging him not to throw away his life when, if he gave himself up and stood trial, he might be judged innocent of the cattle-theft charges. Finally he persuaded the outlaw. Thompson walked outside with his hands in the air.

Now only Gatlin remained, but from inside the shack he shouted defiance. Garrett yelled back that he did not want to kill him, that Gatlin would be given the same day in court as Thompson. All day the arguments went on, until finally Garrett's patience faded. He ordered Charlie Reason and Ed King to slip to the rear of the dugout house and strip the poles from the lean-to type roof. Then they could shoot down on Gatlin if he still refused to surrender.

The rangers removed three of the timbers, and Gatlin called to Sheriff East, offering to discuss terms if East would come inside. The two senior lawmen conferred for a moment, East saying that he was willing to take the risk and speak to Gatlin. The sheriff had once punched cattle with the young gunman and did not think that Gatlin would kill him.

[11] *Ibid.*, 137.

East may have convinced Garrett that he was in no danger, but he did not quite convince himself. He crept cautiously to the half-open door, using a maximum amount of cover. When he was only a step or so away, he could see the rim of Gatlin's hat and the tip of his six-shooter, both projecting beyond the door edge. Taking a deep breath, East waited until the gun tipped low and the outlaw coughed, and then he jumped inside. "Lay 'em down, Billy," he cautioned.

"All right, Jim," Gatlin said, and he placed his pistol on a cot.

The two prisoners were quickly secured, and everyone relaxed long enough to make coffee and fry some bacon. Next was the long ride to Tascosa, where Gatlin and Thompson were ironed and placed in jail. Their stay was only a matter of hours. On the first night someone slipped them a file, the chains were cut off, and the men escaped. They were never recaptured.

Garrett hardly seemed to care that the outlaws had vanished. For some weeks disillusionment had been eroding his desire to do a good job. He suspected that he had been paid to kill men, not to bring them in for trial,[12] and that was not Pat Garrett's style. In the spring of 1885 he disbanded his rangers and became interested once again in the cattle business.

Sparking this renewed activity was a soldier of fortune named Captain Brandon Kirby, who claimed to represent Scottish ranching interests in the West, particularly New Mexico. During the last decade Europeans (especially Scotsmen, Englishmen, and Irishmen) had been sinking their fortunes into western cattle ranches, and most of them lost everything. (John Tunstall, whose death set off the Lincoln County War, was one of the first to lose both his money and his life.) Naturally, with all this cash around waiting for someone to invest it, Captain Kirby lost no time in preparing to present his qualifications. Apparently his glib tongue was qualification enough. James Cree, a wealthy Scotsman, hired Kirby to select some choice cattle lands in southeastern New Mexico.

Kirby was an enigma to New Mexicans in 1885, and to this day he presents an interesting puzzle. According to reports he was tall, handsome, well dressed (perhaps too well dressed to suit the simple folks of Lincoln County), and he always referred to himself as an "English Gentleman."[13] Usually he could be found around Santa Fe, wearing a heavy fur overcoat and signing checks on the Cree

12 Hough, *The Story of the Outlaw*, 299.
13 Mrs. Eve Ball, interview with author, May 14, 1969.

145

funds.[14] Where he came from and where he eventually disappeared to are not known.

As it turned out, New Mexico was not Cree's first choice for the location of a cattle ranch. He and Kirby had investigated the northwestern part of the United States, found the section not to their liking, and narrowed their search to Texas and New Mexico. In Tascosa a chance meeting occurred between Garrett and Kirby, with the result that Garrett took him to Lincoln County, where more ranges were investigated. In August, 1885, Kirby appointed Pat Garrett as his agent to purchase a large amount of property near Fort Stanton.

Pat Garrett closed some fast deals on Kirby's behalf. Captain Brazel on Eagle Creek sold his lands and four hundred head of stock. S. J. Slane, who ranched on the Ruidoso, received fourteen thousand dollars for his cattle and grazing lands. John Poe sold his ranch, fifteen miles southeast of Fort Stanton, for eighty thousand dollars. Even Garrett disposed of his personal holdings on Eagle Creek for an undisclosed amount of money. The *Río Grande Republican* noted that "$300,000 would be a low estimate for money spent."[15]

As the ranch holdings grew, the Crees took a deep interest in their investment and moved to the Southwest to look it over. Upon arriving, they tore down the old Poe home and ranch buildings and used the lumber to build their headquarters in an area in New Mexico now known as Angus.[16] The Crees were a rich, haughty family, used to being looked up to and respected because of their wealth and breeding. They did not regard their association with people of an inferior position as important to them. In the proud, free land of New Mexico they treated their cowboys as they had the Scots peasants—with condescension. They were cold and inaccessible, making themselves no more popular with their help than did Brandon Kirby, their ranch manager. Sam Jones, a neighboring rancher, summed up the reaction of the New Mexicans when he said, "I wouldn't go so far as to say that we look down on anybody, but we shore as hell don't look up to anybody."[17]

Since the purchase of the Cree Ranch had originally included many cattle, it seemed to manager Kirby that the calf crop was not

---

[14] Poe, *Buckboard Days*, 231.
[15] *Río Grande Republican*, August 8, 15, 1885.
[16] Angus now lies beneath Bonito Lake near Ruidoso, N. Mex.
[17] Mrs. Eve Ball, interview with author, May 14, 1969.

as heavy as it should be. Brandon was right. He suspected that the calves were being rustled, although he never understood why. This time the thefts were perpetrated not out of greed but because the cowboys resented being treated as "poor and ignorant help." Picking up a stray calf was their way of showing that the Crees were not as smart as they thought they were.

The Crees were concerned about the losses, and their answer to the rustling was to import Black Angus bulls from Scotland. All the New Mexico livestock were red steers, and breeding them with the Angus cattle would produce two results: the beef would be improved and the calves would be black and thus easily identifiable as Cree property.

Kirby went to Scotland and brought back 150 bulls. The animals were quarantined at a company farm in Canada and then shipped to Socorro, New Mexico, the railhead nearest to Lincoln County. In Socorro the owners of the Cree spread learned to their dismay that Black Angus bulls were not used to walking. While the red steer could easily cover fifteen or twenty miles a day (and the tough, stringy meat proved it), the Angus bulls had never walked a quarter-mile in their lives. The only alternative was to ship the stock to the ranch by buckboard, a trip of over a hundred miles.

Even this attempt to identify the Cree stock failed. The cowboys, still smarting with resentment under the treatment of the high and mighty, caused the final indignity. One by one they surreptitiously castrated the bulls.[18] Brandon Kirby retaliated by discharging many of his men, and Pat Garrett initiated an order forbidding the carrying of six-shooters on company property.

Tensions mounted, and conditions were not helped by the continued invasion of foreign money, which put the small rancher at a serious disadvantage. The choice rangeland—property that had water on it—was rapidly bought up by the moneyed interests.

The weather finally destroyed nearly all the ranchers in the region, thereby forestalling outright bloodshed. The worst drought in years struck Lincoln County in 1886, and the Angus ranch water holes quickly dried up. So many cattle expired that the commanding officer at Fort Stanton finally ordered sixty miles of barbed wire to fence in the reservation and keep the Angus cattle from dying in the military water holes.[19]

[18] *Ibid.*
[19] *Río Grande Republican*, May 15, 22, 1886.

Pat Garrett

The Cree outfit faltered and finally expired. The Crees died or moved back to Scotland, Brandon Kirby went his way, and Pat Garrett, always on the lookout for ways to make money, cast his eye on one of the biggest irrigation schemes ever to hit the South-west.

13.

A Pecos Visionary

Many muddy rivers flow and meander across the red-colored caliche of the Southwest. At times they rush and slash new beds in the sedimentary rock, and at other periods they slumber in near stagnation or vanish entirely beneath the porous sands. Of these streams the Pecos is the Río Grande's principal tributary—is, in fact, the second largest river in the Southwest. It rises in the misty Sangre de Cristo uplift in north-central New Mexico and rolls lazily southward until it joins the Río Grande eight or nine hundred miles away. In the process it drains approximately twenty-five thousand dry square miles in New Mexico and some nineteen thousand equally thirsty square miles in Texas.[1]

That portion of the Pecos known as the Middle Basin lies roughly between Las Vegas, New Mexico, and the Texas border, and is bounded on the west by the Jicarilla, Capitan, Sierra Blanca, Sacramento, and Guadalupe mountains. The Staked Plain keeps it from slipping farther east. Principal tributaries, when they bother to flow, are the Spring, Salt Creek, Río Feliz, Río Peñasco, Seven Rivers, Río Hondo (formed by a union of the Bonito and the Río Ruidoso), Black, Delaware, and Dark Canyon. Except for the heavily wooded mountain country (a very small portion of the Middle Basin), the area drained is generally considered semiarid, suitable for farming only with irrigation.

Farming and ranching were, and still are, the two stable occupations of the Pecos Valley. Post–Civil War immigrants took a long, greedy look at the valley and envisioned bountifully growing fruit and crops. They set about building irrigation systems, recklessly borrowing money to finance their schemes and just as recklessly repudiating their obligations to pay it back. In this way they

[1] Robert T. Lingle and Dee Linford, *The Pecos River Commission of New Mexico and Texas*, 3.

established a never-broken financial pattern for irrigation projects. It is no wonder that most of the early schemes failed; it is a wonder that any were successful at all.

In 1862 the Homestead Act became federal law, and settlers gradually moved into the Pecos Valley to acquire 160-acre farms. They soon realized that private irrigation financing was beyond their meager means, and they asked the government for assistance. Washington responded on July 26, 1866, by passing the Desert Land Act, which granted rights of way for canals and ditches on public lands to holders of valid water rights. The act boosted the authorized sale of land to 640 acres a person at a cost of $1.25 an acre to anyone willing to irrigate his property within three years.[2]

In 1887 New Mexico passed legislation proclaiming that "any five persons who may desire to form a company for the purpose of constructing and maintaining reservoirs and canals, or ditches and pipelines, for the purpose of irrigation, mining, manufacturing . . . shall make and sign articles of incorporation."[3] The act further allowed these corporations to raise money through the sale of stock.

While the territorial and federal governments were passing laws and trying to make the desert bloom through legal means, Pat Garrett was residing quietly in his eighteen-hundred-acre ranch three miles east of Roswell. His home was a comfortable two-story adobe house in a grove of oak and pecan trees. Bluegrass and roses near the wooden front porch added a cozy touch. In the fields grew alfalfa and grapes. Over eight hundred apple and peach trees, planted in straight rows, stretched toward the sun. Pat Garrett had finally become a gentleman-farmer.[4]

But if he lived the quiet life, it was quiet only in the sense that he was in no physical danger. He was still restless, but his energies had turned from the pursuit of badmen to the pursuit of a vision. He dreamed of seeing the Pecos Valley flourish with crops, with businesses, with schools. He envisioned room for both the lion and the lamb to lie down together. Here was a sand-hills empire waiting for a strong man with vision. Properly handled, the entire area could bloom like the Promised Land. Unfortunately, like most dreamers, Garrett was broke.

[2] *Ibid.*, 54.
[3] *Ibid.*
[4] *Roswell Daily Record*, undated article found in random papers of Mrs. George Redfield. The article was written by Major Maurice G. Fulton and was entitled "Roswell In Its Early Years."

On January 15, 1887, he purchased a one-third interest in the Texas Irrigation Ditch from William L. Holloman, a pioneer Roswell citizen. On August 15 the two men formed a partnership, calling themselves the Holloman and Garrett Ditch Company. Capital stock consisted of what they said was five thousand dollars, divided into fifty shares of one hundred dollars each.[5] Their articles of incorporation stipulated that the ditch water come from the North Spring River (less than a mile from Garrett's house), and that the ditch be no less than twelve feet wide at the mouth and no less than ten feet wide at the terminal. The depth could not be less than eighteen inches. Necessary work for improvements and repairs was charged in proportion to the stock held by each individual, and payment could be made in money or in labor. The finances, of course, existed solely on paper. Records are almost nonexistent, and what happened to the corporation is not known. No doubt it simply disintegrated.

Although the company dissolved, Pat Garrett's enthusiasm did not die with it. Thomas B. Zumwalt, Roswell resident, sold him a one-sixteenth interest in the Pioneer Ditch Company, and he paid $1,050 for one and one-half shares in the same company from Captain J. C. Lea and C. D. Bonney, Roswell farmers and businessmen. Once again it was probably a paper transaction.[6]

Still, Garrett was only marking time, investing in other men's enterprises while he studied methods of getting his own irrigation project under way. Just a couple of years earlier he had devised a grandiose scheme that would completely transform irrigation in the Pecos Valley. The thought had occurred to him as he wandered upstream along the Río Hondo. It was the most reliable river around, and the idea of tapping it for irrigation purposes made sense. But how? More astute men than Pat Garrett had sought the answers, and they had been baffled. The Hondo had deep channels, and a ditch dug to the water level would be impracticable, as well as financially unsound.

As Garrett approached the junction of Berrendo Creek, he jumped across the Hondo in a couple of long strides. Then a thought occurred. Why not dam the Río Hondo about a mile and a half below this intersection? When the water level rose to a certain

---

[5] Book G, Deed Records, 460, Carrizozo, N.Mex.; Book 2, Deed Records, 427, Roswell, N.Mex.; *Eddy* (New Mexico) *Argus*, September 29, 1893.

[6] Book 2, Deed Records, Roswell, N.Mex., 424.

height, it could be flumed across the desert.[7] The canal would be longer than any other regional ditch and would be more reliable on a year-round basis. Remote sand hills could be purchased for a modest price and resold to settlers, along with a promise of an unfailing water supply. A small profit could be made off the land sales, but the big money would come from annual renewal of water rights.

Pat needed a partner to finance the project, and Charles B. Eddy, a wealthy New Mexico cattleman and financier, expressed excitement about the idea. He dreamed just as much as Garrett—and possessed just as little practicality. Soon both men were neglecting their ranches and becoming enthusiastic promoters. They quickly learned that money was easier to count than to make.

Pat Garrett's former publisher, Charles Greene, also wanted a chunk of the financial action. He was in the Roswell neighborhood gathering material for a new book (apparently he had learned nothing from the *Billy the Kid* publishing disaster) and called on Garrett for some historical information. Pat obligingly took Greene to the Eddy-Bissell Ranch near present-day Carlsbad, New Mexico, and told him what he needed to know. The talk then turned to irrigation.

Garrett and Eddy drove Greene around the countryside and explained their plan to flume the Hondo. They promised that a fortune would be made once additional capital was obtained. Thus the two local dreamers—Pat Garrett, the taciturn former sheriff whose imagination in the promotional field completely outran his abilities, and Charles B. Eddy, the tireless, frequently quarrelsome cattleman—began work on the credulity of the equally imaginative (and nearly as broke) Greene. Slowly a plausible but far-too-expensive plan to irrigate the entire valley began to take shape.

On July 18, 1885, they organized themselves into the Pecos Valley Irrigation and Investment Company. Details about this outfit are skimpy, but it appears that Garrett and Eddy agreed to handle the promotional work and ditch rights. Charles Greene would be general manager. He and Garrett would travel to Chicago and seek more funds.[8]

It took three years and several trips back east before the company found the necessary backers and incorporated on September

---

[7] *Lincoln County Leader*, December 8, 1888, untitled article by Ash Upson. The *Leader* gave a Roswell dateline of November 23, 1888.

[8] Ralph Emerson Twichell, *Leading Facts of New Mexico History*, III, 225–29.

15, 1888. During these years Pat Garrett kept the idea alive. He sponsored the reorganization, knowing that with the advent of new financial blood he would no longer be a substantial stockholder. The new men were, besides Greene and Eddy, Luther P. Bradley, David L. Hough, James R. McKay, and Charles A. Gregory. There were nine directors, names unknown; presumably Garrett was one of them. The company cited assets of six hundred thousand dollars, divided into six thousand shares of one hundred dollars each. It bought out a small concern with the impressive title the Pecos Valley Land and Ditch Company and obtained control of the Halagueño Canal.

Garrett tied his operation into this ditch, and all together it became known as the Northern Canal, extending for approximately forty miles. It was completed in 1889 or 1890, and several branch canals and pipelines were connected to it. Huge, earth-ripping plows outlined the path, followed by twenty-mule teams dragging ditchers that further gouged out the dirt. These were followed by scrapers pulled by four to six animals. It was the biggest construction project ever to hit the Pecos Valley, and people came from miles away to observe it.

Expenses began to pile up. Construction time lagged. Payrolls were heavy and consistent. The stockholders had underestimated the costs and overestimated their ability to pay for everything. Their assets were more paper than cash. In late 1889, Charles Eddy went to Colorado Springs, Colorado, and talked to Robert Weems Tansill, the Punch Cigar manufacturer. Tansill invested a modest amount of money and helped talk James John Hagerman, a retired businessman living in Colorado Springs, into taking over the company. Hagerman was a promoter, a builder of railroads. Graybearded and grumpy, he disliked being called by his first name. While he did associate with his social and financial peers (and Eddy qualified), he did not consider the poor, half-educated Pat Garrett one of them.

Eddy chartered a special train to take Hagerman and a small party to Toyah, Texas, the nearest railroad stop to Roswell. As the capitalists piled off the train, Pat Garrett met them with a string of hacks, buggies, and buckboards, all ready for the three-day journey.

For Eddy the expenses were worth the effort. Hagerman wrote a forty-thousand-dollar check and bailed the company out of its difficulties. As for Pat Garrett, this infusion of new capital spelled the end of the ditch for him. Hagerman reorganized the corporation without consulting Garrett and changed its name from the Pecos Valley Irrigation and Investment Company to the Pecos Valley Irrigation and Improvement Company. Pat had sunk all his money and energy into these dreams and his assets were now drier than some of the local canals. With no fanfare, with no return on his investment, with no acknowledgment of his contributions, he was dismissed.

After Garrett's departure the company seemed strong. The Northern Canal—now renamed the Hagerman Canal—was completed, and settlers streamed into the Pecos Valley. Then Eddy and Hagerman began to quarrel over policy and methods of management. Eddy left the company.

In 1893 the entire country underwent a depression, and the Pecos Valley reacted in financial agony. Bankers refused to lend more money for irrigation schemes. In October the Pecos roared into a flooding fury and burst several dams. Farmers went bankrupt and could not pay their debts. Hagerman, fumbling to recover his losses, invested an additional $150,000 in repairs. It merely delayed the end. For another five years the company staggered along and in 1908 fell into receivership.[9]

Ironically, the irrigation men overlooked the most significant source of water in the Pecos Valley: artesian wells. While these dreamers struggled to make water flow uphill, to flume it across obstructions, no one drilled downward and watched the water bubble up from the ground under its own pressure. The first well was finished in 1891. By 1900 over 150 wells were operating near Roswell. With such heavy use the water table did finally drop, although better methods of pumping and new conservation laws helped equalize the remaining resource.[10]

With irrigation schemes closed to him, Pat Garrett turned to politics. For years the Roswell area had been an unwilling part of Lincoln County, eager to go its separate way. The reasons were economic and racial. The dry Pecos Valley had little in common with the moist and certainly more mountainous area of Lincoln and White Oaks. To serve on a jury, to register a deed, to handle

[9] Keleher, *The Fabulous Frontier*, 180–207.
[10] Lingle and Linford, *The Pecos River Commission*, 100–102; and G. Y. Fall, "A Study in the Development of Town Government in Hagerman, New Mexico, 1905–1948," M.A. thesis, Eastern New Mexico University, 1951, pp. 4–15.

any of the numerous and time-consuming chores that required a county seat, Roswellians had to travel by stage, horseback, and buckboard across the barren, windswept mesas to Lincoln.

The Pecos Valley and the rest of Lincoln County were substantially two different worlds in occupation and racial structure. The valley people, primarily Anglos, raised cattle and farmed; the mountain people, largely Mexican-Americans, raised sheep. Although there were a few scattered outbreaks of racial violence, such as the Horrell War in 1873–74,[11] the two ethnic groups coexisted tolerably well.

Evidently there were no serious disagreements about the wisdom of dividing the county, but controversy did break out concerning the name of the new one. The New Mexico legislature had jurisdiction over such matters, and several councilmen of Mexican origin were on its rolls. Since they controlled the necessary votes, they insisted that the new county be named in honor of Colonel J. Francisco Chávez, a distinguished member of a pioneer Spanish family who had several times served with distinction as president of the territorial council. Roswell Anglos, dismayed by the name Chávez, tried to compromise and did get the last word—or rather the last letter. They insisted that the final letter be an *s* instead of a *z*. It was reluctantly agreed to, and the county is now called Chaves.[12]

County officials were nearly all Republicans and appointed by the legislature. When the elections of 1890 rolled around, the Democrats, with Pat Garrett taking a strong interest, were determined to change things. Garrett hoped to become the new county's first elected sheriff. But he had not counted on heavy opposition in the primaries. His old friend and occasional nemesis John W. Poe had resigned as sheriff of Lincoln County and moved to the Pecos Valley. Poe successfully thrust forward Campbell Fountain, a young ranchman, to be the Democratic party nominee for sheriff. Garrett angrily tried to run as an independent, but was rejected by the voters.

Bitterly he made plans to leave New Mexico. He disposed of part ownership in an Eddy (now Carlsbad) livery stable and stageline and set his eyes toward Uvalde, Texas, southwest of San Antonio, where he planned to begin new irrigation projects, raise fast

---

[11] Fulton, *History of Lincoln the County War*, 22–25.
[12] Shinkle, *Fifty Years of Roswell History*, 109–13; Curry, *Autobiography*, 64–66.

horses, and live the good life. In April, 1891, bundling up his family, as well as Ash Upson, he moved to his new home.[13]

In Uvalde he settled down to the happiest and certainly the most peaceful period of his violent and controversial career. The country was gently rolling, with high, luxuriant grasses, large oak trees, and a few meandering streams. Pat shucked his work clothes, donned a city suit, and laid his six-shooter on the mantel. It would be a new life in a new part of the country. At his side tagged the ever-faithful, always crusty, heavy-drinking, profane Ash Upson. Seemingly he lived out of a liquor bottle, and his bouts with the demons were a continuing source of embarrassment to the Garrett family. Nevertheless, Apolinaria held her tongue and always set a place for him at the table. Obviously she was a very remarkable, tolerant, and understanding woman.

As for Ash and Pat, they continued their close relationship, although it was seriously strained at times. Once, when Pat had been out of town, he wired Upson to meet him with a buggy at Pecos Station, Texas, and drive him home to Uvalde. The train was late, and the old newspaperman wandered off to Toyah, Texas, farther up the track where he could more easily get liquid refreshment. Two days later Garrett showed up at the Pecos Station and found no Ash Upson. A hot-tempered exchange of telegrams followed:

"Come on the first train as I am in a hurry to get home," Pat wired.

"Can't leave here. Owe every man in town," Ash replied.

"If you don't come on the morning train, I will strike out and leave you," Pat threatened.

"Go to hic, hell, damn you," was Upson's response.[14]

Pat sighed, went to Toyah, and paid Upson's saloon bills. He poured him back on the train, and together they went to Pecos Station and home to Uvalde.

In 1890 there were four Garrett children. Pat fathered eight altogether, humorously referring to them as his "first crop" (those born by 1890) and his "second crop" (those born after 1896).[15] He

---

[13] The *Eddy Argus* and the *Roswell Record* carried many small articles about the coming, and going, of Garrett and Upson.

[14] Charles Siringo, *A Texas Cowboy*, 189.

[15] The children are Ida (born 1881), Dudley Poe (1886), Elizabeth (1885), Annie (1889), Patrick Floyd, Jr. (1896), Pauline (1900), Oscar (1904), and Jarvis Powers Garrett (1905). Jarvis Powers Garrett, interview with author, November 18, 1968.

gave most of his attention to Elizabeth, his blind daughter. The reasons behind her blindness, and whether or not she was blind at birth or became so shortly afterward, are and will always remain a mystery. It is also a mystery why such a rash of incredible rumors have become a part of Garrett's tradition and legend. These stories have such wide acceptance and circulation that it seems justifiable to mention them here and explain them away where possible.

The most common story is that Elizabeth was blind at birth because her father had syphilis. Pat Garrett had a yen for women outside the family circle, but there is no evidence that he had venereal disease. Another grisly tale is that he blinded her with his thumbs during a drunken rage. This is too ridiculous even to consider. And, finally, there is the charge that Elizabeth lost her sight as a result of improper medicine administered to her eyes when she was an infant. This is a possible, even probable, explanation.

Whatever the truth, and whatever the circumstances, her blindness is one of the most poignant episodes in Pat Garrett's career. If Elizabeth ever blamed her father for her condition she never mentioned it. On the contrary, all of the evidence indicates that she adored him. She became his best-known and most famous child. She was a close associate of Helen Keller, a popular public speaker, and an accomplished musician. She wrote "Oh Fair New Mexico" (the official state song) and a host of other melodies. Her spirit was vibrant and inspiring, and she never felt sorry for herself because she was too busy helping those who were less fortunate. She was a credit to her father and an asset to New Mexico.

Elizabeth penned her recollections of Pat Garrett, and, unlike most writers, she gave him a good press. She described him as "devoted" and determined that

> I should live as normal a life as possible . . . [and] have as much education as he could give me. Both of these determinations he carried out to the best of his knowledge and ability. Consequently I climbed trees, rode horseback and went freely over the place alone. In due time I received a high school education and fundamental music training at the Texas School for the Blind in Austin.[16]

She wrote that her father shared with her "all of the wonders and beauties and secrets of [the universe]. This intimacy brought me to the tender side of his nature. There was never a time when my

[16] Shinkle, *Reminiscences of Roswell Pioneers,* 183–85; *Roswell Record,* October 7, 1937.

questions were rebuffed. Instead he met them with patience and truth as nearly as he knew it."

Elizabeth claimed that her father liked the kind of music that "he could pat his foot to." He was not musically inclined but frequently asked her to sing to him. One of his favorite songs was "Sing, Smile, Slumber" by Charles Gounod, which for some reason he insisted upon calling "Six Miles Longer." Once he asked her to sing something about a rose, and she sang everything she could remember about the flower. When she finished, he calmly remarked, "Well, I just wondered how many songs you knew about roses."[17]

Elizabeth related a story that he once told on himself. Back when Lew Wallace was governor of New Mexico, several cowboys gave him an Indian blanket. Garrett was chosen to make the presentation and a speech to go with it. When the governor appeared at the ceremony, the cowboys respectfully lined up in front of him. Pat stepped forward, choked, and said, "Governor Lew Wallace of the Territory of New Mexico, I ——" Then he grew self-conscious, stopped, gulped, and stepped backward onto the toes of a cowboy behind him.

In that awful moment he realized that the carefully memorized speech had fled his mind. He quickly dug into his shirt pocket for a copy. It was not there. Determined to see his talk through, he stepped forward again, turned red, stammered, and said exactly the same thing. Turning in desperation, he grabbed up the blanket and with long strides walked up to Wallace. "Here Guv," he blurted out. "Take the damn thing."[18]

Little is known about the childhood relationship of Pat's other children with their father. There is a small glimpse of Ida, his firstborn, who insisted on tagging along beside Pat as he showed neighbor J. H. Carper his Roswell irrigation ditches. The six-year-old Ida darted frequently between his long legs, provoking a warning to stay out of the way or he would toss her into the canal. The little girl ignored the warning, and he shoved her in with his boot. Since the water was only a foot or so deep, she came out sputtering and wringing her clothes.

"So your father kicked you in the ditch," Mr. Carper said and grinned.

"Yes," the little girl replied. "I didn't think the old —— would do it."[19]

---

[17] *Ibid.*
[18] *Ibid.*

Always following Pat Garrett around were his memories of the Lincoln County War. In Uvalde he reached out to help a participant of that struggle, one who had fought against him. Garrett learned that Billie Wilson, the counterfeit-money passer who had been captured with Billy the Kid at Stinking Springs, was working as a United States customs inspector near Langtry, Texas. Billie had been convicted, but had escaped from jail, run to Texas, reformed, married, and started a family. When Garrett learned of Wilson's presence and that he was a law-abiding citizen, he sent word that he would use his influence to obtain a presidential pardon. Over a year later, after Pat had become sheriff of Doña Ana County, New Mexico, Wilson received his full pardon. Quietly Garrett had talked to several prominent New Mexicans, obtained their signatures on a petition, and forwarded it to President Grover Cleveland. The president thought that Garrett's judgment of the youth was correct and he promptly approved it.

Garrett's judgment was, in this instance, excellent. Billie Wilson never again drifted into trouble. He became a lawman and was destined to die tragically in the line of duty. On June 14, 1918, while sheriff of Terrell County, Texas, he attempted to arrest a drunken cowboy at the railroad station. Wilson was acquainted with the youth and thought that he could handle him without firearms. However, as he approached the baggage shed, the man fired. Sheriff Wilson, a reformed counterfeiter and gunman who had gone straight thanks to Pat Garrett, died with an outlaw's bullet in his heart.

But Pat Garrett was not in Uvalde just to chat with his children or to save outlaws with prices on their heads. He was there to do many things, especially to race horses at the well-known fairgrounds racetrack just west of town. He made many friends, one of whom was Herbert "Hub" Bowles, a respected local rancher. Bowles thought that Pat had the best "mile horse" in central Texas, but the animal was hard to match because few race horses could run a mile. Finally someone brought in an out-of-town horse specifically to challenge Garrett's animal. The betting was heavy.

Contest rules were simple. There would be three races of a mile each, with a rest period in between. The best horse would have to win twice.

[19] *Ibid.*, 48. Carper related the story as happening to a Garrett boy. Since none of the boys were old enough at the time, it must be assumed that he was mistaken and that a Garrett girl was involved.

Garrett's horse lost the first race, but his opponent's horse could not be reined in after the first lap, and it continued on around the track for another turn—one that did not count—while Garrett's animal rested. Pat then won the second and third heats and collected the money, even though his horse had run only three miles while the other had run four.[20]

Pat named one of his best mares after John Nance Garner, who eventually became vice-president of the United States under Franklin D. Roosevelt. Little is known about this friendship. Few records are available, and neither man mentioned the other very often after parting in 1896. In the early 1950's, in response to a query from Oscar Garrett, who asked about his father, John Garner scribbled shakily, "I knew your father as an honorable, honest, patriotic American. When movies slander him, they slander their betters."[21]

In spite of his many friends, however, Pat Garrett was restless in Uvalde. On March 22, 1894, he wrote his wife from New Orleans, where he had gone to race horses: "There is no chance in the world to make a dollar in Uvalde. When I get home we will think the matter of leaving the country over, and see what we think best."[22]

Events were moving fast, perhaps too fast. Ash Upson died on October 6, 1894, and was buried in Uvalde. Pat Garrett paid the funeral expenses. For the next fifteen months Garrett continued to talk about moving. He wanted to leave, to start his dreams again. But where? Then on February 1, 1896, Colonel Albert J. Fountain, the man who had defended Billy the Kid at Mesilla and who had been a political bedfellow of Garrett's during the 1882 elections, mysteriously disappeared in New Mexico's White Sands. Henry, his young son, vanished with him. The authorities feared murder. Once again the Territory of New Mexico needed Pat Garrett.

[20] Florence Fenley, *Oldtimers of Southwest Texas*, 107, 138.

[21] John Nance Garner to Oscar Garrett, undated letter, copy in Sonnichsen Papers, University of Texas at El Paso Archives.

[22] Garrett, *Life*, 24.

14.

Murder and Mystery in White Sands

Almost nobody in modern times associates the White Sands of southeastern New Mexico with Pat Garrett, murder, high tragedy, or mystery. Travelers whizzing down Highway 70 in their high-powered automobiles pointed toward the pleasant city of Las Cruces rarely reflect that less than a century ago this area swarmed with Garrett-led posses, that the sheriff hoped to find new fame and fortune for himself here, that he planned to cap an already remarkable career with an exploit even more notable than the killing of Billy the Kid. Instead he found only more frustrations and ruined dreams. His own death in these parts was to become as big and as controversial a mystery as the one he was trying to solve.

The White Sands has not always been a vacationland. Today children happily slide down the gleaming mountains of white gypsum, filling the air with laughter and their shoes and trousers with the gritty, sandlike mineral. Honest citizens of bygone days usually avoided the eighteen-mile-long, three-mile-wide stretch of awesome wasteland. In winter the wind whistled across its naked dunes as if blowing off a glacier. In summer the intense heat drove out the rattlesnakes and most other forms of life. It was to be near this treeless, waterless, remote site that the United States was to explode the world's first atomic bomb in 1945.

The region is ruffled in waves like a frozen lake and sprawls in a natural basin a few miles from the eastern slope of the San Andres Mountains. Less than a dozen miles to the northeast lies Tularosa. On the southwest is Mesilla. Though the wind-sculptured sands never gave more than temporary rest to local or migrating outlaws, people feared the lonely stretch of rutted road that gouged its way through the mesquite-covered dunes between Tularosa and Mesilla. The area's remoteness provided sanctuary to the lone, or nearly alone, bushwhacker. Many travelers simply rode into the sands and never rode out again.

Several well-known murders took place in or near the White Sands, one of the earliest being that of George Nesmith, his wife, and his eight-year-old adopted daughter. Nesmith was an honest, hard-working Scotsman who owned a portion of Blazer's Mill, the scene of the Buckshot Roberts fight with Billy the Kid's bunch. When Dr. J. H. Blazer bought out the Nesmiths, the family moved to Three Rivers, fifteen miles north of Tularosa, and began farming.

Situated near the Nesmiths was the ranch of Pat Coghlan, the fiery, muscular cattle-rustling "King of Tularosa." A transplanted, ambitious Irishman, Coghlan had migrated to Three Rivers in 1873. Within the next few years he and Billy the Kid had a hand-shaking agreement to pool their nefarious talents in money-making opportunities. Billy would rustle John Chisum's stock and deliver them to Coghlan. The cattle king would butcher or sell them live on the hoof.

The months passed, and Coghlan prospered. He yearned for more land to expand his enterprise and hide his operations. Vainly he tried to purchase the Nesmith farm. Finally he gave up and offered Nesmith and his wife employment as general caretakers, hoping that this would keep them quiet. Coghlan thought every-one's principles were as easily purchased as his own. He was mis-taken. The old couple were naïve and thus considerably shaken when they learned that Pat Coghlan was not an honest man, that he was the object of suspicious scrutiny by the Panhandle Cattle Association. When cowboy detective Charles Siringo came nosing around, the Nesmiths told him what they knew. Siringo soon be-came convinced that he had enough evidence to change Coghlan's address to that of the territorial prison.

In April, 1882, Pat Coghlan went on trial in Mesilla. Witnesses were John William Poe, deputy United States marshal at Roswell; Charles Siringo; and Pat Garrett. Subpoenaed to testify were the Nesmiths, two terrified people who feared retaliation from Cogh-lan. Mrs. Nesmith in particular dreaded the one-hundred-mile wagon trip to the county seat. "I'm afraid to go by the White Sands," she whispered. "So many terrible things have happened there."[1]

Her worries were well founded. On August 17, while traveling to court, the family disappeared. Three weeks later their bodies

[1] Sophie Poe, *Buckboard Days*, 100–101; C. L. Sonnichsen, *Tularosa*, 252–56.

were found near White Sands, decomposed and almost unrecognizable. While no one accused Coghlan of the actual killing, everyone suspected that he had had a hand in the murders. A manhunt spread across the Southwest and Mexico. Eventually the hunters were successful, although it took several years of diligent effort to capture the two slayers, Máximo Apodaca and Rupert Lara. Lara was tried and hanged. Apodaca stoically accepted a life sentence, but committed suicide shortly afterward, allegedly to stop a dead child's cries from haunting him at night.

Both murderers implicated Pat Coghlan as the paymaster. He went to trial, but a jury set him free. Yet he was at liberty in name only. Almost from the very moment he walked out of the courtroom, his world went into a financial spin. Only death put a permanent end to his troubles.

Coghlan had never understood bankers. Ledger sheets confused him. Lawyers demanded and took a large portion of his estate for defense costs. The rustling business began drying up, especially when Pat Garrett buried Billy the Kid, Coghlan's prime source of illegal income, under several feet of Fort Sumner caliche. The former cattle king began to borrow money, ignoring the vital statistics of interest rates. He died penniless in El Paso on January 22, 1911, and is buried in Concordia Cemetery.

But while the Nesmith killings created headlines, and while the entire Southwest reacted with shock and outrage, the crime was not sufficiently heinous to prevent an even more notable slaying in the White Sands within a decade. Involved were local feuds, politics, and personalities. Unlike those of the Nesmiths, the bodies of the next victims were never found; also unlike the Nesmiths, the mystery of their deaths was never solved in a court of law. Yet at least one of the murderers did not go unpunished. Folklore says that he too heard a child crying out at night. Troubled by conscience, the killer confessed to friends before his death.

The area around Mesilla, New Mexico, is a quiet, placid land. Generally it has always been this way, that is, except in the late 1800's, when violent and controversial men invaded it. From the east came Albert Bacon Fall, eventually destined to become President Warren G. Harding's secretary of the interior and then to sink into ignominy as a result of the Teapot Dome scandals. But as of now he was simply a young attorney searching for political soil in which to sink his roots. From Texas came the soft-spoken but dangerous Oliver M. Lee, cattleman and gunman. Although a familiar figure around Mesilla and Las Cruces, he was actually a resident of the Tularosa Valley and was said by a Pinkerton detective to be a "cold-blooded murderer."[2] And from California came Albert Jennings Fountain, also an attorney seeking a political berth. These giants of their time would eventually collide, and the shock wave of that collision would not subside for generations.

Colonel Fountain was supposedly born in 1838 on Staten Island, New York.[3] His place of birth cannot be pinpointed any more than the manner of his death can be proved for certain. Like the enemies who opposed him, he was, and still is, a controversial figure. His way of life, the good he did, if any, and whether or not his death was the result of a conspiracy, are still matters for speculation and argument. Even now no two men seem able to agree on whether he was the most loved or the most hated man in Mesilla Valley. Passions are as everlasting as the sands that hide the mystery.

A strange fact about this remarkable individual is that his name was not Fountain at all but simply Albert Jennings. Probably he took the Fountain from his mother's maiden name, Fontaine. As a youthful fiddlefoot he traveled around the world, settling in California in 1859, where he became a newspaperman for the *Sacramento Union*. The paper soon hustled him off to Central America for a firsthand report of William Walker's filibustering expedition. After returning to the States, he wanted to take part in the Civil War and moved east with the First California Infantry Volunteers. By 1862 the unit had straggled into New Mexico, where the twenty-four-year-old soldier met and married the fourteen-year-old Mariana Pérez. Many claim that Fountain was ashamed of his Mexican wife, a common attitude, for many Anglos took a condescending view of anyone whose skin pigmentation was darker than their own. If true, his shame did not affect his performance as a husband, for Mariana bore him twelve children.

Pocketing his discharge at war's end, Fountain, sporting a droopy mustache and a stocky frame, organized a civilian volunteer company of militiamen to fight Apaches. When an uneasy peace had been restored, the restless Fountain moved forty miles south of Mesilla to El Paso, Texas, and started his legal and political career.

[2] Pinkerton Reports, March 6, 1896, Sonnichsen Papers, University of Texas at El Paso Archives.

[3] See Arrell M. Gibson, *The Life and Death of Colonel Albert Jennings Fountain*, for a thorough, though onesided, biography of Fountain.

He was elected a state senator, although his quarrelsome nature involved him in numerous political controversies. One argument blazed into a gunfight. Fountain caught a bullet and staggered off, returning the same day to shoot and kill his adversary. Fearing that his political future in Texas had waned, he returned to Mesilla in 1875.[4]

In New Mexico local violence was growing. Victorio and his Warm Springs Apaches had been marauding, particularly in areas farther north near Lake Valley and Piños Altos. As the Indians were gradually exterminated or forced back into Mexico, desperadoes whom the Rangers had chased out of Texas moved into the territory. Practically all these fugitives reverted to their former practices, striking in sudden raids from such outlaw strongholds as Rincón, Silver City, Seven Rivers, Kingston, and Socorro. The renegades had a success story that even the most dishonest Santa Fe politician might envy.

With rustling rampant on the cattle ranges and with killings as regular and almost as dependable as the spring floods along the Río Grande, Fountain reorganized the militia to bring law and order back to southern New Mexico. Very few Anglos joined the volunteer, semimilitary group, principally because Fountain considered the Texans as the significant lawbreakers who needed jailing. He thus recruited primarily from citizens of Mexican descent and ignored the Americans who jeered at his followers as "Fountain's Greasers."[5]

The militia first chased down the John Kinney gang, perhaps the most dangerous band of rustlers ever to operate in New Mexico.[6] Doroteo Sáenz, one of Kinney's lieutenants, and a gunman who boastingly called himself the "Human Tiger" were shot and killed while "trying to escape." Few people mourned their passing, even though rumors drifted about that the deaths were more on the order of executions than justifiable homicide.

With the breakup of the Kinney outlaws, Fountain turned his fury on the Farmington gang, who hid out and operated near the Black Range above Silver City. In no time at all the members of this wild bunch were dead, scattered, or in jail. A triumphant Fountain returned to Mesilla.

---

[4] Sonnichsen, *Tularosa*, 59.

[5] *Mesilla Independent*, July 14, 1877; *Río Grande Republican*, August 29, 1885.

[6] Philip J. Rasch, "John Kinney: King of the Rustlers," *English Westerners Brand Book*, Vol. IV (October), 1961.

The colonel now resumed his law practice, taking as clients several noted criminals. If his judgment in doing so confused and confounded ordinary citizens, as an attorney he understood his own motives perfectly well. The law was the law; a dollar was a dollar; and as long as a man rested in jail, he was entitled to as fair a trial as his finances would permit. In 1881 he defended Billy the Kid for the murder of Sheriff William Brady. Though the Kid lost and was sentenced to be hanged, Fountain seems to have argued the case as best he could, considering the circumstances and the Kid's reputation. In 1882, James Patterson, Anthony Price, and Cris Moesner were charged with separate acts of vicious murder. Public opinion demanded that all should be hanged, but defense attorney Fountain talked the juries into recommending short prison sentences.

Fountain's successes were so notable that the *Río Grande Republican* could not resist an angry comment: "Give us a Mexican jury, with Fountain for a lawyer . . . and we can murder any man we please with impunity."[7]

Though Colonel Fountain relished the rough-and-tumble of courtroom drama, his political ambitions led him in 1877 to help establish the *Mesilla Independent*, a Republican party newspaper which he coedited. Under his leadership a campaign was begun against fashionable sins, ranging from crooked politicians to the priestly hierarchy. Nothing was sacred except motherhood, his own opinions, and those of other Republicans. He wrote long columns of reminiscences, all describing himself as a combination frontier Solomon and Horatio at the bridge. Modesty was not one of his virtues.

In 1887 the political fortunes of Colonel Albert Jennings Fountain began to slide. That was the year Albert Bacon Fall came to southern New Mexico. Fall was born in Kentucky on November 26, 1861,[8] and for a while settled in Texas before moving to New Mexico to begin practice as an attorney and Democratic party figure. For a short time Fall and Fountain got along together. Then the relationship ended, and the two men not only sought a political and personal separation but complete destruction of each other. Both men were personally ruthless, quick-tempered, and convinced of their own righteousness. They were proud and egocentric, and

---

[7] *Río Grande Republican*, April 22, 1882.

[8] See Albert B. Fall, *The Memoirs of Albert B. Fall* (ed. by David B. Stratton).

each had plenty of raw courage. And both men had staked their lives on the forthcoming Mesilla Valley political struggle.

Fountain was a born entertainer, a ham actor, a showoff who loved to wear his militia uniform in court. He loved speeches and parades. Fall was more somber, not as exhibitionistic. With his long wavy hair and broad-brimmed Stetson setting off his slender frame draped in a Prince Albert coat, he was the master of the underplayed role. He possessed a remarkable sense of timing, both inside and outside the courtroom.

Fall was a southerner; Fountain a Yankee. This fact alone gave them reason to hate each other. Fall was young, ambitious, and power-hungry; Fountain middle-aged, ambitious, and already a political power. Fall sought to topple his adversary from his high position; Fountain struggled to hang on.

As Fountain continued to make life difficult for the Texans, most of whom he considered outlaws or men with criminal connections, many members of the Anglo minority became suspicious of his motives and sought legal and moral support elsewhere. In addition to this "outlaw business," they distrusted him because he drew most of his political strength from the Mexican community. To make matters worse he had married a Mexican girl and thus had "gone native."

Fall recognized the needs of the Anglos and solicited their patronage. He also sought to broaden his power base by establishing the *Independent Democrat* in Las Cruces, a predominantly Anglo town about five miles northeast of Mesilla. Naturally, the views of Fall's newspaper did not coincide with those of Fountain's.

From their newspaper podiums the two men clashed in the 1888 elections for a seat in New Mexico's house. Fountain won. Though the results were close, they were humiliating to a man as sensitive as Fall. The winner congratulated himself and rode off to Santa Fe, where he became speaker of the house. In the meantime Fall stayed in Las Cruces, studying his mistakes and gathering more insight about his prospects for future political glory. Albert Fall needed a change in strategy. In order to get moving his Texans would have to become more active, both inside and outside the polling places. They would have to influence voters.

In 1889, Oliver M. Lee stepped through Fall's doorway and introduced himself. Lee had a reputation of being a good man with a gun. He owned a sprawling ranch near the mouth of Dog Canyon at the western base of the Sacramento Mountains. An iron-nerved individual who backed down from no man, Lee often had need of a good lawyer. A remarkable friendship began with this meeting.

With Lee supporting Fall, Democratic party fortunes took an upswing. In the 1892 elections Fall did so well that the alarmed Republicans called on the militia to guard the polls. Fall countered by sending for Lee and his fighting men. Two of the gunmen were Bill McNew, a hardened Texan with ice-blue eyes, and Jim Gililland, much younger than his companions but prone to whisky and motivated by a desire to prove that he feared no one.

Lee's riders filtered into town all night long and by morning had taken up positions on the Las Cruces rooftops. When the militiamen under W. H. H. Llewellyn and Captain Thomas Brannigan marched up the street, Fall stepped into the road and yelled, "Llewellyn, get the hell out of here with that damned militia or I will have you all killed!"[9] The militia hesitated, stumbled about for a few minutes, and left. The Republicans lost the election—and cried foul. Democratic officeholders were not about to investigate themselves. The matter was tabled and regional attention turned to other troubles.

During the last few years drought had spread death and financial panic across the Tularosa and Mesilla valleys. Water and range rights, always important, became legal and literal battlegrounds where desperate men took desperate chances to survive. Large and small cattlemen alike maneuvered for more moisture and room. Everyone felt the economic pinch, and men of varying factions cocked their guns and began lining up against each other. Already the big operators were accusing men like Oliver Lee of rustling and murder.

It is difficult to analyze and judge these antagonists: As C. L. Sonnichsen, the authority on southwestern feuds, has expressed it: "In real life the villains and the honest men seemed to get mixed up together. The more one knows about what went on, the more one hesitates to pass positive judgments about who was right and who was wrong. And always one has to remember that this was a game in which each side used a different rule book."[10]

Oliver Lee struggled against the big cattlemen until he gradually became one himself, extending his range and line shacks past the southern tip of the Sacramentos. His cattle multiplied and wan-

---

[9] Keleher, *The Fabulous Frontier*, 215.
[10] Sonnichsen, *Tularosa*, 84.

dered across the entire Tularosa Valley. It was only a question of time before rustlers moved in on him too.

In February, 1893, Lee killed Matt Coffelt and Charley Rhodius for rustling his cattle along the high mesa about ten miles northeast of El Paso. Afterward he used the reliable old plea of self-defense.

Far above the Lee ranchhouse, in the Sacramento's Dog Canyon, lived a French recluse named François Jean Rochas, better known as "Frenchy." On December 26, 1894, three unidentified riders came calling. They greeted the old man with rifle fire, and the recluse, who had clung so tenaciously to his clear-water rights and his fruit orchards, died. Lee was suspected as an assassin, but no court action materialized. Within ten years Lee had taken over Frenchy's holdings and was piping water to the valley below.[11]

Lee's troubles were mounting, however. Before Rochas' death, twenty-one cattle barons had met in Las Cruces in March, 1894, and formed the Southeastern New Mexico Livestock Association. Objectives were to stop the rustling. Lee joined. Colonel Albert Fountain became association lawyer and accepted an assignment for the infighting and prosecution. He began his task quickly and reportedly sent several outlaws to the penitentiary. Criminals captured or run off were primarily individuals of little consequence in the over-all rustling panorama. Rustlers still operated freely.

Colonel Fountain set his prosecution sights on Lee. For a long time evidence and rumor had linked him to disappearing cattle; his neighbors' accusations ranged from thefts of one stolen steer to entire herds. His reputation as a gunman indicated that here was a man accustomed to taking what he wanted. The tough companions often seen in his company did not lessen the suspicion.

Because of Lee's and Fall's close association, a conviction of Lee might have serious political consequences for Fall. So, with his two-pronged emotionalism gathering momentum, Fountain channeled all his recent frustrations and bitterness into a legal and moral drive to rid southern New Mexico of outlaws and put an end to Fall's career.

As the net of investigation began closing in on the Lee Ranch,

[11] On June 16, 1908, Oliver Lee testified concerning water piped down from land he "owned" in Dog Canyon and made available to the railroads. He made no mention of Frenchy. See *Hill and Shepherd* v. *Alamogordo Water Works Company*, Case No. 454, Sixth Judicial Court, Otero County, N. Mex. The case file is in the University of Texas at El Paso Archives, Southern Pacific Railroad Collection.

Fountain wrote a long letter to the home office of the cattle association. In it he accused Lee's men of stealing and selling, or killing hundreds of animals.[12] However, only one bona fide case of cattle theft had to be proved, and cowboy detective Les Dow furnished it.

Dow pretended to be representing one of the roundup crews working a large herd of cattle south of the Sacramentos. When he noticed Bill McNew of Lee's outfit cut a steer whose brand looked suspicious, he rode up and inquired if McNew owned that particular animal.

"Yes," said McNew.

"Well, I'll buy him from you. I'll give you twenty dollars."

"All right. I'll take it," McNew said, and he stuck the money in his pants.[13]

Dow herded the steer away, killed, and skinned it. Sure enough, the original brand showed up on the flesh portion of the hide. This identifying mark was all that Fountain needed. He decided to move against Lee.

Fountain realized that he was now entering the most dangerous time of his life. The Lees, the Falls, and their associates had not become local powers by being passive bystanders. All were tough, dangerous, courageous men. Sometimes they had killed to get where they were. If necessary they would not hesitate to kill again.

It was a cold January 12, 1896, when Fountain left Mesilla for Lincoln to secure the necessary indictments. He believed that an attempt on his life would come soon. His wife, Mariana, sensed his concern and looked half-sick with worry. She insisted that he ask a few neighbors to tag along for protection. He laughed her aside. As a last resort she pleaded that he take nine-year-old Henry Fountain. "They wouldn't take a chance on hurting a little boy," she said.[14]

The two Fountains rode out of Mesilla, heavily bundled against the cold. Slowly the buckboard bounced past familiar landmarks—San Augustine Pass, Chalk Hill at the point of White Sands, Pellman's Well, La Luz, Tularosa—and on into Lincoln.

Inside the courthouse, from which, about fifteen years before, Billy the Kid had made his sensational escape and killed two guards, Les Dow stepped before the grand jury and spread his

---

[12] Pinkerton Reports, September 16, 1896.

[13] Sam Fairchild, Alamogordo, N. Mex., to C. L. Sonnichsen, November 8, 1942, Sonnichsen Papers, University of Texas at El Paso Archives.

[14] Sonnichsen, *Tularosa*, 116.

cowskin on the rough floor. Slowly evidence and testimony began accumulating against the area's leading rustlers. Finally, when nothing more could be presented, thirty-two indictments were handed down. The most important were Case No. 1489, *Territory of New Mexico* v. *William McNew and Oliver Lee*, Charge Larceny of Cattle; and Case No. 1890, *Territory of New Mexico* v. *William McNew and Oliver Lee*, Charge Defacing Brands. As the hearing ended, an unidentified person handed Albert Fountain a piece of paper. On it he read: "If you drop this we will be your friends. If you go on with it, you will never reach home alive."[15]

On Thursday afternoon, January 30, Colonel Fountain and his son drove to the home of Dr. J. H. Blazer, just outside Mescalero, eighteen miles from Lincoln. After outlining to Blazer his fears about his safety, Fountain spent an uneasy night. Early the next morning, as the sun broke through the heavy mist, he noticed two men riding behind his buggy. They never approached close enough to be recognized. He hurried on, lashing his horses into a swift pace. That night he and Henry stayed in La Luz, a fig-growing community nine miles south of Tularosa.

On Saturday, February 1, the Fountains began the last lap of their journey. They drove, generally silent, across the wide and lonesome valley toward Chalk Hill, each nursing his own thoughts about the warmth and safety of home or the silent danger that rode near them. Once the colonel looked back and saw not two men but three. The riders still made no attempt to get closer.

Toward noon Fountain stopped and talked to Santos Alvarado, the mail carrier from Las Cruces to Tularosa. Fountain expressed some concern about the riders but nevertheless pushed on to Pellman's Well, where he paused briefly to feed and water his horses. Before him loomed the long cut through Chalk Hill, and beyond that the San Augustine Pass and Mesilla.

As Fountain trotted his horses away from the well, he paused to chat with Saturnino Barela, another mail carrier. Barela noticed the same three men and pleaded with Fountain to return to Luna's Well and go with him to Mesilla the next morning.

Fountain hesitated, considered the suggestion, and then declined. His wife expected them, and besides, little Henry had a cold. Turning his team into the icy blast whipping down from Chalk Hill, he and his son drove on—and disappeared forever.

[15] *Ibid.*, 117.

15.

Pat Garrett Answers a Call

By noon Sunday, February 2, Colonel Fountain and his son had not arrived in Mesilla. As darkness neared his waiting family grew more tense and fearful, pacing restlessly, asking the same unanswerable questions over and over, listening for familiar hoofbeats on the road. Finally a wagon rumbled to a corral gate at the rear of the house. Everyone rushed outside, expecting to see the colonel's bulky form. Instead they greeted the shaggy, hulking figure of Barela, the mail carrier. He hesitantly asked whether the two Fountains had arrived safely.

Mariana Fountain fainted. Her sons carried her inside the house and returned to hear Barela's story. He explained his meeting and conversation with the colonel on the previous day and then described how only a couple of hours before, on the Mesilla side of Chalk Hill, he had found tracks indicating that the Fountain buggy had swerved off the road and stopped. Nearby were signs that several horses had nervously shuffled about. Nothing now remained: not the animals, the wagon, or the Fountains. Barela suspected that the colonel and the three unknown riders had finally met.

Albert Fountain, Jr., hastily organized a small posse, composed primarily of Mexican friends. They hurried under overcast skies and through threatening weather to the east side of San Augustine Pass. An hour later Major W. H. H. Llewellyn led a somewhat better-equipped posse into the same vicinity. By the time everyone arrived, the cloud cover had partially broken away. A cold, brisk wind blew through the mesquite, and a few stars poked sparkling holes in the black canopy.

Without any logic the posses began a disorganized search for the Fountain trail, wandering back and forth, sideways, up and down the dark road, sometimes bumping into one another. Finally, half-frozen and weary, the men rested. Early the next morning, February 3, they found the spot Barela had described.

Nothing remained to tell a complete story. The buggy tracks cutting through the small sand- and brush-covered dirt hills indicated that the Fountain horses had suddenly swerved off the road and galloped madly for nearly a hundred yards. Their pause had been a long one: scattered about were animal droppings, cigarette papers, and many hoofprints. It was clear that three men had intercepted the Fountains.

Behind a clump of bushes near the roadside were two empty cartridges, a knee print, and a footprint. The posse figured that a bushwhacker had knelt there and fired warning shots at the figures in the buggy, forcing them off the main thoroughfare and onto the desert. The searchers further assumed, because of a lack of bloodstains on the road, that the rifleman had not shot anyone, at least at that moment. Later a more thorough search of the entire scene revealed a huge pool of dried blood where the buggy had stopped. The waist-high bushes had hidden the stains in the initial, superficial search.

The posses wasted little time combing the area. As yet no one knew for certain what had happened. Possibly the Fountains might still be alive. After taking some boot measurements with a broken stick, the searchers rode due east, following wagon-wheel tracks across the rough country.

That afternoon, twelve miles from Chalk Hill, they came upon the abandoned buggy. They also found Henry's hat, the rebozo given to the older Fountain by his wife, the threatening note he had received in Lincoln, and his cartridge belt with twelve bullets missing. The belt had been full when he left Tularosa.[1] Missing were practically all of Colonel Fountain's possessions, including the court papers he carried in his wooden dispatch case.

No positive evidence turned up proving that the Fountains were dead, though the abandoned buggy led to that conclusion. The posse pushed on, grimly trailing hoofprints that pointed east toward the Jarilla Mountains, in remote, desolate, mineral-rich country fifty miles north of El Paso, fifty miles south of Tularosa, fifty miles east of Las Cruces, and twenty miles west of the Sacramento Mountains. Between the Jarillas and the Sacramentos lay Wildy Well, soon to be the scene of a gunfight between Pat Gar-

[1] Pinkerton Reports, April 13, 1896, Sonnichsen Papers, University of Texas at El Paso Archives.

rett and Oliver Lee's bunch. A few miles north and east of Wildy
Well was Lee's Dog Canyon ranchhouse. The members of the posse
hunched in their saddles, suffering from the bitter weather and
paying heavily for their haste in leaving Las Cruces and Mesilla
without properly equipping themselves. The icy wind cut sharply
through their outer clothing, their woolen ponchos growing heavy
and damp from hours of alternating sleet and snow. Only two or
three men had tied blankets and tins of food behind their saddles.
And so they rode until it became too dark to go on. Sliding stiffly
from their saddles, they huddled in aching misery around a couple
of small, flickering campfires that frequently died during the gusts
of raw wind.

The next morning the posse staggered on, freezing, thirsty, and
hungry, but unrelenting in their drive, determined to catch and
force an accounting from the three unknown riders. To the east
the pursuers trudged to within sight of the Jarillas. Here the fugitives had divided their trail. One man had turned in the direction
of Wildy Well. The other two had veered toward the Sacramento
Mountains. The posse split up too. Carl Clausen, Fountain's son-
in-law and a former Indian fighter, and Luis Herrera, a friend,
peeled off from the main group to pursue the lone rider. Major
Llewellyn and five volunteers trailed the other two. The remaining
possemen took the buggy and returned to Mesilla.

Llewellyn's searchers were too cold, too tired, too hungry, and
too thirsty to think out the purpose of their journey or to carry on
effectively any longer. They pursued their men until they were
within two or three miles from Oliver Lee's ranch where, instead
of going farther, they paused to argue about asking Lee questions
concerning the Fountains. During the discussion two of Lee's cowboys drove a herd of cattle between them and the ranchhouse,
effectively obliterating the trail. The discouraged posse turned
and, without considering Lee any further, rode back to Las Cruces.

The ride home was even more brutal than the trailing. The cold
grew more intense, forcing the men to dismount every few miles,
build fires, and exercise painful circulation back into frostbitten
hands and feet. At about four in the morning, they reached the
W. W. Cox Ranch on the east slope of the Oregon Mountains.
They were in pathetic physical condition and no closer to a solution
to the Fountain disappearance than they were when they started.[2]

Clausen and Herrera had only slightly better luck. Doggedly

[2] Sonnichsen, *Tularosa*, 129.

174

they clung to the lone horseman's trail until it terminated at the Wildy Well line shack. Inside were Oliver Lee and four other men —all unfriendly and all unsympathetic to the posse's plight. Lee sneered when Clausen asked him to help search for the Fountains. He claimed no personal interest in their disappearance, regardless of what might have happened. Indicating that he had better things to do with his time, Lee left. As he rode away, Clausen carefully inspected his horse's tracks, finding them to be the same set of hoofprints that he had been following. He and Herrera returned to Mesilla and reported their findings.[3]

During the following days and weeks southwesterners reacted in confusion about the Fountains. No bodies were ever discovered, and it became a popular pastime to speculate about where the graves might be. Everyone from Indian scouts to fortunetellers had a theory, but time passed and nothing ever turned up.

Of course, not everyone agreed that Fountain was dead. His wife was regarded as "somewhat jealous,"[4] and perhaps she had reason to be. Maybe her husband had simply grown tired of her and entered a new life.

Fall's *Independent Democrat* took advantage of these rumors, publishing tales that Fountain had been seen in Chicago, St. Louis, San Francisco, and so on. One story had him joining the revolutionists in Cuba. Articles hinted of a younger woman whom he had taken for a mistress. Other southwestern newspapers were appalled by these statements. The *El Paso Daily Herald*, the *El Paso Times*, the *Eddy* (New Mexico) *Argus*, the *Las Vegas* (New Mexico) *Epic*, the *Santa Fe New Mexican*, and the *Denver News*, among others, denounced such allegations. Most pointed out the lack of law and order in southern New Mexico. They argued that unless the Fountain mystery was solved statehood for New Mexico might be postponed for decades.

Governor William T. Thornton shared the territory's humiliation. He offered a two-thousand-dollar reward and a promise of "full and complete pardon to any party connected with the crime —except the principal—who will first turn state's evidence and furnish the testimony for the arrest and conviction of his associates."[5] The Doña Ana County commissioners upped the offer by five

---

[3] *El Paso Daily Herald*, June 7, 1899; *Río Grande Republican*, April 15, 1898.

[4] Pinkerton Reports, March 5, 1896, Sonnichsen Papers, University of Texas at El Paso Archives.

[5] *Río Grande Republican*, February 21, 1896.

hundred dollars, and the Masonic Lodge of New Mexico pledged ten thousand dollars more. Several businessmen said that they would contribute their "fair share." The total reward money amounted to over twelve thousand dollars—enough to make the most famous manhunter in the West take notice.

And back in Uvalde, Texas, Pat Garrett was indeed taking notice. Comments and stories reaching him from the territory indicated that he was regarded as the logical lawman to become sheriff and hunt down and capture the Fountain killers.

Although Pat Garrett had been in semiretirement for several years, he still had his uses. Disregarded in times of peace, in times of violence he was the man on horseback. With the reputation of a loner, he never allowed politics or friendship to interfere with a job. Fifteen years earlier he had proved it by destroying the Lincoln County outlaws. Without aligning himself beyond redemption with either faction, he had accomplished his task and stoically accepted the natural consequences. When the bloodletting was over and the dangers past, voters discouraged any thoughts he had about re-election. Their memories were long and untroubled by gratitude. Regardless of how good his intentions, he had antagonized too many businessmen, politicians, and ordinary citizens in bringing about the tranquillity that everyone desired.

Now a desperate situation again required a man like Garrett. The Doña Ana County sheriff's office was political and not geared toward law and order. The sheriff was first of all a tool of the politicians, and his deputies were often hired gunmen, on hand if necessary to bully the opposition into submission. When a significant murder did happen, such as that of the Fountains, the sheriff was unable to handle it because of politics or lack of experience. Genuine law enforcement languished, and in southern New Mexico it could truthfully be said that crime did indeed pay.

Many people believed that only Pat Garrett, an outsider, could put a stop to all that. He could end the petty bickering that surrounded the mystery of the Fountains. He had the experience and the iron will to knock aside all obstacles and solve what was rapidly becoming New Mexico's greatest murder mystery.

Wanting Pat Garrett for sheriff and legally getting him were, however, two different matters. First some very confused and some very controversial Doña Ana politics had to be straightened out. And in New Mexico the game of politics was as complex as any in the nation. In addition to the already mentioned reasons for having a sheriff favorable to one faction or the other, the position offered an almost unlimited financial opportunity to the holder.

Pat Garrett, still far away, thought the job worth six thousand dollars for one year,[6] but the newspapers in Las Cruces estimated the position to be worth fifteen thousand dollars, with a skillful manipulation of funds. Politicians could and did protect the sheriff by pointing out all the law's loopholes (and by not sealing them off),[7] and the sheriff protected the politicians by ignoring evidence of violations of the law, particularly those concerning gambling, racing, prostitution, and taxation, which might hurt them or their powerful business friends.

The most recent troubles had started in 1894, when Guadalupe Ascarate, supported by Fall and the Democrats, ran for sheriff against Numa Reymond, supported by Fountain and the Republicans. Both Fall and Fountain regarded the post as worth any effort to obtain. On election day both factions were suspicious and watched the polls closely. By noon, with eighty-eight votes cast, everyone relaxed, closed the polls, and went to lunch. Then the ballot box vanished, only to turn up at the post office, the ballots still there, but strangely rolled up, not lying about separately folded. All were marked Democrat.

Instead of declaring the election void, both sides agreed to go ahead and worry about the controversial ballots later. That night when the afternoon votes had been tabulated, the Republicans were declared the winners, unless the morning's eighty-eight votes were counted.

[6] Pat Garrett to Apolinaria Garrett, February 25, 1896, Jarvis Garrett Papers, Albuquerque, N. Mex.

[7] A sheriff often came into office substantially a poor man but usually retired to a ranch after serving just a few terms. He had made a great deal of money by utilizing some or all of the following sources of income: (1) He was paid a small salary. (2) He was paid approximately five dollars a day for court appearances. When he did not show up, he always sent a deputy, paid him one or two dollars of the fee, and pocketed the rest. (3) Sometimes he took bribes, but this was dangerous and not nearly as prevalent as one might think. It was too easy to make money in "legal" ways. (4) Deputies would round up the local drunks after supper, keep them overnight, feed them breakfast, and turn them loose. Legally this was considered as two days spent in jail, and the sheriff collected fifty cents a day a prisoner —while spending about fifteen cents for each man's breakfast. (5) The sheriff would accept scrip for back taxes. He took it for sixty to eighty cents on the dollar, and then held it until it could be redeemed at full value. The extra money went into his pocket. (6) The sheriff paid himself "informer fees." After reporting the presence of illegal gambling to the proper authority (meaning himself), he collected fifty per cent of everything. Adlai Feather, interview with author, Mesilla Park, N. Mex., March 2, 1969.

To settle the dispute, the commissioners' court held a meeting of supposedly unarmed men. Into the room, however, strolled Oliver Lee, a United States deputy marshal's badge on his shirt, his six-shooter protruding from a holster. No one contested his presence, perhaps because he intimidated the commissioners. When the meeting adjourned, the eighty-eight votes were allowed, and the Democrats and Ascarate were declared the winners.[8] Fountain cried foul and appealed to the courts. The appeal was still pending when he disappeared.

The struggle for the sheriff's office, combined with the festering mystery of the Fountains, prompted Governor William T. "Poker Bill" Thornton to go to El Paso, where he could talk with Pat Garrett. Pat was in town to see the on-again, off-again heavyweight championship fight between Bob Fitzsimmons and Peter Maher.[9] On about February 20, Thornton called for a conference in his hotel room with every significant political figure on Doña Ana County.

He outlined the embarrassment of the murder to the territory, claiming that such an unsolved crime hurt its chances for statehood. He asked detailed questions concerning the sheriff's office litigation. Finally, he recommended that Pat Garrett be assigned as chief deputy, given jurisdiction in the Fountain case, and be paid five hundred dollars a month.

Ascarate sneered, saying that he "was able to take care of the sheriff's office and would not let anybody dictate who his deputies should be." Numa Reymond snapped that he would drop his court suit if Ascarate would resign and allow Pat Garrett to be appointed sheriff. This proposal brought Fall into the argument, breaking the gathering up with the claim that there was "some political scheme

[8] *Ibid.*

[9] The El Paso fight was scheduled for February 14, 1896. Newspaper reporters were on the scene, the fighters were training in Las Cruces and Juárez, Mexico, and tickets sold for twenty-five dollars and up. However, Governor Charles A. Culberson said that no fight could be held in Texas, and he sent in eleven Rangers to enforce his orders. Mexican troops were dispatched to Juárez to stop any fight plans there. The New Mexico legislature barred it from being held in the territory. The fight was canceled and then rescheduled in a town on the Gulf of Mexico. That too was canceled, but in late February, Judge Roy Bean invited the participants to Langtry, Texas, where the fight was held on an island in the Río Grande. Fitzsimmons knocked Maher out in the first round. See Virginia Klaus and Opal Wilcox, "The Bob Fitzsimmons–Peter Maher Fight," *Password*, Vol. X, No. 2 (Summer, 1965), 63–67; C. L. Sonnichsen, *Pass of the North*, 358–62; C. L. Sonnichsen, *Roy Bean: Law West of the Pecos*, 174–89.

to the entire meeting."[10] During the discussion Pat Garrett sat in as an observer. If he made any comments the newspapers did not record them.

On February 24 he attended another meeting in El Paso, this one comprised of a "committee" of unnamed persons whom Pat Garrett referred to as "the most prominent men of New Mexico." Governor Thornton headed it. They asked Garrett to work on the Fountain case as a private detective. He told his wife in a letter dated the twenty-fifth that the committee and Governor Thornton had promised an "opportunity for me to make money, and a chance to get the Sheriff's office of Doña Ana County." They also agreed to "pay my expenses of $150 a month, and $8,000 in case I succeed in arresting and convicting the murderers."[11]

This letter, long and rambling, makes no mention of the supposed Fountain killers, nor does it indicate that he was eager, as some writers have alleged, to recapture the fame he had achieved as the slayer of Billy the Kid. His motives were clearly financial, for as usual his gambling and his horse racing had drained the family coffers of whatever small amounts they might once have possessed. He told Apolinaria, pregnant with the fifth Garrett child, not to be despondent but "be the good and brave little wife that you have always been . . . . If it were not that we are so poor, I would not be away from you for a moment. So, if I am successful we will get located in this country, and I will never be away from you and the children again."

Although Garrett hesitated until 1900 before finally selling his Uvalde property to John Nance Garner,[12] he never again lived in Uvalde. Instead, he rented a home on West Court Street in Las Cruces and brought his wife and children from Texas to live with him. Soon his buggy became a common sight churning through the caliche and sand streets around town, interviewing anyone who cared to make a statement.

[10] *Río Grande Republican*, February 21, 1896; *El Paso Daily Herald*, February 28, 1896.
[11] Garrett, *Life*, 25.
[12] Deed Records of Uvalde County, Texas, Vol. XXVIII, p. 120.

16.

The Trail Lengthens

Pat Garrett fumed at his lack of total command, of being unable to make final decisions about when, where, and how to strike. He was powerless to make arrests, powerless to coax co-operation from reluctant and sometimes fearful citizens, powerless to do anything except wait, watch, talk, and ask questions.

He wanted to be sheriff immediately, or at least to be a chief deputy with a promise of being in complete command before long. It stung his pride to be so confined. He knew that the governor, the newspapers, the entire Southwest were watching him, all expecting quick results.

Others observed him too, and at least one individual coveted the position that Garrett found increasingly humiliating. Efrego Baca, a loud-mouthed *pistolero* who possessed little of Garrett's stature as a lawman, complained from his home base at Socorro, New Mexico, that Governor Thornton had chosen the wrong man to solve the Fountain mystery. Baca scowled and hinted that he was in possession of certain facts concerning the slayings and that he alone could bring the killers to justice. All he needed was for Thornton to give him the authority to act—and, naturally, furnish the necessary funds to do so.[1]

Governor Thornton ignored Baca's entreaties and hired Garrett, possibly because Pat was not the braggart that Baca was. Garrett kept his own confidence and made his moves only after figuring all the odds, possibilities, and angles. He growled at those who wanted Oliver Lee jailed immediately, just as he ignored those who claimed that Fountain was still alive and no crime had been committed.

[1] Pinkerton Reports, March 25, 1896, Sonnichsen Papers, University of Texas at El Paso Archives. Pinkerton operative J. E. Fraser apparently did not like Baca, for reports to Pinkerton headquarters reflect his opinion that the Socorro gunman was little more than a frontier confidence man.

Numa Reymond, sheriff of Doña Ana County, New Mexico. Courtesy Doña Ana County Sheriff's Collection, University of Texas at El Paso Archives.

Wildy Well, near Orogrande, Texas, scene of the Garrett–Oliver Lee gun-fight. Courtesy Madison Collection, University of Texas at El Paso Archives.

Norman Newman (alias Billy Reed?), killed by Garrett and his deputy José Espalin at the San Augustine ranchhouse. Courtesy Hal Cox Collection, University of Texas at El Paso Archives.

183

Refugio Espalin, twin brother of José Espalin, about 1910. Courtesy
Anita Espalin.

ABOVE: The San Augustine ranchhouse about 1900. The Organ Mountains can be seen in the distance. BELOW: The corrals behind the San Augustine ranchhouse. In the back, left to right: Tom Rhode, Hester, Will Craven, Ince Rhode, and Ed Cox. FOREGROUND: W. W. Cox (standing), Sterling "Park" Rhode. Both photographs courtesy Hal Cox Collection, University of Texas at El Paso Archives.

W. W. Cox. Courtesy James Cox
Collection, University of Texas at
El Paso Archives.

Oliver Lee. Courtesy C. L. Sonnichsen Collection, University of
Texas at El Paso Archives.

Oliver Lee as a servant of the people in the New Mexico territorial legislature. Courtesy C. L. Sonnichsen Collection, University of Texas at El Paso Archives.

James Gililland. Courtesy R. L. Madison.

William "Bill" McNew. Courtesy C. L. Sonnichsen Collection, University of Texas at El Paso Archives.

Miguel A. Otero, governor of New Mexico Territory, about 1902. Courtesy Collections in the Museum of New Mexico.

The plaza in El Paso, Texas, 1904, during the time Garrett served as collector of customs. Courtesy M. G. McKinney.

Pat Garrett (right) and his brother Hillary. The photograph was probably taken in El Paso about 1900. Courtesy Jarvis Garrett.

Pat Garrett (right) and his brother Alfred. The photograph was probably taken in El Paso about 1900. Courtesy Jarvis Garrett.

Tom Powers with two Appaloosa horses, about 1908, in front of the El Paso County Courthouse. Courtesy Powers Collection, University of Texas at El Paso Archives.

The Coney Island Saloon, about 1910, Pat Garrett's hangout while he was collector of customs in El Paso. The saloon was owned by Tom Powers. Courtesy Tom Kolberson.

Mannen Clements, close friend and father-in-law of "Killin'" Jim Miller, killed in 1908. Courtesy Western History Collections (Rose Collection), University of Oklahoma Library.

George Gaither (center) and Sheriff James H. Boone (far right) of El Paso. The photograph was taken in El Paso about 1900. Courtesy Martin Merrill.

The Rough Riders Convention in San Antonio, 1905. ABOVE: Theodore
Roosevelt is seated third from the left; third and fourth on the right are
Tom Powers and Garrett. BELOW: Pat Garrett is second from the left.
Theodore Roosevelt is fourth from the left. The man in the sombrero is
Tom Powers. The other men are unidentified. These photographs helped
cost Garrett his job as collector of customs. Both photographs courtesy
University of Texas at El Paso Archives.

The governor employed Garrett in order to have him on hand when the sheriff's office was vacated. In all likelihood Thornton did not expect that Garrett would uncover any significant evidence. Garrett was hired because he was a one-man striking force, a fearless individual who made arrests. But since Garrett was not a professional investigator, Thornton sent for the Pinkerton men.

The Pinkerton Detective Agency had begun operations in the 1850's, and ten years later the founder Allan Pinkerton had become Abraham Lincoln's part-time personal bodyguard. He also organized and became chief of the United States Secret Service. After the Civil War the Pinkerton agents expanded out of Chicago and gained a dubious reputation as strikebreakers, solving labor disputes in the typical time-tested manner: with bricks, muscles, clubs, shovels, and shotguns. The battles were always bloody, the after-effects always long-lasting and bitter. Organized unions justly hated Pinkerton's. In the late 1800's their reputation improved with the successful shattering of several western gangs, particularly train robbers. Business became so good that Pinkerton's opened a Denver branch office to handle criminal investigations.

In early March, 1896, Thornton sent a telegram to Pinkerton's manager, James McParland, in Denver, urging him to assign one of his best detectives to assist Pat Garrett. On the tenth, agent J. C. Fraser stepped off the train in Las Cruces.

The techniques and personalities of Garrett and Fraser were too different for them to collaborate closely. Fraser was a trained team man; he worked with others and thought it no dishonor to ask for or receive assistance. Garrett was quieter, inclined toward grouchiness, and rarely gave information about evidence that he had uncovered, where he had been, or where he was going. Thornton eventually had to ask Fraser for a progress report on Garrett.

Fraser considered the lanky Garrett an enigma. He furnished Pat leads he had developed and information he had come across and could not understand why Garrett did not reciprocate. Several times he wrote Governor Thornton in frustration that Garrett was too tight-lipped, that information could not be obtained except through the most detailed questions. Fraser's reports were generally objective and relatively clear, except when they mentioned Pat Garrett. Then his sentence structure became awkward, his statements uncertain and strained. The Pinkerton agent was having trouble pegging this very difficult, very complex individual.

Nevertheless, most of their disputes were minor, concerning matters of procedure rather than basic beliefs about guilty parties. Fraser wanted indictments promptly sworn out for the arrest of Lee, James Gililland, Bill McNew, and Bill Carr, the last a cowboy associate of the others. The agent also yearned to jail Fall as an accomplice after the fact but realized that he could never prove Fall's complicity.

Pat Garrett advised Fraser to shelve these ambitions temporarily. The political climate needed changing; he had to be sheriff. Besides, more evidence was needed for a conviction, and rash public comments about allegedly guilty people might weaken the case. Fraser countered that the case would never get stronger until he or Garrett obtained statements from Lee and his men. He argued that Garrett's knowledge stemmed primarily from supporters of Colonel Fountain. Fraser considered their affidavits necessary, but obtainable any time.

Garrett growled in return that the men would be hard to find and might be dangerous if they were tracked down. Far better, Pat said, to forget about those interviews, which would probably be lies anyway. Would Fraser expect Lee to admit killing the Fountains? Logically it would be better to build the case slowly. As the evidence mounted, he expected someone within Lee's inner circle to break and confess. Discussions had already taken place among the Fountain partisans regarding whether Gililland or McNew would be the easiest to break.

One method of increasing the pressure was to infiltrate the gunmen's female campfollowers. Garrett suggested that Fraser contact a Mrs. Richardson in Tularosa and a Mrs. Stevens in El Paso. He did not know their first names, but the Tularosa woman regularly slept with McNew and probably had access to much of the gang's secrets. The Stevens woman owned a roominghouse in El Paso and had a long-established bedroom relationship with Lee.[2]

Fraser hurried to interview Mrs. Stevens but obtained no useful information. Evidently he did not see Mrs. Richardson, but he did find and talk to a Mrs. Taylor, who spoke of being on the Tularosa stage on the morning of the Fountains' disappearance. According to her, Lee, McNew, and a man whom she could not identify rode weary horses across the road in front of her.

Garrett shrugged his shoulders and dismissed the statement. He had investigated the story and learned that Mrs. Taylor had not been on the stage at all. She had traveled the lonely road in a pri-

[2] *Ibid.*, March 12, 1896.

vate rig with the stagedriver, who stopped several times for some clandestine romance. Anyway, Garrett had much more reliable information placing Lee in another location at the time.[3]

And that was how the investigations progressed. The detectives had little to work with, but they hoped eventually to persevere and gather enough evidence for indictments. As of then, even if they could make arrests, political officials such as Sheriff Ascarate and Fall could undermine the case before it went to court. Arrests would have to wait until the sheriff's office changed hands and Garrett moved in. (Oddly enough, Fall became one of Garrett's staunchest supporters, not because Fall suddenly became an advocate of law and order but because he realized that Garrett would eventually get the position anyway.)

On March 15, Fraser strolled into Garrett's Las Cruces hotel room and was surprised to find Garrett and Fall talking. Pat introduced the two men; they shook hands and exchanged a few weather pleasantries. That night Fraser wrote in his report: "Mr. Garrett told me afterwards that Fall . . . wanted him [Garrett] here as deputy sheriff." Fall said that, regardless "whether Numa Reymond became sheriff or Ascarate remained in office, he [Garrett] should have a commission . . . and he should have any amount of assistance that he might need."[4]

Although Garrett realized that Fall would never be elated with him as sheriff, he did sense that the attorney bore him no ill will. With a political change obviously blowing in the brisk, dry spring winds, Fall was smart enough to bend in the right direction. It would not hurt to have Garrett a little more friendly, even though Pat would never yield in his determination to send Lee to prison or the scaffold. In the meantime, Fall promised to go to Santa Fe and throw his support behind Garrett.[5]

A few hours after this discussion Garrett told Fraser what had happened and implied that Fall represented his last hope for becoming sheriff. If he did not get the office quickly, he might soon drop out of the Fountain investigation altogether. This possibility worried Fraser. Pat Garrett might not be the West's best detective, but he was the only effective individual capable of bringing the

[3] *Ibid.*, March 15, 1896.
[4] *Ibid.*
[5] During the Lee trial, Fall forced Garrett to admit that he (Fall) had been largely responsible for Garrett's appointment as sheriff and that this appointment had come about because of Fall's trip to see Governor Thornton in Santa Fe. *El Paso Daily Herald*, June 7, 1899.

Fountain murderers to justice. If Garrett withdrew, who would swear out the necessary warrants against the Lee bunch when the time came? Who would make the arrests?

Fraser wrote to Governor Thornton and explained the crisis. He pleaded for action from several influential persons in Las Cruces and Mesilla. The wire pulling worked. On March 19, District Judge Gideon Bantz finally declared Numa Reymond the winner. He took office on the following day.

Reymond was just as ambitious and stubborn as Ascarate. When Pat sought an understanding about when Reymond would make him chief deputy and then resign and turn the office over to him, the new sheriff hardly blinked. His reply was that he had no intention of giving up the job. He also had no intention of making Pat a chief deputy but did offer to hire him as an ordinary deputy and give him full authority in the Fountain case. Reymond adamantly declared that he had already guaranteed the post of chief deputy to Oscar Lohman, a Las Cruces businessman.[6] Garrett snapped that he would never accept any of this. He stormed out of the office and told Fraser what had happened.

The Pinkerton agent agreed that Reymond's attitude was unacceptable. Even if Garrett changed his mind and accepted a minor position, he would have to serve under two superior officers. Not only would this destroy the flexibility of his investigation but he would not likely be appointed sheriff when and if Reymond resigned. The post would automatically fall to Lohman, and he would also get the necessary party support in the next election.

Fraser asked Major Llewellyn to use his influence and straighten out the situation. No one openly admitted what happened, but rumors indicated that Las Cruces businessmen raised one thousand dollars and paid it to the two officials. Predictably, Lohman suddenly lost interest in becoming a chief deputy, and Garrett took his place on the twenty-second. Several weeks later, in late April, Reymond finally resigned and Garrett became sheriff.

As sheriff, Garrett had to reappraise his political position. He had been a lifelong Democrat and possessed a strong sense of party loyalty. Yet he was a practical man. New elections would be held in a matter of months. He could not seek office as a Democrat because he owed his position to the Republicans, who were his only supporters. He solved his dilemma by running as an Independent. After winning easily, he registered as a Republican.[7]

[6] *Ibid.*, March 19, 1896.

For a time after Garrett's initial appointment, a genuine break seemed imminent in the Fountain case. While Pat had been worrying about becoming a politician, Pinkerton's agents had been hard at work interviewing southwesterners who knew, or claimed to know, something about the murders. One of their best leads concerned Slick Miller, whose residence was the New Mexico penitentiary at Santa Fe. Colonel Fountain had arranged his stay there several years before on the basis of rampant cattle stealing.

Fraser was transferred to England on a new case, and so Miller told W. B. Sayers, another Pinkerton agent, of an earlier plot to kill Fountain in 1884. Lee, McNew, and Bill Carr had been involved, although the ringleader had been Ed Brown, a Socorro resident reputed to be dabbling in small-time rustling. Before Brown's plans for ambushing the colonel could become effective, Fountain scattered the gang with one of his periodic outlaw drives. Miller claimed the actual Fountain murderers were the same ones who set up the association. He offered to induce Brown to talk provided the governor would pay for the information with a full pardon. Thornton agreed.

First, the authorities wanted to create a climate whereby Brown would find it in his best interest to tell what he knew. And where could a better atmosphere be found than in jail? Consequently, Brown was picked up on a rustling charge and promised a long prison term if he did not identify the Fountain killers. The ruse did not work. He remained silent behind bars, denying that he knew anything about an assassination.

The New Mexico authorities finally gave up on him. What had been their best and most promising lead dissolved like the summer mist hovering over the Organ Mountains. Miller went back to the penitentiary, and Pinkerton's completely dropped out of the investigation on May 16, 1896. Pat Garrett was now on his own.

Garrett seemed more timid as sheriff than as a private detective. Through 1896 and 1897 and into 1898 he did little except remain taciturn and moody. Sometimes he spoke of developing his case but said little else.

In the meantime Governor Thornton had served out his term and had been replaced by Miguel Otero. The new governor prodded Garrett to act. The grand jury was scheduled to meet on April 1,

[7] *Rio Grande Republican,* October 9, 1896.

1898, and rumors swept the Mesilla Valley that Pat Garrett was finally going to seek indictments.

He rode to notify prospective jurors in Tularosa, and while there he dropped into the back room of Tobe Tipton's Saloon and General Store. Tipton, Oliver Lee, Fall, and District Clerk George Curry were playing stud poker. Garrett might have turned and left, but in the presence of enemies his pride would not allow it. Instead, he took Tipton's vacated chair and called for a fresh deck. What formerly had been a modest game with modest stakes now became a contest of grit, nerve, and endurance between two pistol-packing frontier gladiators: Lee and Garrett. All others in the adobe-and-wood saloon sat silent, worrying not so much about wins and losses, as about how to stay alive should the game terminate in gunsmoke.

For seventy hours the marathon contest continued with no one dropping out except to eat or nap. Garrett and Lee hardly budged, quietly sparring with carefully chosen words as well as cards. Each spoke coldly and politely to the other, being careful not to turn his back or close his eyes.

George Curry finally broke the impasse. "I've been hearing," he said, "that the Doña Ana grand jury is going to indict somebody in this crowd for doing away with the Fountains. My guess is that somebody in this bunch may want to hire a lawyer before long, and I have an idea that the lawyer he is going to hire might be sitting at this table."

Years later Tobe Tipton remarked that "there was more dynamite gathered around that poker table than could be found in any other room in New Mexico. There we were, sitting on a powder keg, and Curry deliberately struck a match."

"Mr. Sheriff," Lee said, "if you wish to serve any papers on me at any time, I will be here or at the ranch."

"All right, Mr. Lee," Garrett coldly replied. "If any papers are to be served on you, I will mail them to you or send them to George Curry for serving."[8]

The two gunmen relaxed and tossed their cards on the table. There would be no killing that day.

Garrett returned to Las Cruces, but Lee did not go home. Instead, he slept for several hours and awoke impatient to see what the grand jury was up to. He went to Las Cruces and shook his

[8] R. N. Mullin, interview with author, December 9, 1969; R. N. Mullin to C. L. Sonnichsen, February 16, 1951, Sonnichsen Papers, University of Texas at El Paso Archives; Sonnichsen, *Tularosa*, 153–54; Curry, *Autobiography*, 106–107.

head in disbelief when the jury adjourned without mentioning either him or the Fountains. Puzzled, he left a package of dirty clothes in town and caught the Santa Fe train to El Paso.

But Pat Garrett had a sound strategy, and he invoked it as soon as the jurors adjourned. He knew that indictments were expected, and if they were not handed down it would throw everyone off guard. Then would be the time to strike.

On the following day, April 2, Garrett went before Judge Frank Parker and requested bench warrants for the arrest of Oliver Lee, Jim Gililland, Bill McNew, and Bill Carr. His deposition promised to prove that these parties were the same men who "murdered Colonel Albert J. Fountain and his son, Henry Fountain."[9] Major W. H. H. Llewellyn and Thomas Brannigan signed a second deposition, swearing that on February 3, 1896, their posse had found "tracks and other evidence [indicating] that the said Fountain and his son were murdered."[10]

Garrett's strategy paid off. The next day he swooped down on McNew and Carr, arresting both without encountering any resistance. They were jailed and held without bond in Las Cruces. Garrett made no effort to arrest Lee, however. The Dog Canyon rancher returned to Las Cruces, picked up his clothes, heard what had happened, and left for his home. He wasn't molested.

When he reached his ranch house, Lee turned to see a posse of eight or ten deputies (he called them a "troop of militia") charging up on his back trail. They halted as he reached his porch. He turned to pull off his glove as he stood glaring at them. Then he went inside.

The possemen huddled uncertainly among themselves. Some wanted to rush the house; others wanted to leave. Before they could make up their minds, however, Tom Tucker, a ranch hand, stepped outside and told the deputies that Lee was not at home. The possemen muttered again to each other and then returned to Las Cruces. As the last lawman disappeared, Lee went again to El Paso, where the newspapers quoted him as saying that he "did not propose to be taken to Las Cruces and kept in jail for an indefinite length of time."[11]

Lee knew that Pat Garrett did not have enough evidence for a conviction—that what he really wanted was a confession. If the

[9] Keleher, *The Fabulous Frontier*, 249–50. Keleher quotes the affidavits in full.
[10] *Ibid.*
[11] *El Paso Times*, April 12, 1897; *El Paso Daily Herald*, June 7, 1899.

law could put Lee in jail and hold him there for a while, that was fine. Perhaps Lee would talk, but a more likely possibility was Mc-New, whom Garrett had already jailed. If he was kept in jail where Lee could not influence him, McNew might make a deal for his freedom. Garrett could at least wait a few months and see. While doing so, it did not particularly matter that Lee ran loose. In the long run it made Lee's chances of hanging just that much more certain.

Fall fully realized what Garrett was hoping for, and he worked frantically to free McNew and Carr. Within a week he had obtained a preliminary hearing for them, but much more rode on the outcome than whether or not two suspected murderers remained in jail. In order to keep the gunmen behind bars, the prosecution would have to display all of its evidence.

In early April, 1898, the hearing began and Garrett's star witness, Jack Maxwell, took the stand. Maxwell testified that he had stayed at Lee's house on the day that Fountain disappeared. Lee, Gililland, and McNew were not at the ranch but came in late at night on horses that staggered with weariness. All three men looked worried.

On the stand Maxwell was scared, confused, and inarticulate. Fall tore relentlessly at him, bringing out the fact that Garrett had promised him a two-thousand-dollar reward if his testimony convicted the prisoners. It was a bad moment for justice. Fall made it look as if Garrett was buying evidence.

When Fall finished, Maxwell was certain only of his own name, and may have had trouble remembering that. The *El Paso Times* of April 10 said that he had "succeeded in contradicting his direct testimony and proving himself a good witness for the defense."

From that point on the hearing was all downhill for Pat Garrett, and it was a very discouraging ride. But for six days he stubbornly sent one witness after another to the stand. Their statements were hazy and mostly opinions. Missing were the sticks used to measure the footprints around the Fountain buggy. The prosecution claimed that they were stolen.

When the hearing ended, Garrett was more surprised than Fall when the judge ordered only Carr to be released. McNew was remanded to jail and denied bond. For nearly a year he remained in confinement while Pat Garrett waited patiently for McNew's confession—a confession he never made.

17

Gun Duel at Wildy Well

Heartened by the detention of Bill McNew, Pat Garrett made no immediate effort to round up Lee and Gililland. Time rode on the law's side. McNew might yet confess. New evidence might turn up. Witnesses could step forth. The Fountain bodies might be found. In the meantime, let the two gunmen remain desert fugitives. Should new leads develop justifying prompt trials, there would be opportunity enough for pursuit and capture. Perhaps by that time the power and influence of Fall might somehow be broken or substantially reduced.

It was Fall that Garrett feared most. Fall was the legal pillar, the brilliant courtroom strategist who straddled and blocked the one-way trail leading from Lee to the scaffold. His profession was defense, usually that of noted outlaws who appealed to him as they stared through the jail windows and saw eternity waiting. Just two years before in El Paso he had eloquently defended John Selman for the murder of John Wesley Hardin, the most dangerous gunman in Texas. Fall could not convince all twelve of the jurymen that Selman was innocent, but he at least confused ten, and that was enough for a hung jury.

This sensational murder trial was not an unusual one in Fall's remarkable career. Years later he would state in his memoirs that in nearly a lifetime spent before the bench he had defended some five hundred accused criminals. At least fifty were charged with first-degree murder, and he "had lost only one case," that man being sentenced to seven years in prison.[1]

But Fall had other ambitions and desires too, and they directly conflicted with his interests in Doña Ana County. In June, 1898, he announced that he was temporarily leaving Las Cruces to march for greater glories against Spain in Cuba. The Spanish-

[1] Stratton, *Memoirs of Albert B. Fall*, 44–45.

American conflict had begun, and for months the Southwestern newspapers had been beating editorial war drums, following the lead of better-known eastern propaganda writers. The message caused an emotional wave in the West that can only be described as "awesome and magnificent," as well as "hysterical and irrational." Recruiting offices were jammed. Standing at the head of the line was a nervous and anxious Fall.

Of course, Fall had many misgivings about leaving. He knew the risk that Lee, Gililland, and McNew took while he was gone. Counterbalancing this fear, however, was the knowledge that, with the exception of McNew, the other two had sidestepped Garrett for months. No doubt they could continue to do so.

So Fall temporarily vanished from the sageland of southeastern New Mexico, although he did not go to Cuba as he had hoped. Instead he served in the military's legal department and remained Stateside while Lee and Gililland hid out in the desert. They grew beards and roamed as far north as the Black Range (about seventy miles from Las Cruces), avoiding everyone except close friends and relatives. Once, while camped near a stream, they heard approaching hoofbeats and scrambled to safety beneath a wooden bridge as Garrett and a posse rumbled across just a few feet overhead.[2]

When they needed fresh horses and supplies, they usually rode to the home of Print Rhode, Lee's brother-in-law, who lived on the east side of the San Andres, or to the San Augustine ranch of W. W. Cox, also a Lee brother-in-law. Sometimes they helped with the branding. In early July, 1898, José Espalin and Clint Llewellyn, two of Garrett's deputies, rode down from the late afternoon shadows of the Organ Mountains and found them in the corral.

Neither lawman seemed surprised at seeing the gunmen there, nor did the outlaws seem disturbed at finding two of Garrett's *pistoleros* in their midst. The only explanation that makes sense is that all these individuals were tough and hard, used to working both sides of the law. Perhaps Lee's service as a former deputy sheriff under Ascarate, plus his experience as a United States deputy marshal, gave him a kinship of sorts with the two men who were supposed to be hunting him.

Espalin was the closest thing to a Mexican hired gun in the territory. He was a handsome, blue-eyed fellow whose only facial

---

[2] Sterling Rhode, interview with Herman Weisner, undated, Organ, N. Mex.

disfigurement came from two missing front teeth, a vacancy he constantly tried to whistle through.[3]

No one acted suspiciously, and before long the men were exchanging conversation and gossip. Lee talked more than he should, mentioning that he and Gililland were spending the night with his employees James and Mary Madison at Wildy Well, twenty-five miles or so southwest of the Dog Canyon ranch. The Madisons took care of Lee's thirsty cattle on this portion of his range and furnished water to the El Paso and Northeastern Railroad, which maintained a spur from the well to the main tracks, less than three miles away.

As Espalin left, he led his horse through the corral gate. Pausing to shake hands with Lee, he whispered, "Cuidado" ("Be careful").

After having convinced Lee and Gililland of his secret support, José Espalin rode to Garrett's ranch, about ten miles away, and explained where the gunmen were headed. For this bit of alleged treachery, the ranchers branded him a traitor and never forgave him. In their rule book, of course, they were correct. In his own book he was merely giving his allegiance to that person who had a claim on it first—in this case, Sheriff Pat Garrett.[4]

Garrett hastily organized a posse composed of Espalin, Llewellyn, Ben Williams, and Kent Kearney, all tough, experienced fighters except Kearney, who had never been tested in battle. He was a tall, good-natured former schoolteacher, brave and eager to do all he could. Of the riders he alone was not a regular deputy but tagged along out of a sense of duty. He was to pay a high price for his enthusiasm.

The posse left before dark and rode thirty-eight miles across the desert. Obviously Pat was still following his own fifteen-year-old advice about pursuing criminals when they were not traveling and were not expecting you to be traveling either.

At about 4:00 A.M. on July 12, Garrett and his deputies reined in about a mile from Wildy Well and went the rest of the way on foot. Before them loomed an adobe house with an attached wagon shed, outbuildings, a pumphouse, and a large galvanized water tank sitting on a low platform with loose dirt shoveled high

---

[3] Emmitt Isaacs, interview with author, October 29, 1967, Las Cruces, N. Mex.
[4] Lee told Keleher substantially the same story as related here. See Keleher, *The Fabulous Frontier*, 253. However, on the witness stand Pat Garrett stated that Espalin had not conversed with Lee and Gililland, but instead had seen them leave the Cox ranch. See *El Paso Daily Herald*, June 7, 1899.

around the bottom. In the corrals were horses belonging to Lee and Gililland.

Cautiously the posse slipped through the early-morning moonlight toward the house. All was silent. Garrett did not know how many people were there, but he expected to find only the two fugitives. He did not know that fifteen or twenty section hands from the Escondido station were sleeping nearby. However, that knowledge would not have mattered anyway. The railroad workers did not participate in the fight and had no effect on the outcome.

As the posse slipped closer, Espalin removed his boots to walk quieter. Soon they were at the front door and had not been challenged. From inside came the sound of heavy snores. Pat nudged the door and found it unlatched.

Motioning Kearney to follow him, Pat shouldered the door open, jumped inside, rammed his six-gun into the nearest sleeping figure, and ordered him to throw up his hands. To his surprise and embarrassment he had thrown a gun on Mary Madison, who bolted straight up in bed and screamed when she saw the gun barrel pointed at her.

Awakened at the same time were her husband and three other people, the Madison children—a boy and a girl who were just barely toddlers—and a stranger named McVey, who had arrived two hours earlier. Garrett asked where Lee and Gililland were and upon receiving no answer ordered everyone to dress while he searched the area.

As he and his men moved cautiously through the outbuildings, McVey overcame his fright and tried to signal someone on the housetop. The posse caught on and quickly found a rickety ladder used by the outlaws to scale the building. Garrett said that since McVey was so anxious to warn his friends he should climb up and tell them to surrender. McVey refused. Next, the sheriff ordered Madison to do the same, but he also refused.

The roof appeared to be a natural fortress dominating the entire vicinity because of its height. Whoever held it held the entire area. Of typical southwestern adobe architecture, it was flat and protected on three sides by a two-foot wall. Small holes where the mud cement had cracked and fallen out provided almost perfect shooting maneuverability.

Since Lee and Gililland could shoot down on everyone without exposing themselves, Garrett positioned his men as best he could.

He ordered Williams behind the water tank and told Llewellyn to guard the people inside the house and keep them neutral.

Garrett, Espalin, and Kearney climbed the ladder to the top of the shed where, by standing at full height, they could see a portion of the roof. Pat could not see anyone, and so he dragged a ladder onto the shed and placed it against the house wall. Kearney climbed the ladder a few rungs in order to see across the top. By his own account Garrett now called upon the fugitives to surrender —a statement, incidentally, vigorously denied by Lee, who claimed that the call to surrender came after the firing had commenced.

As Garrett yelled, Kearney saw a rifle silhouetted against the sky-line and fired. Pat, realizing that it was too late to discuss surrender terms, opened up with his own rifle. Two bullets knocked dirt, twigs, and gravel from beneath Lee's stomach. Garrett shot and ducked. As he did, a slug from Lee's gun whistled across the empty space where his head had been. Lee said later that he thought Garrett had been hit.

Jumping to the ground, Pat ran inside an outbuilding from which he continued the battle. Espalin also clamored down, but was pinned beside the house and found himself unable to move across the clearing in order to get into a fighting position. For the remainder of the two minutes that the battle lasted, he simply stayed where he was.

As for Kearney, he had no sooner fired the first shot than a responding bullet broke his shoulder. Another slug buried deep in his groin as he tumbled in agony to the shed roof and then to the ground.

From inside the house Madison yelled at Garrett, demanding permission to take his family to safety in the root cellar. Garrett yelled back, "Go ahead!" Madison grabbed those near him and sent them scurrying below, but in his haste he overlooked his daughter. She continued to wander around the small house amid all the gun-fire, and once or twice just missed getting accidentally shot.[5]

Williams tried to do his part from beneath the water tank, shooting at the gun flashes on the roof. Answering bullets flew back. Several slugs ripped through the galvanized tank, and Williams, unable to escape, lay there and froze as the cold water poured down.

[5] R. L. Madison, interview with author, El Paso, February 28, 1967. Madison is the son of the Wildy Well Madisons. Although he had not been born when the fight took place, both parents repeated the story to him many times.

Garrett was now the only available fighter left in his posse. All the others were immobilized, especially Kearney. As he pondered his predicament, Lee called down, "You are a hell of a lot of bastards to order a man to throw up his hands, and shoot at him at the same time."

"Kearney fired without orders," Garrett replied. "Are you ready to surrender?"

"I don't think I will. I've heard that you intend to kill me."

"You need have no fear. You will be perfectly safe in my hands. Any story that you might have heard that I wanted to kill you is false. Now, will you surrender?"

"Who do you think has the best of it?" Lee taunted. "You have got yourself into a hell of a close place."

"I know it. How are we going to get out of here?"

"If you pull off, we won't shoot you."[6]

Garrett yelled back an OK and said that he was depending on them to hold their fire. He went immediately to Kearney and winced when he saw the ragged wounds and the amount of lost blood. Still, there was nothing he could do. From the roof, Lee and Gililland impatiently ordered him and the others to move on. Kearney could stay where he was.

Thus began the most humiliating episode of Garrett's life. Although outnumbering the fugitives two to one, he and his posse had been forced to surrender, lay down their arms, and walk away, leaving one of their own behind. Beside Garrett walked Llewellyn, who said little. Williams was too busy wringing water from his clothes to say much. Only Espalin swore. His bare feet were picking up thorns and cactus stickers.

After reaching the horses, Garrett and his posse rode to Turquoise Siding, just a few miles from Wildy Well, and sent a section crew back for Kearney. As the men appeared, both Lee and Gililland spoke a few words to the wounded man and rode off.

Kearney's suffering was so intense that he apologized to Mrs. Madison for any trouble he had caused her and begged her to remove the bullet from his groin. She complied, asking the section crew to pick him up from the ground and lay him in a buckboard. Then, using the only scalpel she had, a dull butcherknife, she per-

---

[6] *El Paso Times*, July 12, 13, 14, 16, 1898; R. L. Madison, interview with author, El Paso, February 28, 1967; Keleher, *The Fabulous Frontier*, 253–55.

formed the operation. A heavy and misshapen copper slug was removed from his body. The Madison family still has it.[7]

Garrett had him taken to Alamogordo on the train that afternoon and then moved to La Luz, less than ten miles away. A resident named Art McNatt listened as Kearney told him how he intended to get well and "go back and get those fellows." He died the following day.[8]

When Garrett and his worn-out deputies arrived back in Las Cruces, the El Paso newspapers picked up the story and printed both versions.[9] Surprisingly, each side tended to agree on specifics. They disagreed over whether or not Garrett called upon the fugitives to surrender before opening fire, whether or not they were asleep when he did begin shooting, and whether or not he intended to kill or to capture the two men.

Lee's story was that he and his partner were asleep and that Garrett tried to murder them. The tale sounded good, and it convinced a lot of people who should have known better. Lee and Gililland were veteran fighters, men who would not sleep soundly even under the most ordinary circumstances, and these were definitely not ordinary circumstances. It is agreed that during the hot summer months many people did sleep on the roof, porch, or even in the yard, and that could explain their being there. Yet it seems significant that the Madison family and McVey, the wandering stranger, slept inside behind a closed door. Assuming that none of this was unusual, that Lee and Gililland were indeed "roof sleepers," it seems impossible to believe that four burly men breaking into a room directly below them, waking three adults and two children, would not disturb the rest of the two men lying less than four feet above. No one could have slept through all that uproar.

Now comes the question whether or not Garrett intended to kill or to capture the outlaws. If he wished to slay them, why did he not shove open the door and commence firing at the Madisons? He obviously thought that the sleeping persons were Lee and Gililland. Here was a perfect opportunity to kill men he believed to be dangerous fugitives. Instead, he risked his life and those of his deputies by jumping inside and ordering everyone to surrender.

[7] R. L. Madison, interview with author, El Paso, February 28, 1967.

[8] C. L. Sonnichsen, interview with Art McNatt, Alamogordo, N. Mex., November 6, 1942.

[9] *El Paso Times*, July 12, 13, 14, 16, 1898; *El Paso Daily Herald*, June 7, 1899.

But whatever the stories were, the certainties were one man dead, one sheriff humiliated, two fugitives still loose and running, and the entire Southwest in an uproar. Garrett vowed that he would never rest until Lee and Gililland were in custody.

18.

The Trial

The Cuban war ended quickly and Albert B. Fall returned to southern New Mexico. In his absence Oliver Lee's and Jim Gililland's situation had deteriorated in spite of their victory at Wildy Well. They were still fugitives from the law, and Kearney's death had brought an additional charge of murder. Sooner or later Garrett would track them down. And while they might be lucky again, they could not expect to be lucky forever.

A big debate centered on Lee's charge that Garrett had been afraid and had intended to kill instead of capture them. Even Fall growled that the gunmen could not surrender until they were certain of their safety. New and assassination-proof arrangements would have to be worked out before the outlaws would turn themselves in.

These allegations split the Southwest into pro- and anti-Garrett factions. Street-corner philosophers argued heatedly over who had the more raw courage and who would win if Garrett and Lee ever met on even terms. But behind Fall's smokescreen of accusations he had a valid, if undisclosed, reason for not wanting his clients jailed. Rumors had been sweeping the Southwest that James Gililland was talking too much. Already the territory had rounded up two relatives who swore that Gililland had been boasting of his part in the Fountain killings. If Garrett ever put him behind bars, Fall doubtless feared that he might confess.

As long as Pat Garrett held legal warrants for the two outlaws, only time and opportunity separated them from capture and perhaps death. Once they were in his custody, the prosecution could take its time about setting a court date and a trial location. This left Fall only three alternatives: he could encourage his clients to continue taking their daily chances; he could turn them over to Garrett; or he could surrender them somewhere beyond the sheriff's grasp. The last could be done only by creating a new county with legal jurisdiction in the matter.

From his political stronghold in Las Cruces the wily Fall sought ways and means to push such an undertaking through the New Mexico legislature. He teamed with W. A. Hawkins, a brilliant attorney for the El Paso and Northeastern Railroad, who happened to have thoughts along the same lines but for slightly different purposes.

The railroad was already kindly disposed toward Oliver Lee. In 1897 he had sold them the upper reaches of his Dog Canyon property (sometimes called the Alamo Ranch) for five thousand dollars. In 1898, Alamogordo was platted and the first locomotive reached the town. Timber became important, and a spur line snaked its way into the Sacramentos to cut and haul out the huge pines. Ditches were dug across Lee's land so that the mountain water could be tapped.[1]

Doña Ana County had jurisdiction over the region, but communications were poor, roads were remote, and the railroads found it difficult to conduct their ever-increasing business affairs. They wanted a new county with a new county seat, Alamogordo. Fall offered his help in creating the county provided that its western boundary extended to the San Andres Mountains. It would thus encompass the Fountain murder area and remove legal jurisdiction for the case away from Doña Ana County.

New Mexican politicians merely yawned over the idea. Thomas Catron, Republican leader in the territorial council (the senate) saw no reason why he should support Fall, a Democrat. Governor Miguel Otero was equally hostile, although he and Catron were not friends. In addition, both Catron and Otero, regardless of their political differences and jealousies, stood together in believing that Lee was seriously involved in the Fountain murders. Neither would smile favorably on new legislation making life easier for the accused.

Fall and Hawkins were not country lawyers, however, awed by those in high places who yielded political power of life and death in such matters. They simply undertook to outsmart the opposition, and they did it with surprising ease.

First, they offered to name the new county Otero, thus appealing to the governor's vanity. Almost overnight he reversed his po-

[1] For the mountain railroad and water struggles, see Dorothy Jensen Neal, *The Cloud Climbing Railroad* and Dorothy Jensen Neal, *Captive Mountain Waters*.

sition and began to suspect that he might have been wrong in questioning the motives of Fall and Hawkins. Anyone could see that New Mexico needed one more county. When Catron learned of the new county's proposed name, he roared with fury but nevertheless consented to the creation of Otero County with the stipulation that everyone support his own pet project, the creation of McKinley County in the western part of the territory. The deal was made, and Otero became an official county on January 30, 1899. George Curry became its first sheriff.[2]

While the legislative bickering had been going on, the two outlaws for whom the county had been created had remained discreetly out of sight. Lee went to San Antonio, Texas, where in October, 1898, he married Winnie Rhode, sister-in-law of W. W. Cox, an Organ Mountain rancher. This coalition of families, the Lees with the Coxes and the Rhodes, would have far-reaching effects upon the life of Pat Garrett.

By March, 1899, Lee and Gililland were back in the San Andres and living with Eugene Manlove Rhodes (no relation to Lee's wife), a small, wiry man whose cleft palate caused him speech difficulties. Perhaps because of this infirmity he had turned his talents to writing, specifically about the southwestern cowman. Sonnichsen wrote of Rhodes:

> He knew more about these people and what made them tick than any other rangeland recorder. He understood their shy kindness, their rock-ribbed reserve, and their special code of ethics. He knew that a man who could kill his enemies could be tender to children, gallant to women, and faithful to a friend. He accepted the fact that you could be loyal to another human being without approving all his actions or analyzing and judging his motives. He sensed a hidden nobility in the most desperate characters and suspected a hidden weakness in the outwardly ultrarespectable. In short, he knew and approved of the rules those cowmen lived by, and he became Oliver Lee's friend and supporter.[3]

By Rhodes's own admission he sheltered more than one outlaw. Before the stranger left after accepting his hospitality, Gene Rhodes always rode off in another direction. Then he could honestly tell the sheriff, who invariably came by within a few hours or days, that "he did not see which way the man went."[4]

[2] For the story of Otero County, see Mrs. Tom Charles, *More Tales of the Tularosa*, 40–44, and Keleher, *The Fabulous Frontier*, 257–59.

[3] Sonnichsen, *Tularosa*, 169–70.

[4] Allan Rhodes, interview with author at Gene Rhodes's gravesite, June, 1970.

Although the cowboy author sided with Lee and Gililland in their struggle with Garrett, that did not necessarily mean that he disliked the lanky sheriff. He understood Garrett also and had considerable respect for him. Years later he penned one of the most eloquent defenses of Pat Garrett's character that ever appeared in print.[5]

It was Rhodes who worked out the surrender details for Lee and Gililland. He wrote to George Curry in Otero County and obtained an agreement to the following terms: the fugitives would not be turned over to Pat Garrett, and they would not be incarcerated in the Doña Ana jail while waiting for a similar structure to be built in Alamogordo.

After Curry had obtained approval of these conditions from Governor Otero, Rhodes appointed himself a peace officer and took the guns of his "prisoners." On March 13, 1899, Rhodes, Lee, and Gililland quietly boarded the Santa Fe–Las Cruces train at the Aleman station, near Socorro. Both fugitives were heavily bearded. Gililland wore a pair of blue glasses, and Lee pulled a section hand's faded blue cap down over his eyes. Their plan was to travel incognito to Las Cruces and turn themselves in to Judge Frank Parker. En route they moved uneasily about the empty smoking car.

On board the same train, unknown to the fugitives, rode Sheriff Pat Garrett and Texas Ranger Captain John R. Hughes. The background for this "coincidence" began several months earlier at the Ysleta Texas Rangers camp ten miles southeast of El Paso, when Garrett wandered over to swap yarns with his old friend Hughes. Gradually the talk turned to business, and Hughes asked Garrett to use his influence to get Geronimo Parra out of the Santa Fe penitentiary. Parra had slain Sergeant C. H. Fusselman at El Paso in 1890, and Hughes wanted to send him to the gallows.[6] Garrett agreed to return Parra if Hughes could arrest Pat Agnew, a small-time New Mexico bandit whom Pat had chased into Texas. The ranger grinned through his heavy gray beard, stuck out his hand, and called it a deal. Soon he had Agnew in chains and was turning

5 W. H. Hutchinson, *The Rhodes Reader*, 305–16.

6 Joe Parrish, "Hanged by The Neck Until Dead," *Password*, Vol. III, No. 2 (April, 1958), 68–75. After being delivered to El Paso, Parra was tried for Fusselman's murder and sentenced to be executed in the city jail. On January 6, 1900, he and Antonio Flores, another convicted prisoner, were led out to be hanged, and a wild scuffle broke out. Several men were stabbed before the famous double hanging took place. Ropes were finally drawn about their necks, and they dropped through the trapdoor to their deaths.

him over to Garrett in El Paso. In return, Pat kept his part of the bargain. He and Hughes traveled to Santa Fe, where the necessary extradition papers were signed and the prisoner was released from jail.

With Parra between them, the two lawmen took the south-bound train for Las Cruces and El Paso. What happened next is difficult to believe. Perhaps some of it should not be believed at all.

According to Gene Rhodes, who told the story, Garrett acted suspicious and cased the train at every stop. All the new passengers underwent a thorough scrutiny. Between Rincón and Las Cruces (about thirty-three miles apart), an unsatisfied Garrett and Hughes chained their sulking captive to his day-coach seat and walked single file into the smoking car, where the three men sat. Rhodes and Gililland were watching one door, while Oliver Lee observed the other.

Suddenly Lee hunched down in his seat and sent a silent message across the car with his eyes. Rhodes, who was reading, buried his face deeper in his copy of *Cyrano de Bergerac*. Across from him Captain Hughes paused and placed one of his scarred boots on the leather seat beside Gililland. He picked up and silently scanned a book left lying on a seat.

Pat Garrett continued to saunter down the aisle until he stopped beside Lee. For a long time he stood there, staring out the window and meditating, "a needlessly long meditation" it seemed to Rhodes. Nobody spoke.

Finally, without bothering to smoke, the lawmen turned and left the car. They never returned during that trip.[7]

Since that day historians and buffs have wrangled over whether or not Garrett and Hughes recognized anyone. Even the outlaws and Rhodes could not agree. Both Rhodes and Lee thought that Pat did not recognize them. Jim Gililland believed differently, bragging that Garrett was too frightened to attempt an arrest.[8] In later years Hughes denied that he recognized any of the three men. In a conversation with Eugene Cunningham, a popular western writer, he expressed doubt that Garrett noticed them either, for Hughes believed that Pat "would have died if necessary trying to arrest them."[9]

Perhaps so. But there are many unanswered questions. Why

[7] Hutchinson, *A Bar Cross Man*, 65.
[8] Hutchinson, *Another Verdict For Oliver Lee*, 3.
[9] *Ibid.*

would Garrett and Hughes not take Parra to the smoking car with them unless they wanted him out of the way in case shooting started? It could be argued that perhaps Parra did not smoke, or did not want a cigarette at the time. But even if so, experienced lawmen would never have taken a chance by leaving a dangerous prisoner alone, no matter how thoroughly he was chained, unless they had a good reason.

Why did Garrett and Hughes not walk into the smoking car and sit together, instead of choosing to stand beside the outlaws? Why did the two lawmen not smoke?

Although Hughes admitted that he did not know either of the outlaws well—and perhaps did not know Rhodes at all—Garrett certainly did. Would he be fooled by beards, a pair of glasses, and a beat-up hat? Also, surrender negotiations had been carried on for weeks among the governor, the outlaws, Gene Rhodes, George Curry, and Judge Frank Parker, could Garrett have failed to know about them?

If Garrett did recognize the men, why did he not attempt an arrest? The question is unanswerable. A guess is that he knew they were coming in to surrender, and out of personal preference, or because he had been ordered not to, he did not interfere. That would not stop him, however, from silently exposing himself to the gunmen to show that he was on to their little game. He and Hughes would have enjoyed that. Neither would worry about his respective chances in a gunbattle. Their nerve ran cooler than the headwaters of the Río Grande. Each possessed that attitude of supreme self-confidence which comes from a long, honorable, and successful career in a notably uncertain profession.

Whatever the truth, when the train pulled into the Las Cruces station Deputy Ben Williams was waiting on the platform. He had learned that Lee and Gililland would be on board, and, although he stood scowling, he did not intrude on the arrangements.

Rhodes hustled his two prisoners to Judge Parker's home, where their formal surrender was accepted. Although the agreement specified that neither man was to be imprisoned in the Las Cruces jail, the Alamogordo jail had not yet been built. Something had to be done, and so Parker ordered them to Socorro and into the custody of Sheriff C. F. "Doc" Blackington. Later, when the Otero County jail was finished, Blackington took his prisoners by train to El Paso, and then north on the El Paso and Northeastern Railroad.

During the layover in El Paso, Blackington told Lee and Gililland to wait in the Union Station while he went for a drink. Evidently it turned into quite a few drinks, for Constable Manning Clements arrested him and refused to believe that he was the Socorro county sheriff until Lee identified him.[10]

Problems were still ahead for the two gunmen. Their defense counsel conceded that the territory could not obtain a fair and impartial jury in Otero County, Lee's stronghold. And the prosecution reluctantly backed down from insisting that the trial be held in Las Cruces or Mesilla, Colonel Fountain's old bailiwick. Finally everyone agreed to hold court in Hillsboro, Sierra County, on May 25, 1899.

Any place as remote as that Black Range community had to have impartial jurors. There was no railroad; a stagecoach provided the only public transportation. Even the telegraph had not arrived. Soon, however, Western Union strung a wire to the outside world so that curious folk from all over the country might know about courtroom events almost as soon as they happened.

Hillsboro was a mining community, a county seat, one of the Southwest's most picturesque places. Huge cottonwood trees draped over the Middle Percha Creek as it meandered through town. Hillsboro boasted a brown brick schoolhouse, a brown brick jail, and a smelter. Stately mansions lined the stream. Today almost all the outstanding architecture, the pillars, the stained-glass windows, the massive doors, the ornate furniture have fallen into ruin or disappeared completely. Rattlesnakes crawl among the scattered stones where once young ladies squealed and giggled at croquet.

The Lee-Gililland trial was the most sensational event that ever happened in Hillsboro. Soon afterward the town lost its position as county seat. The mines began to play out. The people moved away. Unchanged, however, was the memory of those eighteen days in 1899, when Hillsboro was the center of the Southwest.

Into Hillsboro came swarms of people who could not have been more pleased and excited if they had been attending a public hanging. The Union Hotel overflowed, and a serious room shortage developed. The territory established a tent city on the north side of town and housed its witnesses, while the defense did the same on the opposite end. Friends and supporters of both factions, plus curious citizens by the hundreds, camped out on the mountainsides.

In this carnival atmosphere Fountain's death remained the focal

[10] Keleher, *The Fabulous Frontier*, 260–61.

point only because it was through him that the two opposing political groups clashed. Lee and Gililland were merely pawns, the means of deciding which party won. If the defendants were found guilty, the decision would be widely interpreted as a setback for the ambitious Fall and the Democrats. If the prisoners were freed, Tom Catron and the Republicans would have suffered a political loss of face, though not an irreparable one. He and the Santa Fe Ring would probably survive and even flourish. A loss to them meant that Fall's political rise would continue with perhaps the governor's seat or a position in Washington as his final destination. Nobody in Santa Fe wanted anything like that.

Entering the arena first was Tom Catron, appointed by Governor Otero as a special counsel to assist the prosecution. For his vast knowledge of law, his courtroom oratory, and his determination to introduce Lee and Gililland to the hangman, a better qualified man could not have been selected. However, overriding these obvious qualities hung the stigma of "Ringism," the common knowledge that the Santa Fe Ring, with Catron as its articulate and crafty spokesman, exercised a political stranglehold on the entire territory, with the possible exception of Fall's southeastern portion. Whether deserved or not, the name Catron was synonymous with corruption. Even his figure, corpulent to an extreme, suggested to the local miners, whose muscles were hard like the minerals they quarried, that here was a man who did not work for a living, but who lived by taxing those who did.

Following Catron into town came Fall, the southern New Mexico dandy who looked and sounded better because Catron looked and sounded so bad. Fall grabbed the initiative immediately, handing out long-winded interviews to bored newsmen eager to justify their presence to faraway, cost-conscious editors. Fall outlined his strategy, one that never varied for the duration of the trial: this was to be a battle of little men against big men, of small interests against large interests, of poor ranchers against rich landholders, of a weak Democratic party against the Republican juggernaut.

Also making an appearance was Pat Garrett, as controversial a figure as anyone there. As usual he remained quiet. He alone is not recorded as calling names or hurling accusations. Though he was a leading witness for the prosecution, his testimony, as reported by the newspapers (trial records were not preserved), shows an unemotional approach similar to what might have been expected if he had been testifying against a couple of itinerant hog thieves.

Finally came Lee and Gililland, the two prisoners, although it may not be correct to call them that. They acted more like celebrities than men accused of a terrible crime. Their well-armed friends did the guard duty, escorting them to and from jail. Anyone who wanted to shake hands or speak a word of encouragement to them could do so. Lee, in particular, charmed everyone. His laugh was loud, hearty, friendly, and unusual. He shook all over when something struck him as funny, and no one who heard him laugh ever forgot it.

Newspaper accounts of Lee's career were never neutral. As with Garrett, Lee was either liked or hated; there existed no middle ground. Most articles before his arrest painted him as a cold-blooded, calculating gunman. But the Hillsboro news dispatches changed that image. Overnight he became a six-gun Robin Hood. In the Southwest Sherwood Forest Gililland was Little John and Garrett the sheriff of Nottinghamshire. Add the ridiculous story that Lee read both Greek and Latin, and it is easy to understand why the prosecution was not optimistic about the outcome.

The territory charged Lee and Gililland with the murder of young Henry Fountain only. The deaths of the elder Fountain and Deputy Kearney were saved for a future time. Meanwhile, McNew, still in confinement at Las Cruces, had obtained a change of venue to Silver City and was scheduled to go on trial one month before the others. Charges were dropped against McNew so that the prosecution need not reveal its evidence to Fall. After all, it was Lee whom the prosecution really wanted. McNew and Gililland were regarded as subordinates who carried out Lee's commands.

Jury selection began on May 25 and took three days. Everything began to go wrong for the prosecution. A supposedly key witness from North Dakota failed to appear. Also missing were three Mexicans who claimed to have been butchering a stolen beef near Chalk Hill at the time of the murders. Reportedly they watched the killers ride away with the bodies strapped to horses.[11] Jack Maxwell was also absent, and Garrett had to bring his star witness from the White Oaks barrooms.

Finally, on Monday, May 29, the trial began and former New Mexico governor Thornton testified to his trip to Las Cruces fol-

---

[11] T. J. Daily to Santa Fe District Attorney, May 14, 1899, Richmond P. Barnes to Tom Catron, May 31, 1899, Catron Papers, University of New Mexico Library, Albuquerque; Pinkerton Reports, March 18, 1896.

lowing the Fountain disappearance. He spoke of viewing the alleged murder site and offering a reward for the slayers.

Theodore Heman, foreman of the Lincoln County Grand Jury in 1896, testified to the cattle-rustling indictments against Lee and McNew, thus establishing a motive for the Fountain killing. Barela, the mail carrier, told of his last talk with the colonel.

On Tuesday a reluctant Jack Maxwell was sworn in. This time he had "forgotten" much of his earlier testimony given during the McNew-Carr hearing. Over Fall's strenuous objections, the prosecution read it back to him. He swore that he had slept at the Dog Canyon ranch on the night of the murder and that Lee, Gililland, and McNew came in the next day riding tired horses and looking extremely worried.

Unable to prevent these statements, Fall relentlessly tore into the hapless Maxwell. He brought forth the admission that Maxwell had written a friend of Lee's, telling him not to worry—that Maxwell would swear the boys "were forty miles away when Fountain disappeared." Fall damaged his credibility even further by bringing up again the confession that Garrett had promised him two thousand dollars for testifying to certain facts. Maxwell began to sweat and look faint. Finally Fall sneered and allowed him to leave the stand.

Other witnesses fell before Fall's harassment. Dr. Francis Crosson went into great scientific detail about the microscopic examination he had made of the blood-soaked earth around the Fountain wagon. His conclusions were that the blood was that of a human being.

"Will you undertake before this jury to test samples of human blood, dog's blood, and rat's blood and tell which is the human blood?" Fall asked.

"No, I wouldn't. Blood testing is so difficult that the best expert in the world would not swear to it."[12]

Attorney Fall asked only a few more questions.

By the end of the first week the prosecution had worked its way down to "Little Jim" Gould, a cousin of Jim Gililland's wife. He swore that Gililland had said that Henry Fountain "was nothing but a half-breed and to kill him was like killing a dog."[13] Fall asked where Gould was in March, 1897. He replied "in jail." Fall asked whether Gould was a friend of Jim Gililland or Bill McNew. Gould

[12] *El Paso Daily Herald*, June 7, 1899.
[13] *Ibid.*

answered that both men considered him an "enemy." The defense attorney had no more questions.

Next came Riley Baker, Jim Gililland's brother-in-law. He, too, spoke of Gililland's boastfulness, saying the gunman had bragged that the bodies would never be found and that no one would ever be convicted of murder. Fall established that Baker was also an enemy of the three accused men and dismissed him.

Finally Pat Garrett took the stand for the prosecution. Of all the men having to face Fall's cross-examination, he alone was unshaken. Instead, he got in a few licks of his own.

Fall questioned Garrett about his initial involvement in the Fountain murder case, specifically asking what had led to his appointment as sheriff. Garrett told of attending an El Paso hotel conference shortly after Colonel Fountain disappeared. There several citizens of Las Cruces urged him to become sheriff, submitting murder evidence implicating Lee, Gililland, McNew, and a Doña Ana county official (the newspapers did not name the official, but it is rather obvious that they meant Fall). As a private detective, Garrett testified, he drew three hundred dollars a month, but he was dissatisfied with the position. The significant factor in his becoming sheriff had been Fall's trip to Santa Fe in his behalf. Shortly afterward two county commissioners (also unnamed) were discharged, and Pat pinned on the badge.[14]

"What was the condition of affairs when you first went to Las Cruces?" Fall asked.

"Well, you fellows had been shooting at one another and cutting up," Garrett replied.

"What fellows?"

"You and Lee and Williams and others."

"What did you say would be your course if given any warrants for the arrest of Lee? Did you not say that you would go after him by yourself?"

"Yes sir."

"Upon what were these warrants based?"

"Upon affidavits."

"When this evidence came into your hands, why did you not apply for a bench warrant?"

"I did not think it was the proper time."

"Why did you not think it was the proper time?"

"You had too much control of the courts." (*Laughter*.)

[14] *Ibid.*, June 7, 1899.

"In other words, you thought I was the administration?"

"You came pretty close to it."

"You base your conclusions on the fact that I procured the sheriff's office for you?"

"Well, you showed your strength then."

"What did you do when these warrants were sworn out?"

"Sent out a posse to serve them."

"Isn't it a fact that this posse was composed of militia—and that they pressed food from citizens?"

"Not to my knowledge."

"What was your object in sending this mob after Lee and Gililland?"

"It was not a mob, it was a posse."[15]

Thus the cross-examination of Pat Garrett progressed. He testified at considerable length about the fight at Wildy Well, noting that he had gone alone to arrest Lee at the Dog Canyon ranch shortly after the skirmish but found no one there except Tom Tucker, Lee's foreman.

As the prosecution witnesses finished trickling to the stand, the defense rose to present its case. George Curry testified that Jack Maxwell, the prosecution's main witness, had earlier told him that Lee, Gililland, and McNew were definitely at the ranch during Fountain's murder—and were not missing as Maxwell had told the jury.

Albert Blevins, a Texas and Pacific fireman, testified that he went to Lee's ranch on the afternoon of the murder and found the defendants there.

Lee's mother, in one of the trial's more dramatic moments, testified that her son was a good boy and had been home all day.

Lee himself swore that he did not know about the murder until several days after it happened. He would have surrendered right away, but there was too much "mob talk and information that I would be subject to violence."[16]

Print Rhode, Lee's brother-in-law, testified that Major Llewellyn had planned to blow up Lee's house with dynamite. Although the prosecution vigorously denied the story, the statement had its planned effect upon Lee sympathizers, who made up most of the audience.

When the time arrived for final arguments, Richmond P. Barnes,

15 *Ibid.*
16 *El Paso Times,* June 10, 1899.

of Silver City, delivered a flowery address for the prosecution, quoting freely from Dickens' *Pickwick Papers*. The *El Paso Daily Herald* of June 15 commented that some of his figures of speech "probably went over the heads of the jury." Even the interpreter, translating for the Mexican jurors who could not understand English, had a hard time with "some of the fancy work" and frequently made Barnes repeat his expressions.

Next came William B. Childers, also for the prosecution, who spoke in a language that everyone understood. He ridiculed Lee's testimony that he was "afraid to come in because Garrett would kill him." Childers angrily snapped that the defendants had no reason to resist arrest, that "Lee went in and out of Las Cruces without fear until March, 1898. McNew was in the custody of Sheriff Garrett for several months and he was not killed, or mobbed, or threatened." Childers defended Garrett's contract with Jack Maxwell, explaining that there was nothing unusual in paying for truthful evidence. After all, had not the governor offered a reward for information leading to the arrest and conviction of the murderers? He closed with a comment upon defense claims that since no bodies had turned up no murder had been proved. Childers noted:

> To hold that you cannot convict of murder because the body cannot be found is to condone murder, to put a premium on crime. It is easy in this country to waylay a man and conceal his body where it cannot be found. There is every evidence that these three men were the perpetrators of this crime. The men have wholly failed to explain any of the incriminating circumstances that form a web we have woven so tightly around them, but instead of refuting our evidence, they have raised the cry of politics.[17]

Fall rose next and talked long and eloquently about the benefits of the jury system and its assistance to human beings in difficulty. He called Maxwell a liar and noted that eight defense witnesses had contradicted his testimony. Either these eight people were liars or Maxwell was. Not all could be telling the truth. He referred to Doña Ana County officials as "a lot of broken down political hacks" who "have gathered together, as does the slimy filth on the edges of a dead eddy." He appealed to the poor of the jury, saying that the territory had spent considerable sums to try the accused but that the defense had to fight out of its own finances. "Our de-

[17] *El Paso Daily Herald*, June 15, 1899.

fense is an alibi, clearly proved," he stated. "You would not hang a yellow dog on the evidence presented here, not less two men."[18] When Fall finished, the courtroom burst into lengthy applause.

Tom Catron made the final speech at eight o'clock that night, probably knowing that whatever he said would make little difference. Nevertheless, he was still determined. One by one he went over every bit of evidence, every suspicious word on the part of the defendants, every action by them not satisfactorily explained. His argument took two and one-half hours, and when he finished he was worn out. So were the jury and the spectators.

The jury had hoped to sleep on the case and debate it the next morning. However, at 11:30 P.M., Fall insisted that they render a verdict before going to bed. They did so, taking exactly eight minutes to reach a decision: not guilty.

The courthouse was an instant bedlam as everybody cheered, yelled, and laughed. Officially it was the end of the case. The heart went out of the prosecution; they did not revive the indictments for Kearney's death or Albert Fountain's murder. The Fountain case is today known as New Mexico's greatest murder mystery. It is not, of course. A good many people know who committed the crime. They have not talked for the record, but they have said plenty in private.

[18] *Ibid.*

19.

Another Verdict: Another Killing

The Fountain murder case will always remain legally unsolved. The perpetrators and those who might have stepped forward and told what they knew are long since dead. No new suspects have turned up in the ensuing years, and the controversy still remains. Were the three accused men actually guilty? Were only one or two of them guilty? Were all of them innocent?

The vast majority of Fountain's friends do not doubt that Lee, Gililland, and McNew were all guilty as charged, and in the intervening years nothing has happened to change their minds. They still regard the jury's verdict of innocent as an appalling miscarriage of justice. Their belief in the guilt of the trio is as implacable and unyielding as their certainty of an ultimate and higher judgment.

One would expect to find an opposite consensus among friends of the accused, but that is not the case. No solid agreement exists. Naturally some of Lee's defenders deny that he or the others did anything wrong, but *most* will admit that there was a lot of truth in the accusations concerning the Fountain deaths. These same friends, however, will quickly exclaim that the colonel was a "troublemaker" and "got what he deserved." Other partisans believe that only Gililland and McNew were involved. They absolve Lee of everything except "guilty knowledge" and say that because of loyalty to his friends he would not take that knowledge to authorities. Accordingly, Lee might have wanted Fountain dead, but he took no part in the slayings because "he would never assist in the murder of a small child."[1]

There seems to be universal agreement on one point: the Fountains were murdered. Their bodies supposedly turned up in a half-dozen places throughout the Southwest. It is whispered that they were crammed into one of the steam-boiler fireboxes that Lee was

[1] Informants who made these statements wish to remain anonymous.

installing at his wells. A Gililland relative allegedly hauled three large wagonloads of mesquite roots to the furnace at Wildy Well for the purpose of cremating the bodies (mesquite roots, as south-westerners know, burn fiercely but very slowly).[2]

There are stories that the bodies were cast into a steep, remote canyon in the San Andres. And there are tales that they were buried in a corral and horses stampeded inside to trample the earth. And Lucy Gililland, Jim's younger sister, has added a gruesome touch. She worked for her board at the Dog Canyon ranch during the time of the killings. One morning while slopping the hogs she found them rooting up the remains of Henry Fountain from a shallow grave near the fence. She went into shock, and the body was removed and buried in another place.[3]

Later Lucy Gililland married Bob Raley, a cowpuncher who was not popular with his peers. He and McNew argued over range rights and water wells, and Raley put a bullet through McNew's ear. He would have killed him if friends had not intervened. McNew's revenge came in 1915 when he lured Raley and his wife from their home near Ore Grande on the pretext that they were wanted on the telephone at a neighbor's house. Both Raleys were suspicious. Bob alighted from the buggy carrying a .30–30 rifle, and Mrs. Raley packed a six-shooter. Neither had a chance. As they approached the house, McNew fired through the screen door and killed Raley with a bullet in the head. Mrs. Raley was wounded in the neck.

When she recovered, Lucy Raley wrote to Albert Fountain, Jr.: "One of the men who killed your father and brother has just killed my husband. If I had done my duty [and taken] the stand (although it would have ruined my brother), it is possible that my husband would still be alive."[4]

It was Mrs. Raley's brother, Jim Gililland, who was the weak link in an otherwise strong chain of silence. He talked even before the trial, as noted by the two relatives who gave sworn testimony regarding his comments. That the jury did not take these statements into consideration does not detract from their possible truthfulness. Certainly no one was ever indicted for perjury.

Jim Gililland was a striking figure, towering six feet four inches

[2] Mrs. Mary Ellis Wright, daughter of Lucy Gililland Raley, interview with author, Redrock, N. Mex., April 23, 1968. The Gililland relative who supposedly hauled the roots has not been identified.

[3] Gibson, *The Life and Death of Colonel Albert Jennings Fountain*, 286.

[4] Lucy Raley to Albert J. Fountain, Jr., October 27, 1915, Fountain Papers, University of Oklahoma Library Archives, Norman.

and weighing nearly 250 pounds. He might have stepped out of a Frederic Remington painting, with his gold tooth flashing below his brushy, untrimmed mustache. In stereotyped cowpoke fashion, his legs were bowed, and he talked with a slow drawl, a limp Bull Durham butt end bouncing between his lips as if punctuating his drawn-out sentences. At the time of the Fountain killings he was little more than a boy, wild and very impressionable.

His relationship with McNew was never good after the killing of Raley and the wounding of Lucy. Gililland constantly worried about her safety. In the fall of 1916 she overstayed a visit to Alamogordo, and some unfounded fears were raised for her safety. Upon finding McNew drinking alone in a local saloon, Gililland warned him to let his sister alone or "it wouldn't be like cutting that Fountain kid's throat."[5]

In the early 1920's or 1930's Gililland underwent a stomach operation in the East. Complications set in upon his return to his Capital Peak Ranch near Mockingbird Gap in the San Andres. The incision became inflamed and he finally had to see a doctor in Alamogordo. The wound was reopened, and inside were several yards of gauze. The old rancher never physically improved much after that. He walked with a stoop and groaned in agony every time he climbed on a horse. Soon afterward he sold his sixty-three thousand acres and retired to Hot Springs (now Truth or Consequences), New Mexico.

The New Mexico State Land Office listed the property and notified a twenty-two-year-old cowboy named Butler Oral "Snooks" Burris that it was for sale. He and his father, Frank, were both interested, but it was the son who consummated the deal. The Burrises knew both the Coxes and the Lees, but not closely. Neither man knew Gililland. However, both Snooks Burris and Jim Gililland were cut from substantially the same western fabric. Both loved the land, both were friendly and highly personable, and both preferred the saddle to the automobile seat. Their meeting in 1937 began an intimate friendship that did not end until Gililland's death almost ten years later. During this period Burris learned to call the old man affectionately "Uncle Jim."

After a selling price had been negotiated, Burris agreed to wait sixty days before taking possession. It would take that long for Gililland to round up his cattle. Thus Burris spent part of his time in Las Cruces and the rest in a tent pitched on the ranch property

[5] Mrs. Mary Ellis Wright interview with author, Redrock, N. Mex., April 23, 1968.

while he helped collect the stock. During those sixty days Gililland and Burris spent a lot of time together in their favorite activities, talking and drinking. Gililland obviously had something on his mind, and since he liked and respected Burris, he guardedly began to call frequent attention to a grave near a remote arroyo in the San Andres. A large rock served as a tombstone. There was no inscription. "Son," Uncle Jim would say, "that grave holds a lot of secrets."[6]

Burris was puzzled, though he asked no questions. Uncle Jim would say more in his own good time. Gradually the old man began discussing the necessity for getting rid of the colonel. Gililland talked about the Fountains and how no one knew exactly what had happened. "Rumor has them buried on my ranch," he would say—and wink. Once, while passing the gravesite and listening to the usual comments about its secrets, Burris asked, "Is that the one, Uncle Jim?" Gililland nodded and said yes. He told how the Fountain bodies had been buried there twenty years before after being removed from another location. Only recently he had marked the spot with a rock.[7]

Back at the ranch the Fountain subject occupied his troubled mind more and more. He often drank heavily for hours. "If I heard him talk about the Fountain killings once, I heard him talk about it a thousand times," Burris says. Gililland's thoughts were simple and uncomplicated. The killing of the boy bothered him; the slaying of the colonel did not. "That old son of a bitch got what he deserved," Uncle Jim would growl.[8]

Gililland always began the subject by laughing, and it was a peculiar laugh. "Har, har, har!" it went. He told how he, Lee, and McNew bore down on the racing wagon carrying the Fountains. The three gunmen simply pulled alongside and began shooting as Fountain frantically lashed his horses in a futile attempt to escape. Many shots were fired; no one knew for certain who finally hit the colonel.

"Har, har, har!" Uncle Jim would laugh. "That old son of a bitch jumped out of that wagon like a big toad. He hopped directly between the two horse riggings, and was dead when we reached him."[9]

[6] Butler Oral "Snooks" Burris, interview with author, Rumsey, Calif., February 23, 1969.
[7] *Ibid.*
[8] *Ibid.*
[9] *Ibid.*

As for young Henry Fountain, his death was not funny. Gililland always wept when he talked about it, and poured the whisky down as if he were trying to burn the memories from his mind. The boy was killed because "dead men tell no tales." Lee, McNew, and Gililland drew straws. Uncle Jim got the short one. Without a word he reached into his pocket, pulled out his knife, opened it, grabbed the boy by his black hair, pulled his head back, and, to use Gililland's own words, "cut the little feller's throat."[10]

The bodies were buried first in an undisclosed location and later removed to the remote canyon north of Lava Gap in the San Andres. Twenty years later, Gililland grew concerned that the gravesite might become lost forever, and so he marked it with a rock.

After Gililland moved to Hot Springs and edged closer to death, he handed Snooks Burris a Masonic pin with an Odd Fellows link on the bottom. He claimed to have taken it off the colonel's body. "Give it to Albert Fountain, Jr., after I'm gone," he instructed. Burris entrusted the pin to his father, Frank, who turned it over to Jack Spence, vice-president of an Alamogordo bank. Spence placed it in a safety deposit box until Gililland died on August 8, 1946, at which time it was turned over to the Fountain family, who pronounced it authentic.[11]

Nothing further happened to clear up the Fountain mystery until November, 1950, when Frank and Snooks Burris led a dozen men, including two Fountains, high into the San Andres to dig up the grave and recover the bones, if possible. When they reached the site, they dug several holes, but found no evidence that a grave had ever existed there. The searchers returned home, puzzled and empty-handed.[12] From that expedition three possible conclusions can be drawn: (1) James Gililland was lying; (2) in the twenty years since the grave was dug, the country had been so overgrown with brush and so laced with arroyos that Gililland mistakenly marked the wrong spot; (3) Burris missed the gravesite almost twenty years after Gililland first showed it to him for the same reasons stated in number two. Whatever the truth, this expedition ended the search for the Fountain bodies.[13] No such quest has been

[10] *Ibid.*

[11] *Ibid.*; Albert Fountain III, interview with author, Mesilla, N. Mex., August 26, 1970.

[12] *El Paso Times*, November 27, 28, 1950; *El Paso Herald Post*, November 26, 1950.

[13] *El Paso Times*, November 28, 1956.

made again, and it is not likely that another will be made in the future.

Jim Gililland's alleged remarks to Snooks Burris are not the only time he is reported to have talked. For years all sorts of confession tales have been handed down and repeated: Gililland supposedly kept a diary and recorded there his part in the crime; another story credits a Las Cruces attorney with taking down his confession and notarizing it. Neither the diary nor the written statement has ever been made public. Nevertheless, before Jim's death, most of his friends said that "someday, before it is too late, Jim will tell all he knows about the Fountain case." William A. Keleher, a southwestern historian, heard the rumors and visited him in Hot Springs. Gililland was polite and responsive up to a point, but "skirted and evaded all efforts . . . to talk about pivotal points in the case."[14]

Toward the end of Gililland's life the only one who really caught his ear was a Nazarene preacher. The old, terminally ill gunman, rambling incoherently, thought the reverend gentleman was Christ. Gililland spoke to him in an "unknown tongue" that no one understood. Those standing nearby were relieved to hear that the preacher did not understand the tongue either.[15]

Of other alleged participants in the Fountain mystery, only one caused any particular consternation. Bill Carr, who won his freedom in the preliminary hearing with McNew, reportedly "got religion" at a revival-tent meeting. Nobody minded that, but when he began to give some expressive testimonials, several people grew concerned. Fortunately, nothing came out of his mouth to which anyone paid any official attention.[16]

Oliver Lee talked little, if at all, about the Fountain case and denied having any part in it or knowing anyone who did. He lived a relatively productive life after the trial, although he had his troubles. In 1914 he sold his ranch to a corporation headed by James G. McNary, of the First National Bank of El Paso, and McNary talked him into becoming manager of a huge ranching enterprise with headquarters near the Sacramento River. The ranch was called the Circle Cross, and for a while it was the largest spread in southern New Mexico. Its boundaries extended from the Mescalero Indian Reservation to Ysleta, Texas. But financial difficulties

---

[14] Keleher, *Fabulous Frontier*, 276.

[15] Lucy Raley, interview with C. L. Sonnichsen, Sunrise Acres, El Paso, Texas, August 13, 1954, Sonnichsen Papers, University of Texas at El Paso Archives.

[16] Gibson, *The Life and Death of Colonel Albert Jennings Fountain*, 285.

were coming. McNary's bank failed and dragged several large El Paso business establishments down with it.[17]

Occasionally other events reminded Lee of how tenuous his hold on life was. In November, 1919, Johnny Hutchings, of Alamogordo, entered his Buick roadster in the cross-country automobile race from El Paso to Phoenix. Lee went along—and later regretted it. When they were about thirty minutes out of El Paso, a bystander fired a shot through the back of the driver's seat. Hutchings received a fatal wound. Whispers indicated that the bullet was actually meant for Lee, for over the years he had made a lot of enemies as well as friends. Major William F. Scanland, a patient in the Fort Bliss Hospital, was arrested for the offense and sentenced to prison.[18]

Lee continued to live in Alamogordo, served as director of the Federal Land Bank, and held other positions of trust. His friends sent him twice to the New Mexico state legislature. On December 15, 1941, he died peacefully of a stroke in Alamogordo.

Not much is known of William Henry McNew. Reportedly he was the meanest and most vicious of the three. Tall and slender, he had eyes like blue marbles. His outstanding characteristic was his huge feet, which required special, handmade boots. A curious story says that in 1937 he suffered a small stroke which at first appeared fatal. No breathing and no heartbeat could be detected, but he nevertheless regained consciousness before the morticians could begin their work. When he came to, he told a blood-curdling tale of having been in hell and standing up to his knees in molten lava. Shortly afterward, on June 30, he suffered another stroke, and this one really did kill him. Before he died, however, the lower parts of his legs blistered, and all the hide peeled off as though they were burned.[19]

Three years had passed since Pat Garrett had gone to Las Cruces. Though his pursuit of the Fountain murderers had grabbed the headlines, the publicity did not slow down his day-to-day enforcement of the law. New Mexico and west Texas newspapers were quick to print the scantiest bit of information about him, and all the stories indicate that he was a very active lawman. On July 3, 1896, he also became a United States deputy marshal. He needed

---

[17] Sonnichsen, *Tularosa*, 199–201.
[18] *El Paso Times*, November 3, 4, 1919, October 20, 1920.
[19] The informant prefers to remain anonymous.

the extra money, and the government wanted someone to help stem the illegal flow of Chinese laborers across the Mexican border.[20]

Garrett managed to stay busy, but his efforts failed to improve his financial outlook very much. Consequently, in early October, 1899, he looked forward to a possible reward for picking up a fugitive at San Augustine Ranch.

San Augustine Ranch is so old that its very beginnings are forgotten. It stands on a picturesque plateau at the eastern base of the Organ Mountains, approximately twenty-five miles from Las Cruces. The first Americans passed that way nearly 150 years ago, and they gazed in awe at the large springs, the ruins of two adobe structures, and miles of crumbling walls. When asked who built it, the Mexicans shrugged. It had always been there.

Thomas J. Bull, an adventurer from Indiana, took possession in 1850, but he sold out within a few years to Warren J. Shedd, an adventurer from St. Louis. Shedd envisioned the ranch as a stopover for wayfarers. He built a hotel, a stage station, and horse corrals. Soon wagon trains were pausing out front, resting, and laying in supplies. Travelers came on foot, on horseback, by wagon and stage. Most visitors spent only a night. A few hung around several days, and many stayed forever. Their tombstones can still be found.

During the Civil War, Shedd temporarily went into retirement. The only recorded activity at his ranch took place in late July, 1861, when the Union Army's Seventh Infantry, commanded by Major Isaac Lynde, surrendered under the San Augustine cottonwoods to a small Confederate force commanded by Colonel John R. Baylor.

After the war, when travelers resumed their journeys, Shedd built a large adobe dance hall and gambling house. Girls were imported to assist the liquor sales and to make sure that no cowboy ever went to bed lonely. Gradually the remote ranch took on a fearsome reputation. Screams were reported late at night. Boarders who talked too much about their cash on hand mysteriously disappeared. Shootouts became common, although San Augustine never had a Boot Hill. Bodies were usually buried where they fell, or shoveled under beside the road. One of the weirdest stories concerned slave girls, whom Shedd allegedly kidnapped from Mexico. When he tired of their charms or they lost their beauty (which happened fast in that depraved atmosphere), they were either sold back into Mexican peonage or murdered and buried in the corrals.

[20] Department of Justice, Number 17113, File No. 5624, National Archives.

Nobody ever proved any of these horrible tales, and Shedd was never legally charged with a crime more serious than selling liquor without a license.[21]

By the 1880's, Shedd was growing old and feeble. He sold out to Benjamin E. Davies, who was much more respected. A Welshman who had ridden into the Mesilla Valley with the California Column in 1862, Davies drastically changed the character of the San Augustine. An era of culture and refinement followed. He became a successful stockman, and huge herds of sheep and cattle roamed his ranges. Gone was the terror that had stalked the ranch during the preceding decades. Lives were happier and brighter—until his four-year-old daughter died of a rattlesnake bite. Davies' death followed a short time later, and since his wife could not operate the ranch alone, she put it up for sale. William W. Cox bought it in 1893.

Cox, known as "W. W." or "Bill" to his friends, was a tall, slender, wiry man with brown eyes and a thick shock of hair. Quick-tempered and a good storyteller, he became known for his odd habit of wearing a white shirt, with a white starched collar, a string tie, and a vest. Except in bed, he never dressed any other way, even when branding cattle or breaking horses. He never ran out of cuss words or tobacco. While inoffensive in his language, he never put a halter on it, even around preachers and women. Most people liked him, and his cowhands were loyal both to the man and the brand.

Cox had grown up on the Texas frontier and had become accustomed to the hardships and violence of frontier life. During his early years he learned that ambushes and bushwackings were a respected way of dealing with enemies. His father, Captain James W. Cox, rode with the hated state police, a law-enforcement body predating the Texas Rangers and installed by the Reconstruction government. Many of these lawmen hid behind their badges while they robbed, killed, and plundered. Whether or not the elder Cox did so is not known, but there were indictments of an unknown nature against him in Karnes County. When he and a friend, Jake Chrisman, went to answer the charges, they stumbled into an ambush by the John Wesley Hardin gang. For some years a strug-

---

[21] Marshal Hail, "The San Augustine Ranch House," *Frontier Times*, September, 1969, pp. 39–40, 64–65; "The San Augustine Springs Incident," *Nike News*, December, 1967, pp. 2–9; James Cox, interview with author, San Augustine Ranch, November 9, 1967.

gle had been raging between the two factions (now known as the Sutton-Taylor feud),[22] and an exchange of gunfire followed. It was W. W. Cox who rode by later and found his father and Chrisman, both dead, the older Cox reportedly having fifty-eight wounds in his body. The boy turned avenger, and soon there were several murder warrants against him.

That region of Texas soon flared into warfare. Cox was captured and jailed. There is a legend that he spent several years behind bars without a trial. He went to jail with a sack of peaches and threw the seeds out the window. One of them sprouted and the tree grew so large that one dark night he slid down it to freedom.

Taking his family, he fled to the Big Bend and became a ranch foreman. In 1890 he moved to Doña Ana County in New Mexico, where he settled, became respectable, and managed to have the Texas charges against him dropped. Three years later he purchased San Augustine Ranch, and the Cox family has owned it ever since.[23]

Although Cox became Oliver Lee's brother-in-law, that had no immediate effect upon his relationship with Pat Garrett. They respected each other, and if Garrett knew about Cox's past, he made no mention of it. The rancher remained law-abiding and was not involved in the Fountain slayings. When the colonel and his son disappeared, Cox freely assisted in the investigation. He gave information to Garrett and Pinkerton agent Fraser concerning the whereabouts of Fall during the early days after the disappearance.[24]

Meanwhile, in Greer County, Oklahoma, Norman Newman, a handsome, boyish-looking man, was returning from town with his farming partner. It was early November, 1898, and the forty-mile trip to sell farm produce was almost ended. Both had money in their pockets, but Newman wanted it all, and so he killed his partner while the man slept. (There is another version which says that the partner attacked him first and that Newman slew him in self-defense with a wagon wrench.) Newman loaded the body in the wagon, drove to the farm, stripped off the dead man's clothes, and threw the corpse into a shallow body of water, where it remained for six weeks. Hastily bundling up his partner's possessions, Newman drifted a few miles away to another job.[25]

---

[22] Sonnichsen, *I'll Die Before I'll Run*, 35–115, has the best account of this feud.

[23] The Cox Collection, University of Texas at El Paso Archives.

[24] Pinkerton Reports, March 7, 23, 1896.

[25] Sterling Rhode, taped interview with Herman Weisner, Organ, N. Mex., undated; *El Paso Daily Herald*, October 9, 1899.

He did not wander far enough, however, for he was caught and put in jail. There he met Perry Cox, W. W.'s brother. Cox was there on a minor charge, but he was in long enough to get to know and like the boy. Within a few weeks he broke Newman out, furnished him with a stolen horse, and instructed him to ride straight for San Augustine Ranch.[26]

The kid arrived travel-worn and dusty as W. W. Cox was branding calves in the rock corral. Newman watched silently for a moment, hopped off his small bay horse, slid his legs over the fence, and pitched in. When they finished, Cox asked his name. "Billy Reed," the man said. Cox told him that he needed no new hands but that Mrs. Cox was pregnant and could use some kitchen help. Reed accepted the job. Nobody asked why a fellow with such obvious cattle experience would be content doing household chores.

Reed aroused interest in other people, too, especially lawmen around the Southwest. Rumors spoke of an undisclosed but substantial reward offered for his arrest. The crime had so outraged Oklahomans that they were determined to track him down.

Sheriff George Blalock[27] of Greer County had followed Newman's trail for months, learned that he lived at the Cox ranch, and accordingly notified Pat Garrett. A warrant was sworn out for Newman, alias Reed, and on Saturday, October 7, 1899, Blalock, Garrett, and Deputy José Espalin left Las Cruces to make the arrest.

Espalin rode horseback, while Garrett and Blalock traveled in a buckboard. Approaching their destination, they hid the horse and buckboard behind a small rise. Blalock was assigned to watch over the horses, and Garrett and Espalin slipped quietly down the road behind the house. The two lawmen cautiously opened the rear gate and quietly crossed the patio. The kitchen door was open and Reed stood facing the sink, washing dishes. Pat stepped through the entrance, leveled his gun, and asked, "Are you Mr. Reed?"

The man nodded yes.

"Well, I have a warrant for your arrest, Mr. Reed."[28]

Reed wiped his hands on an apron as Garrett holstered his pistol. Then Reed's fist smashed Garrett in the face. The sheriff retaliated by striking the outlaw a vicious blow across the head with the

[26] Sterling Rhode, taped interview with Herman Weisner, Organ, N. Mex., undated.

[27] The name has been incorrectly spelled Blaylock.

[28] Sterling Rhode, taped interview with Herman Weisner, Organ, N. Mex. undated.

handcuffs. Reed staggered and went down, but as Garrett and Espalin attempted to straddle and secure him, a new factor entered the brawl. Old Booze, A. B. Fall's pet bulldog who had been sleeping on the porch, heard the commotion and figured he was not doing his job unless he became involved. With a snarl he jumped through the open French window.

The struggle turned into a wild melee of yells, barks, growls, profanity, and the clatter of bodies crashing into the walls and furniture. Reed's clothes (which had belonged to the man he murdered in Oklahoma) were almost torn off as Garrett and Espalin repeatedly knocked him to the floor. Finally he broke away and raced frantically for the meathouse, a roofed-over breezeway near the kitchen. A pistol lay on the shelf there. Reed jerked open the meathouse door and lunged inside. Two gunshots roared. One bullet lodged in the wall beside him, and the other went into his back and tore through his heart. He died instantly.

Gunfire frightened the dog, and he quit chewing on the officers and returned to the porch. For a long moment the only sounds were labored gasps of heavy breathing. Then Garrett and Espalin entered the breezeway and dragged Reed's body outside. Carrying him to the small buckboard, the two exhausted men pitched him in, sliding his head under the driver's seat and allowing his lower legs to dangle over the tailgate. On reaching Las Cruces, they found that his heels and feet were badly mauled from being dragged on the high center of the road.

On October 8 the body arrived in El Paso for embalming, and from there it was sent to Oklahoma. An inquest was held in Las Cruces on the ninth; Deputy Espalin admitted firing both shots, including the fatal one. Neither law officer was found at fault. No reward—if one was ever offered—was collected.[29]

Cox was in Mexico during the battle and did not learn of it until several days later. He was not pleased that Reed had been killed in his house—especially with his pregnant wife sitting terrified in the next room—but there is no convincing evidence that Cox was bitter or outraged toward Garrett as a result. Afterward Pat borrowed money from Cox and worked for him on a cattle roundup (of which more later).

Print Rhode, Mrs. Cox's younger brother, was perhaps the most

[29] Robert N. Mullin, "Pat Garrett—Two Forgotten Killings," *Password*, Vol. X, No. 2 (Summer, 1965), 29–62; James Cox, interview with author, "San Augustine Ranch, November 9, 1967.

furious at Garrett over the killing. A short, stocky individual with a ruddy complexion, Print boasted of his strong hands and muscular arms. He loved to fight with his fists, and while he did not necessarily look for trouble, plenty of it seemed to follow him around. This young slugger rode with Cox up the trail from Texas, and the rancher considered him completely loyal and dependable.

Rhode was not at San Augustine Ranch when Reed was killed, but he happened by a few hours later. In almost a frenzy he paced about as he listened to the story. It was not Reed's death that bothered him. He resented the fact that it had occurred in front of his sister, who could have been seriously injured. Rhode swore that if Garrett were not so far away he would kill him.[30]

During the next few months Pat Garrett continued to busy himself as sheriff. On February 12, 1900, the George D. Bowman & Son Bank was robbed in Las Cruces. The bandits got away with fifteen hundred dollars, and Garrett spent many days on horseback trying to solve the crime.

But Pat was rapidly tiring of the sheriff's life. Now nearing fifty, he was too old to be spending so much time in the saddle. He wanted different work, something free from financial liabilities. With the dismissing of the territorial case against Lee, Gililland, and McNew, his prospects vanished for a share of that reward money. The work of five years had been for nothing.

Pat had been an honest and frugal sheriff, as the *Río Grande Republican* stated.[31] During his first year in office expenses had totaled about three thousand dollars, whereas the county ordinarily spent between ten and fifteen thousand. But even with these savings, the Doña Ana commissioners were reluctant to pay him his day-to-day pittance. By 1900 the county owed him almost four thousand dollars, and he needed it. When he finally made a tax collection of three thousand dollars, he held it up while he asked Fall for suggestions. The lawyer advised him to keep it and allow the district attorney to file a charge of misappropriation of funds so that the entire matter could be aired. Fall represented him, and Garrett won his case. Not only did he keep the three thousand dollars, but the county commissioners ordered a special tax levied so that an additional eight hundred dollars due him might be raised and paid.[32]

[30] James Cox, interview with author, San Augustine Ranch, November 9, 1967.
[31] *Río Grande Republican*, February 16, 1897.
[32] *El Paso Herald*, December 26, 1901.

Pat Garrett

His collection troubles represented the final indignity for Pat
Garrett. He announced that he would not seek re-election. The job
was too difficult, the authorities too ungrateful, the pay too meager.
Instead, he cast his eye on a government job in El Paso.

20

El Paso Customs Collector

El Paso, Texas, in 1901 was emerging from its bloody past. For thirty years it had been a haven, a refuge for the gunman and outlaw with no place to turn except the graveyard. Such awesome gunslingers as Dallas Stoudenmire, John Wesley Hardin, and John Selman had been tolerated for a while and then buried. Old-time little-known gunmen such as Mannen Clements were still around, reduced to shaking down prostitutes and bullying the meeker citizens. They were relics of another age, trapped in an atmosphere of change, and gradually being ground under as they failed to adjust to a new era.

No longer was El Paso just a backroads border community. Its three banks had not been robbed in years, and its five railroads hustled, rumbled, and screamed day and night, unloading and taking on new cargos and passengers. Four international bridges spanned the muddy Río Grande. Ten newspapers alternately published and went out of business, but the *El Paso Daily Times* and the *El Paso Herald* consistently met their payrolls. Servicing El Paso's ten thousand residents were two electric plants, an opera house, and nineteen churches. Offsetting these evidences of peace and prosperity were innumerable saloons, a flourishing red-light district called the Tenderloin, a half-dozen opium dens, drinking water full of sand, and politicians who bribed Mexican citizens to wade across the Río Grande and vote in American elections.

Across the Río Grande sprawled the ornate, poverty-stricken community of Juárez (formerly Paso del Norte), Mexico. A bustling border town somewhat larger than El Paso, it funneled goods in and out of both communities. South of Juárez bawling herds of cattle were driven across the sandhills, where fine dust slipped beneath neckerchiefs and brought gritty oaths from sweat-soaked vaqueros. Railroad cars loaded with copper, gold, and silver ore

241

from Mexican mines—largely owned by American and British interests—rattled into El Paso and halted near the smelters. On a smaller scale the farm produce of both countries was bartered back and forth across the river. Citizens of Mexico purchased hard-to-get items in El Paso, while in Juárez, American ladies pinned yards of high-quality imported cloth beneath their voluminous skirts and, with looks of total innocence, rode mule-drawn streetcars back to the American side. They were rarely searched.[1]

Overseeing this border trade on the United States side was the collector of customs, whose operation centered in the $150,000 customhouse on the southeast corner of St. Louis and North Oregon streets. The Customs District of Paso del Norte, established in 1853, took in all of west Texas, plus the Arizona Territory (present New Mexico and Arizona). Caleb Sherman supervised this frontier of nine hundred miles as the first customs collector. With his headquarters at Frontera, Texas (less than ten miles northwest of El Paso), he earned his wages of two thousand dollars annually. In 1855 he collected $10,319.29 in duties.[2] Las Cruces took over the office in 1858, but the headquarters was transferred back to El Paso in 1863. By 1886 there were twenty-five employees in seven different offices, although in 1890 this number was reduced when Arizona became a separate collection district.

The collectorship at El Paso appealed to Pat Garrett, even though H. M. Dillon had been there for nearly three years. Pat had no way of knowing Dillon's exact status (the position was a presidential appointment), but he planned to keep himself as well known as possible and hoped that political lightning would strike.

In May, 1901, Garrett led a delegation of citizens from Las Cruces to El Paso to meet President William McKinley. The President arrived on a Sunday morning and gave the committee a private audience aboard his train. The group pleaded the cause of statehood for New Mexico, citing the population increase, the cattle and agricultural resources, and the mining and railroad interests. Garrett's party also asked McKinley to remove Governor Miguel Otero from office. The president nodded, noncommittally. He promised his support for statehood but cautioned that he would have to take Otero's dismissal under advisement.

---

[1] Mrs. Hugh White, interview with author, El Paso, Texas, June 3, 1968.

[2] Lee A. Riggs (chief inspector of El Paso customs), "A Short History of the District of El Paso," unpublished manuscript, 1938, copy in the possession of the author.

Explaining that he was on a vacation trip, McKinley declined to expedite any business before returning to Washington. He dismissed his audience, picked up his tall hat, bounced his cane on the oak floor, and took a buggy tour of El Paso. Late that afternoon he attended Sunday services at Trinity Methodist Church and then bade farewell to the sand, the barren mountains, and the prickly mesquite of El Paso.[3]

While McKinley may have seriously considered statehood for New Mexico, he had very little time to work toward it. Within five months he died from an assassin's bullet and the presidency passed to the exuberant and aggressive Theodore Roosevelt.

In late 1901, Roosevelt exercised the prerogative of his office and chose not to reappoint Collector Dillon. He sought a rugged, fearless man who might qualify, and his thoughts turned to Pat Garrett, though the two men had never met. Pat's chances were not hurt by the fact that four years earlier he had switched his political allegiance from the Democratic to the Republican party.

The nomination might have gone smoothly except that Roosevelt soon had disquieting second thoughts about Garrett. Letters and telegrams quickly piled up on the President's desk, protesting the former lawman's appointment. Most of them were from disappointed Republican office seekers who, when referring to Garrett, used the old cliché, "unfit for office." Very few of the correspondents bothered to explain their charges, and those who did furnish details wrote substantially the same message as George A. Knight, a former delegate to the Republican Convention in Philadelphia. Writing on stationery labeled the Fifth Congressional District in Texas, Knight objected that to appoint a man "who had made a record for himself as a 'killer' would . . . seriously reflect on any administration." Knight said that he had never met Garrett but had lived for several years in west Texas near the New Mexico border and knew the former sheriff "quite well by reputation."[4] Knight said that the position should go to some "competent and worthy Texas Republican." In times past the appointees had not "generally been the choice of the people." The local organization had never been "strengthened to any extent" by these appointments. Knight concluded by urging that the President seriously reconsider the matter.

[3] *El Paso Herald*, May 7, 1901.
[4] George A. Knight to President Theodore Roosevelt, December 13, 1901, General Records of the Department of the Treasury, Record Group 56, National Archives.

Outnumbering these protests, in numbers of signatures, were words of praise from citizens endorsing Garrett. Nearly all these letters and telegrams were from El Paso businessmen and city officials. But Garrett did not let his future rest on the uncertain influences of letters and wires. He presented his case directly to the President in early December, 1901. Former New Mexico Governor Wallace and Fall also threw their support behind him.[5]

Roosevelt still expressed some doubt about Garrett's "sterling qualities." Garrett traveled to Washington, D.C., to plead his case. Reportedly the President handed the former sheriff a printed note and asked him to read it aloud. If it suited Garrett, he was to sign it. The note stated: "I, the undersigned Patrick F. Garrett hereby give my word of honor, that if I am appointed Collector of Customs at El Paso, Texas, I will totally abstain from the use of intoxicating liquors during my term of office." After finishing, Pat beamed and replied, "Mr. Roosevelt, it suits me exactly," and he scrawled his signature beneath it. Within seconds Garrett had demolished three of the more obvious objections against him: by repeating the words aloud, he proved he could read; by signing the statement he proved that he could write; and by both these acts he took an oath not to drink.[6]

On December 16, 1901, Roosevelt nominated Pat Garrett collector of customs at El Paso and sent his name to the United States Senate for confirmation. Immediately the Senate Committee on Finance called Pat to its chambers and inquired into his alleged gambling. When questioned by Senator John C. Spooner of Wisconsin, Pat replied convincingly, with hardly a smile on his thin, straight lips, that he did not know the difference between a "straight flush" and "four of a kind." No senator could foresee, of course, that within two months Garrett would be guest of honor at an El Paso luncheon where the toastmaster would joke: "Here is the man that President Roosevelt worried about because he had the reputation of being a poker player. Everybody in El Paso knows that Pat Garrett isn't a poker player. He only thinks he's a poker player."[7]

Others knew of Garrett's card-playing habits. His old friend John

---

[5] *El Paso Herald*, December 26, 1901.

[6] Henry F. Hoyt, *Frontier Doctor*, 120. This book mistakenly refers to Garrett's position as that of "internal revenue collector." Many writers have perpetuated the error.

[7] This statement has wide but undocumented circulation around El Paso. Also see Keleher, *The Fabulous Frontier*, 86.

Nance Garner wrote him from Uvalde on December 14, exclaiming that everyone was "jubilant over the appointment." Garner noted that most folks expected Pat to make a lot of money, but "I am confident that at the end of your term . . . you won't have a cent more than you have now. Because in [one] big game . . . you could lose a year's salary . . . and you always imagined you could play poker."[8]

The Senate committee waved Garrett through, and confirmation came on December 20. Garrett hurried over to pay his last respects to the White House, and as he and the President walked to the door, Roosevelt said, "Mr. Garrett, I am betting on you."

Pat replied, "Mr. President, you will win that bet." Jubilant over his good fortune, he quickly left on the train for El Paso.[9]

At the Grand Hotel, Pat called his wife and children to his side and, with Fall as his counsel, held a press conference. Garrett publicly thanked both Wallace and Fall for their support and declared that in making his appointment the President had considered the sources rather than the substance of the charges against him. Fall now took over the proceedings. He chatted about how Roosevelt had considered Garrett's record and ability and found him competent. He also smoothed over and explained the embarrassing charge of misappropriation of funds recently lodged against Garrett in Las Cruces.

But Garrett did not go to El Paso to make speeches or to explain away old rumors and charges. He was there to work and, as he wrote Roosevelt, "to administer the law justly and conscientiously to all."[10] Pat Garrett meant exactly what he said, and although he was sometimes accused of incompetence, he was never accused of dishonesty. Most of his difficulties, as in the past, boiled down to his grating personality. The Corralitos calf case gave his supporters their first cause to worry.

Cattle coming into the United States from Mexico had always been appraised according to age. The duty was $2.00 a head for calves one year old or under and $3.75 for those above that age. Naturally it took a person knowledgeable about cattle to act as inspector. Normally this duty would have been carried out by a specialist hired by the government, but Garrett vetoed that sugges-

---

[8] Garrett, *Life*, 37–38.

[9] *El Paso Herald*, December 26, 1901.

[10] Pat Garrett to Roosevelt, February 8, 1903, quoted in biographical introduction, by Jarvis P. Garrett, in Garrett, *The Authentic Life of Billy the Kid*, 39.

tion. He was well qualified to inspect cattle, and since he had worked with livestock off and on most of his life, there was no reason to dispute his contention. A politically wiser and less stubborn man might have foreseen the difficulties involved and appointed a specialist for the job. But Pat's pride stood in his way, and he operated on a slim budget. There was no reason to pay a person for work that he could do, and his refusal played directly into the hands of his enemies.

In April and May, 1902, J. D. Campbell, representing the Corralitos Ranch near Casas Grandes, Mexico, shipped four separate herds of young cattle, totaling 3,132 head, across the Río Grande to El Paso. He described all of them as calves, but Pat judged that a little over half—1,866, to be exact—were more than one year old, and he charged duty accordingly. Campbell angrily questioned the decision and appealed to the Board of Appraisers in New York.

Unfortunately, the New York officials considered El Paso to be at the end of the earth.[11] During the next few months a series of letters, telegrams, documents, and instructions raced back and forth between El Paso and New York while the cattle grew older each day. Finally, on August 22, the board agreed to a "fair average estimate." Only 10 to 30 per cent of each shipment was judged to be over one year old, a total of 587 head. Campbell was not pleased with the decision, but it was an improvement over Garrett's tally, and he accepted it. Garrett, however, took the loss personally. He promptly appealed, vowing to fight to the United States Supreme Court if necessary. He did go as far as the United States Circuit Court, where his case was either dismissed or dropped.[12]

In official Washington the dispute with the Corralitos Company was a small part of a louder series of complaints reaching the office of Leslie M. Shaw, secretary of the treasury. The El Paso collector was accused of being contentious and difficult to reason with. In February, 1903, I. A. Barnes, representing an American importing firm doing business in Juárez, circulated a petition calling for Garrett's removal—and Barnes's own appointment to the position. Few people in El Paso were fooled by so blatant a tactic; even the news-

[11] Suit 1542, Board of General Appraisals, New York, August–December, 1902. Since there was not enough appraisal business in the Southwest, the New York board handled such cases. Records are in the Federal Records Center, New York, N.Y. The records on Garrett's appeal are missing.

[12] *El Paso Herald*, August 27, September 17, 1902.

papers laughed, pointing out that the petition had "received the merry ha ha and the cold shoulder."

One unidentified correspondent wrote the *El Paso Herald* on February 24, 1903, predicting that the uproar would "come to nothing." Garrett was conscientious and trying "to serve his government without fear or favor." The Corralitos Company had been after the collector from the first because "they knew he would do his duty and play no favorites." The Juárez merchants were after him because "he enforces the law and does not allow the importation of goods duty free. It hurts their business and they howl." Certain persons, the writer continued, have said "that Mr. Garrett wanted to collect all the revenue he could in order to make a good showing." This charge, he said, was ridiculous. Garrett was "a genuine American who enforces the laws because he was put here for that purpose and because they were made to protect American interests."

Nevertheless, Barnes's petition had its effect. Secretary Shaw sent Garrett a reprimand, bluntly telling him to practice politeness while on the job. This rebuke so humiliated Garrett that he by-passed Shaw and wrote directly to President Roosevelt. "It has been my ambition," the angry collector stated, "to treat all persons doing business with this office with the upmost courtesy, and if in any case it has not been done I certainly did not know of it."[13] Obviously Garrett had a direct line to the President's office, and Roosevelt, though growing uneasy about his controversial appointment, showed no inclination to terminate it.

Shaw sent Joseph Evans, a special treasury agent, to El Paso with instructions to check into Garrett's operations. Evans and Garrett began their relationship like two wary dogs sniffing at each other. The inspector asked Garrett to appoint George M. Gaither to do the cattle inspecting. Pat objected, for he knew Gaither as a small-time political hack who drifted from one government job to another, and not particularly competent at any of them. Accordingly, Garrett told Evans that he considered Gaither "absolutely unfit for any position under the government."[14]

Then Garrett had second thoughts. Why not put Gaither on as a cattle inspector? Give him a thirty-day trial period, and if he did not work out, everyone could see that Garrett had at least

---

[13] Garrett to Roosevelt, February 8, 1903, quoted in Garrett, *Life*, 39.
[14] Garrett to Secretary of the Treasury Leslie M. Shaw, April 7, June 20, 1903, Treasury Records, National Archives.

tried. Gaither began his duties on March 9, and at the end of a month Garrett did not reappoint him. When Gaither asked why not, Pat simply said that he had no authority to employ him full time. Then Gaither stormed away, vowing to his friends that he would have Garrett's job.

There the matter rested until the morning of May 8, when Garrett approached Evans and Gaither, who were slouching near the doorway of the Nation's Meat and Supply Company on San Antonio Street.

"Did you tell [anyone] that I said [your] . . . position was permanent?" Garrett demanded of Gaither.

"No, I did not," Gaither replied, "but said that you promised, with the assistance of Colonel Evans, if possible to make it permanent."

"You are a God-damned liar!" Garrett roared. Turning to Evans, he snarled, "You are a God-damned liar too!"

With that, Gaither struck Garrett, and the two men stood toe-to-toe, swinging wildly at each other. County Attorney Maury Kemp and Chief of Police Peyton J. Edwards, followed by about twenty-five spirited citizens, charged in and separated the gladiators. The corner was mass confusion, and the *El Paso Evening News* chuckled that the scene bordered "on the comic opera style for a few moments." There were no knockdowns, but Gaither had a trickle of blood on his face. Both men were arrested, and the next morning each paid a five-dollar fine for disturbing the peace.[15]

At this point the Treasury Department, trying to intimidate and humiliate Garrett, appointed I. A. Barnes as a special investigator (a reward for circulating the petition?) and ordered him to investigate the affair and submit an impartial report. Barnes apparently did an honest job; he hardly needed to do anything else. Affidavits were taken from witnesses Maury Kemp, Joseph Evans, J. C. Peyton, and J. H. Biggs. Barnes asked Garrett to present his side too, but Pat replied that he had already "been tried and adjudged upon malicious statements" and "respectfully declined" to make any further comments. On May 27, Barnes submitted his report to Secretary Shaw, concluding it with the remark that "many of the citizens considered the fight a very disgraceful affair."[16]

---

[15] *El Paso Evening News*, May 8, 1903; *El Paso Herald*, May 8, 1903; *El Paso Daily Times*, May 9, 1903.

[16] I. A. Barnes to Secretary Shaw, May 27, 1903, Treasury Records, National Archives.

Shaw had already asked Garrett to explain the scuffle. On May 14 Shaw had written him: "You are directed to submit a prompt and full report upon the subject, and you are advised that such conduct upon the part of a person holding the office of Collector of Customs is regarded as indefensible and deserves censure in the strongest terms."[17]

Garrett replied on May 21, and his comments were as blunt and to the point as Shaw's had been: "While there are extenuating circumstances connected with this unfortunate affair, your letter would indicate that . . . I was entirely in the wrong, no defense could be made for my actions, and that I might expect no consideration. Consequently, I do not deem any report I might make would be construed as justifiable for my conduct."[18]

That ended the episode, except for some good-natured kidding. A couple of hours after the fight Pat passed Fall on the street.

"Hello, Pat," said Fall. "I hear that you had a fight with Gaither this morning. You'll learn not to come down here and tangle with these Texans."

Pat grinned and replied, "Albert, do you remember that time up at Cox's ranch when that little Gene Rhodes chased you all around the corral and beat you up so bad that we had to pull him off and take you to the house for a drink of whiskey to bring you back to life?"

"I don't remember a thing about it," Fall said. He repressed a grin of his own and walked on.[19]

Garrett knew that, though his troubles were being laughed about in El Paso, there was no smirking in Washington. Shaw was obviously out to get him, and the proof was not long in coming.

"Reports from many sources," Shaw wrote on one occasion, "indicate that you are not doing your full duty in fixing the correct market price of cattle admitted to the United States." The Secretary urged Garrett to give "personal attention to and require indication on every entry of the specific class of cattle imported sufficient to enable our special representatives [Evans and Barnes] to trace actual conditions in each case." Shaw said that there was too much laxity in the admission of cattle.

[17] Assistant Secretary of Treasury to Pat Garrett, May 14, 1903, Treasury Records, National Archives.

[18] Garrett to Secretary Shaw, June 20, 1903, Treasury Records, National Archives.

[19] Maury Kemp, interview with C. L. Sonnichsen, El Paso, undated, Sonnichsen Papers, University of Texas at El Paso Archives.

Garrett struck back on June 20. The cattle question was "connected with many details which are difficult to explain when investigation is conducted with the view in mind to make the most of trivial discrepancies that arise in the transactions of business." Garrett blamed the entire difficulty on the "adverse and exaggerated reports" which Treasury agent Evans had made to Shaw. The statements, based on "stories poured into the ear of ready listeners for the purpose of causing conflict," had tainted Garrett's administration with "gross neglect and suspicious dealings." When he acted "in favor of the government interest," he had been opposed by Evans, and was "embarrassed and annoyed in his judgment for fear of making mistakes."[20]

Barnes also jumped on the appraisal issue. In his report for July he stated that among other things Garrett has consistently undervalued Mexican cattle—the direct opposite of what Evans was trying to prove. Garrett must have smiled when he heard this argument. It was the first time, he wrote Secretary Shaw on July 20, that he had known owners to complain about the duty being too low. Barnes, somewhat flustered, struggled to explain his statements but only made matters worse. He said that Mexican cattle were of such poor quality that they could compete on the American market only by being admitted with low duty rates, and thus the collector was illegally subsidizing them. Garrett retorted that Barnes "has had but a few weeks experience in the cattle business, and that consists of what he has gained from cattlemen antagonistic to this office."[21]

On another occasion Barnes complained that Garrett had, apparently for no reason, dismissed Frank G. Presnell and Charles B. Read as ore samplers in the customhouse. When this report reached Washington, Shaw wired Garrett and asked for an explanation. Pat said that the men were too slow in running tests and that he was eager to improve the service. He added that Barnes and Read were personal friends, that Read had been instrumental in circulating a recall petition, and that Barnes was trying to repay a debt by having Read reinstated. In this instance, Garrett's actions were upheld.[22]

Occasionally a letter supported Garrett. On November 5, 1904, a correspondent (whose name is not decipherable) wrote Secre-

[20] Garrett to Secretary Shaw, June 20, 1903, Treasury Records, National Archives.
[21] *Ibid.*
[22] *Ibid.*, March 17, March 23, July 18, 1903.

tary Shaw testifying to Garrett's character. He claimed to know Pat Garrett and said that he had "never seen [Garrett] under the influence of liquor." Furthermore, the former lawman always told the truth, something, he added, "few men in this part of the country appear able to do." Garrett's difficulties, he said, stemmed from a lack of identification with the local Republican organization, "whose members seem more anxious to fight each other than to build pride in the party."

As Garrett's position became increasingly untenable, two friends stood by him. One was Emerson Hough, the well-known western writer. Hough went to see Garrett in El Paso and said that he would like to make a southwestern tour to find material for a new book he was writing. In October, 1905, Pat took him through Lincoln County, New Mexico, and into Roswell. Garrett showed Hough the irrigation canals and explained how close he had come to being a wealthy man. As they drove their buggy out onto the mesas an antelope crossed the road in front of them. Garrett grabbed his rifle, swung it into line, pulled the trigger, and heard only a click as his gun misfired. He swore, remarking that he had once had Oliver Lee in his sights and the same thing had happened then.[23]

Hough and Garrett discussed reprinting Garrett's *Authentic Life of Billy the Kid*. Pat admitted that the job had been poorly done, that much of it was in error, and that he wanted to see the truth about the Kid published. Hough liked the idea and agreed to rewrite Garrett's version, but, after sleeping on the matter and consulting with his publishers, he decided that a new and complete history of the Lincoln County War was needed. This plan was later discarded, and Hough's manuscript became part of a series entitled *The Story of the Outlaw*. Garrett read, made changes in, and finally approved the Lincoln County portion, but his efforts were largely wasted when the script underwent heavy editorial cutting in order to present a more dramatic effect.[24]

Garrett counted on making some money from the book for his services as narrator and adviser, and his letters to Hough indicate that he believed a verbal financial contract existed between them. Hough's replies are very vague on the subject of an agreement to share literary proceeds. It is evident that his conscience was both-

---

[23] James Shinkle, interview with author, Roswell, N. Mex., August 8, 1968; *Roswell Record*, October 23, 1905.

[24] The Hough, Garrett, and Roosevelt correspondence that follows is in the Emerson Hough Collection, Iowa State Department of History and Archives, Des Moines.

ering him as he wrote, but whether or not he ever sent a check to ease his mental suffering is not clear. There is no definite mention that he did so in the correspondence.[25]

Another friend of Garrett's, Tom Powers, a one-eyed, happy-go-lucky Irishman, owned the Coney Island Saloon in El Paso. Powers had left Wisconsin in a hurry after "beating hell out of his father," and in the Southwest he became a well-known bar owner and gambler. Pat spent considerable time in the Coney Island Saloon, and even gave Powers the revolver that he had used when he killed Billy the Kid. "One-Eyed Riley," as Powers was often called, already had an impressive gun collection with a number of weapons hanging in a place of honor above the bar. Years later, after Pat's death, the Garrett family filed a civil suit asking for the return of the gun. They won their case, although whether or not the wily Powers actually surrendered the correct six-shooter is debatable.[26]

Powers asked Garrett for an introduction to President Roosevelt at the 1905 Rough Riders convention in San Antonio, Texas. Pat complied, and referred to Powers as a "cattleman." He lied not because Roosevelt would have been angered by the presence of a gambler and bar owner mixing with his hard-drinking and poker-playing Rough Riders but because such an intimate association of these two west Texans might have been misconstrued as proving that Garrett's close friends were men of disreputable character.

At the gathering Roosevelt walked amicably about the encampment, cheerfully chatting and posing with his famed clenched-teeth grin among his former comrades, many of whom were now engaged in all sorts of questionable occupations. None of these photographs caused any comments except those taken with Powers and Garrett. Almost before the negative had dried, an uproar started when the photos were leaked to the press. Roosevelt was

[25] Shortly after Garrett's death, New Mexico Territorial Attorney General James M. Hervey contacted Hough and asked whether he would help finance an investigation into Garrett's death. Hough replied that "Garrett owed him considerable money" and that he could not help. James Madison Hervey, "The Assassination of Pat Garrett," *True West*, March–April, 1961.

[26] Mrs. Tommy Powers Stamper, interview with author, Virden, N. Mex., July 10, 1968. Mrs. Stamper, who was Tom Powers' favorite daughter (he had no sons and he named her Tommy), claims that her father gave an identical model to the Garrett family. She claims that the original Garrett pistol is still owned by the Powers descendants.

[27] R. N. Mullin, interview with author, El Paso, August 5, 1968. Mullin claims that secret-service men went to El Paso, collecting and destroying all the controversial photographs that they could find.

reportedly shocked upon learning that Powers was a gambler, and he growled furiously about being misled.[27]

El Paso newspapers flashed the story that Garrett's next two-year appointment was in danger, and they were certainly correct. Pat's had been a controversial nomination from the beginning, and, though Roosevelt had had many second thoughts about the wisdom of his choice, he had nevertheless stood by Garrett. The photo, coming on top of everything else, threatened to be too much even for the President's generosity. Garrett's friends strongly advised that he promptly apologize to the President and forsake Powers. Garrett did apologize, but he stubbornly refused to repudiate his friend. He could no more turn his back on a friend than he could appraise cattle for less than he thought fair.

Garrett reasoned that, if the President would talk to him and Powers, Roosevelt would recognize Tom as a responsible individual. With this conviction in mind he took Powers to Washington in early December, 1905. For a day or two the situation did not look desperate and Powers thought that they could win their case with a string of local endorsements. He wired Numa G. Buchoz, chief deputy collector in El Paso, and Charles Kinne, secretary to the Civil Service Board and chief clerk in the customhouse, to see what they could do. The men went to work and soon rushed off a bundle of petitions urging that Garrett be reinstated. In the meantime, neither Garrett nor Powers was permitted an audience with the President. On December 13, 1905, Pat learned that he would not be reappointed.[28]

Garrett still did not fully comprehend what was happening. Hough was asked to intercede, or at least ascertain the real reason for his dismissal. Hough tried, and, after several exchanges of correspondence with the President, learned that Secretary Shaw had finally accomplished what no gunman had previously been able to do—he had brought Pat Garrett down. Roosevelt had simply taken responsibility for the act, and the photo had provided the perfect excuse. Roosevelt summed it all up in a letter to Hough, dated December 16. Shaw had taken a strong stand against Garrett's reappointment on the grounds "that he was an inefficient collector; that he was away a large part of the time from the office; that he was in debt; and that his habits were bad." Roosevelt said that the photo incident "had nothing to do with these reports."

28 Issues of *El Paso Times, El Paso Herald*, and *El Paso Evening News*, December, 1905.

However, the President admitted that he was displeased to have Garrett "bring up as his intimate friend a man who . . . was well known as a professional gambler, and then have myself, Garrett and the gambler taken in a photograph together." Theodore Roosevelt described the entire affair as "not a happy incident."[29]

An interesting footnote is that Powers and Roosevelt became friends on March 15, 1911, when Roosevelt visited El Paso. They shook hands, exchanged a few pleasantries, and once more had their picture taken together—this one being much clearer and in better focus than the one taken earlier in San Antonio. Roosevelt graciously thanked Powers for a bear cub that the barman had captured in Mexico while on a hunting trip. It was shipped to Roosevelt in Washington, D.C., and the President was delighted. The reporters promptly dubbed it "Teddy's bear," and from this expression sprang "teddy bear" and a new industry.

But on December 22, 1905, Roosevelt again wrote Hough, making no mention of the photograph incident. He quoted Secretary of the Treasury Shaw as saying that he "either had to give up any attempt to secure good service . . . [at El Paso] or let Pat go." The President then revealed more of his personal philosophy. "I am refusing to appoint man after man," he said, "who I think is inefficient. This is a hard thing for me to write . . . but I want you to understand that Pat Garrett was my personal choice, just as . . . Seth Bullock in Deadwood and Ben Daniels in Arizona, both of whom are much of the Pat Garrett stamp, are my personal choices." If the Department of Justice has found that "either of these men does not do his duty, why, he will have to go out."

With the news of his dismissal, Pat Garrett left El Paso and returned to Doña Ana County, New Mexico. Perhaps it was a death wish that led him back to Las Cruces, within rifle shot of his old enemies. Whatever his thoughts and desires, he knew that he was returning to die.

[29] Roosevelt to Hough, December 16, 1905, Emerson Hough Collection, Iowa State Department of History and Archives, Des Moines.

21.

Financial Miseries

A very disillusioned and depressed Pat Garrett climbed aboard a rickety Santa Fe Railroad coach and rode back to Doña Ana County and to his dilapidated ranch twenty-five miles east of Las Cruces. The circumstances of his return remain, to this day, inexact and subject to controversy. Some southwestern history buffs believe that he went back to search for the Fountain bodies, to avenge his Hillsboro humiliation, and to make another try for the reward money. That is nonsense. The reward probably was not collectable at that late date, although it had never been officially disavowed. Most of it had been offered by private individuals and corporations, not by the territory. Even if someone was convicted (and another trial of the three accused would be highly unlikely, even though territorial officials still thought them guilty), getting the committed firms and people to honor ten-year-old obligations and promises would be difficult indeed.

The Garrett place was near the area where the Fountains had disappeared, but the ranch had been selected by coincidence, not by design. Garrett had simply wanted to raise horses on the land, not necessarily to use it as a headquarters for chasing criminals. And he returned there now because he had nowhere else to go.

Most assertions that Pat intended to reopen the Fountain mystery when he returned in 1906 stem from a statement made many years later by Hough to James Madison Hervey, attorney general of New Mexico. After Garrett's death, Hervey asked Hough to contribute money for a thorough examination of all the facts and theories. Hough demurred with the excuse that "Garrett got killed trying to find out who killed Fountain and you will get killed trying to find out who killed Garrett."[1] The extensive correspondence be-

---

[1] James Madison Hervey, "The Assassination of Pat Garrett," *True West*, March–April, 1961.

tween Hough and Garrett contains no mention of the Fountains, the Lees, the Coxes, or anyone else who might have been connected with Garrett's death. Their communications dealt solely with personal matters, Garrett's irrigation schemes, his discharge as customs collector, his mining ventures, his many debts, his agricultural aspirations, and his thoughts concerning Hough's forthcoming book, *The Story of the Outlaw*. That Garrett had no lingering professional interest in the Fountains is further demonstrated by his many absences from the ranch both during and after his tenure as collector. He would have remained forever in El Paso if Roosevelt and succeeding presidents had continued to reappoint him. To him the ranch was an investment and a place to keep his family.

He had begun ranching in 1898 or early 1899 by homesteading 160 acres on the east slopes of the San Andres, about seven miles from San Augustine Pass.[2] Gradually he built a small wood-and-rock house, a couple of outbuildings, and a few corrals. A large pool of water (now called Garrett's Spring) bubbled out of the brush-covered mountain about eighteen hundred feet northwest of the main building, and Garrett piped it downhill to his living quarters. Various breeds of livestock roamed the high, rolling country, and Garrett's animals were branded with an O on one or both jaws. His steers stocked a Las Cruces butcher shop, a few Holstein cows were kept for the benefit of Organ and Gold Camp miners, and, oddly enough for a man who loved quality stock, he grazed a large herd of small, inferior horses for use in his Las Cruces livery stable and feed lot.[3]

Garrett's pride, however, was his race horses. With his son Poe acting as both jockey and trainer, the Garrett O became a familiar sight on tracks all over the Southwest and Mexico. In Las Cruces he sponsored a horse in almost every heat, and during off-racing days a crowd would gather to watch his animals train.[4] These activities created some undesirable side effects. While horse racing did not hurt his popularity with the townspeople, neither did it arouse any rapture among his ranching neighbors. When their mustangs and quarter horses mixed with Garrett's racing

[2] There are no records of the exact date of his homestead deed, but the *Río Grande Republican* occasionally made a brief mention of his ranch in the San Andres.

[3] Sterling Rhode, taped interview with Herman Weisner, Organ, N. Mex., undated; *El Paso Herald*, October 19, 1899.

[4] H. M. Dow to author, January 24, 1967. Dow lived in Las Cruces during the late 1890's and often watched the Garrett horses run and train.

stock and inferior breeds, the results were often colts with weak backs and spindly legs.[5]

On May 24, 1899, Garrett paid one David Wood two hundred dollars for a quit-claim deed to Sinking Springs (often called Stinking Springs), in the center of Bear Canyon, seven miles northeast of the home ranch.[6] Since he controlled the water, this deed gave Garrett title to the entire canyon, a wild, remote area sheltered on the south by Black Mountain and on the north by what later became known as Goat Mountain. A small rock house and corral were included in the purchase. Garrett planned to raise horses there, as well as exploit the canyon's mineral possibilities.

Garrett's two ranches adjoined each other and hugged the northwest rim of Gold Camp, the richest mining community in southern New Mexico. Fall had large interests there, as did speculators from all across the nation. The famous Torpedo Mine alone was valued at over a quarter of a million dollars in 1904, and eye-popping hauls of silver and copper ores were blasted and hauled from its rich veins.[7] Though Garrett dabbled some in Gold Camp investments, he was financially unable to become deeply involved. Instead, he reasoned that his own property might have fabulous wealth too, and he delegated Poe Garrett to swing the miner's pick every time he found a shiny place on a rock. Pat believed that their personal bonanza always lay just beyond Poe's next shovelful of dirt. One of their most promising claims was the Bear Springs Mine. Another was the Nellie Lode with over fifteen hundred feet of shafts.[8] Neither claim did much more than meet expenses, and Pat gradually wearied of digging and assigned his fifteen-year-old son to that task alone. Garrett turned his attention to the selling of mining investments.

Pat had always been a speculator at heart. During his years in the customs service the newspapers made frequent mention of his trips into Mexico as he led gullible eastern capitalists to check on mining and ranching possibilities. Pat gradually became so well known below the border that as late as October, 1905, his friends were booming him as the next "Ambassador to Mexico."[9] He might have made it had not Secretary of the Treasury Shaw complained

[5] Emmett Isaacs, interview with author, Las Cruces, N. Mex., October 29, 1967. A Doña Ana County rancher, Isaacs knew Garrett and all Pat's neighbors.
[6] Quit Claim Deeds, Book 24, 497–98, Doña Ana County, N. Mex.
[7] Fayette Jones, Old Mines and Ghost Camps of New Mexico, 73–80.
[8] Mining Deeds, Book 3, page 3, Doña Ana County, N. Mex.
[9] Roswell Register, October 23, 1905.

to Roosevelt about Garrett's frequent trips away from the office (and, of course, there was that black mark acquired when he took Tom Powers to San Antonio).

In May, 1898, Pat and John Meadows, former buffalo hunter and cowboy, paid one hundred dollars to W. H. Hawkins, a brilliant El Paso and Northeastern Railroad attorney, as a down payment on the "Tennessee claim." The claim was in Ore Grande, a bustling miners' camp in the Jarilla Mountains north of El Paso. Six months later, under threat of repossession, the two men kicked in another one hundred dollars on the note for one thousand dollars. That was their last payment, and the mine shortly reverted to Hawkins.[10]

Garrett's experience with the Tennessee claim further convinced him that the profit in mines came not from hard work but from sale and speculation. Accordingly, he and the two Llewellyns, W. H. H. and Clinton B., organized the Alabama Gold and Copper Mining Company, whose articles of incorporation charged them with "acquiring, holding, working, and operating gold and silver mines." Ore Grande was again the area of operation. The partners' assets were listed at an incredible two hundred thousand dollars, divided into twenty thousand shares of ten dollars each.[11] The firm's actual purpose was to sell worthless stock. For ten dollars a share the buyer purchased pipe dreams and fast talk—all of it guaranteed by only a few words of assurance, a smile, and a beautifully etched piece of paper with Pat Garrett's signature boldly scratched across the bottom as secretary of the organization. The records do not say when this company went out of business, but it evidently folded about 1900 or 1901.

When Pat grew disenchanted with his mining ventures, he noted the success of A. B. Fall and suspected that lawyers invariably made large amounts of money. In 1905 he paid a small fee and became a bona fide Mexican attorney.[12] His first case (and evidently his last) involved defending an accused murderer near Santa Rosalia (now Ciudad Carmargo), Mexico, in the winter of 1905. The weather had been unseasonably cold, several inches of snow had fallen, and twenty miles from town, at the *Los Asabuches* (The Hackberries) Ranch, owner O. E. Finsted had a poker game

[10] W. A. Hawkins to P. F. Garrett, May 10, 1899, Hawkins Papers, Southern Pacific Collection, University of Texas at El Paso Archives; Deed Records, Book 15, 270, 311, Otero County, Alamogordo, N. Mex.
[11] Corporations Received Book, No. 2474, Volume 5, 38, New Mexico State Archives, Santa Fe.
[12] *Las Cruces Citizen*, August 18, 1906.

going. An argument broke out, and Finsted shot his two companions, known only as MacMurray and Rutherford. A ranch employee named Anderson poked his head inside to see what was happening, and was also shot. Anderson's fourteen-year-old son saw his father fall. The boy rode to *Estacion Diez* (Station Ten) on the Mexican Central Railway and wired the authorities in Santa Rosalia.

The *rurales* and Dr. G. B. Calnan, on vacation from the United States, went to investigate. Inside the house they found MacMurray sprawled dead on the floor. Rutherford had managed to drag himself into bed, where he had covered himself with a comforter before he died. Only Anderson survived, but he did not see who shot him. Finsted swore that the house had been attacked and robbed by bandits, but authorities discounted this tale because a considerable amount of cash was found scattered across the playing table, and in a corner sat an open safe, its contents untouched. Since there were no fresh hoofprints in the snow, the police charged Finsted with murder. Finsted hired Pat Garrett to defend him.

Garrett somehow talked Dr. Calnan into supporting Finsted, and the two men visited Washington in hopes of obtaining United States intervention. Failing in their efforts, they returned to Mexico, where Finsted was convicted of murder and sentenced to life in the penitentiary at Chihuahua. Revolutionaries freed him a few years afterward and he continued living in Mexico.[13]

His legal efforts having brought him no success south of the border, Garrett returned to Doña Ana County and to a financial situation growing more desperate by the day. He was so poor that Organ grocer L. B. Bentley refused him credit and wrote his name in a "deadbeat" book. Pat owed him less than ten dollars at the time.[14]

Liabilities continued to pile up, and Garrett was occasionally forced into civil court because of unpaid debts.[15] Even Tom Catron pressed him to honor a five hundred-dollar note signed on February 20, 1901. In two and a half years Catron had not been able to collect a single payment. He wrote Garrett many letters, citing

[13] *Río Grande Republican*, March 16, 1906; Geddes W. Mabee, Jr. to C. L. Sonnichsen, January 11, 1961, Sonnichsen Papers, University of Texas at El Paso Archives.

[14] Book in possession of Herman Weisner, Organ, N. Mex.

[15] District Court Records, Case No. 2637, Doña Ana County, N. Mex. On April 11, 1906, the Las Cruces firm of F. Brunschwig & Co. won a civil suit against Pat Garrett for $284.

impending poverty and claiming that "my account in the bank is overdrawn, and it is difficult for me to get money." He laid heavy stress upon their former close relationship and said that he could not understand why Garrett treated him in such an ungrateful manner. "There should be different actions from those you are showing me. I have always looked upon and considered you one of my best friends. Please answer my letters."[16]

Catron occasionally threatened legal action, but he saw the futility of that after he sent a note in May, 1904, to W. G. Walz, an El Paso importer who specialized in Mexican and Indian curiosities and souvenirs. He asked Walz to discount the note to a local bank, send him what he could get, and ask the bank to collect from Garrett. Walz's prompt reply was sympathetic but discouraging:

> I went to three or four local banks, and they all offered to take it if I would endorse it, and they each and every one told me that he was no good and that the endorser would have to pay. They did not even want to take it for collection as they have plenty of their own against him. He gets a salary [as customs collector] advanced to him as early as the 5th of the month. The First National Bank has a $100 note of his three years old that he will not even pay the interest on. He owes our company a small amount that he begs off on. I do not know any way for you to collect this from him. He might pay for politics or some other reason, but he pays no one down here. He figures in a lot of deals, but I do not think he puts a cent up on any of them.[17]

Perhaps it was Walz's comment about paying for political reasons that persuaded Catron to make one more try. On June 1 he wrote a final letter to Garrett:

> You surely do not owe much money and you ought to try to pay what you owe, especially as you hold a responsible position. The time will come when there will have to be a reappointment, and then all these businessmen will turn loose against you, and you may find it somewhat difficult to get a party to stand by you.

Garrett did not respond to this hint of blackmail, but before another year had gone by he must have wished that he had done so. Why Garrett refused to honor most of his obligations cannot be

---

[16] Thomas Catron to Pat Garrett, June 17, July 21, 28, September 24, October 12, 1903, Catron Papers, University of New Mexico Library, Albuquerque.
[17] W. G. Walz to T. B. Catron, May 31, 1904, *ibid.*

Emerson Hough, the renowned western writer, a close friend
of Pat Garrett. Courtesy Iowa State Archives.

The gold-and-silver-washed revolver presented to Pat Garrett by his associates at the El Paso Customs Office in 1902. It is a Colt Thunderer, double-action .41, serial No. 138671. Courtesy Bob McNellis, El Paso.

Jarvis Garrett, Pat Garrett's youngest son, holding the .41-caliber Colt given to his father in 1902. This photograph was taken in Albuquerque in 1972. Courtesy Bob McNellis, El Paso.

Pat Garrett, all 6′5″ of him. This photograph was taken either in El Paso or in Las Cruces, New Mexico, near the end of Garrett's life. Courtesy Gary Roberts.

Martin Lohman. Pat Garrett mortgaged his ranch to Lohman, who in turn mortgaged it to W. W. Cox. Courtesy Doña Ana County Sheriff's Collection, University of Texas at El Paso Archives.

Court scene at Organ, New Mexico, when Wayne Brazel and Print Rhode were charged by Pat Garrett with running cattle illegally on his land, 1907. Courtesy Herman Weisner.

ABOVE: José R. Lucero, sheriff of Doña Ana County, New Mexico. BELOW: Felipe Lucero, sheriff of Doña Ana County. Felipe arrested Wayne Brazel for the murder of Pat Garrett. Both photographs courtesy Doña Ana County Sheriff's Collection, University of Texas at El Paso Archives.

George Curry, governor of New Mexico Territory, about 1908. Courtesy Collections in the Museum of New Mexico.

Fred Fornoff, captain, New Mexico Mounted Police. Courtesy Western History Collections (Rose Collection), University of Oklahoma Library.

Jim Miller (The son-in-law of Mannen Clements), lynched at Ada, Oklahoma, April 19, 1909. Courtesy Western History Collections (Rose Collection), University of Oklahoma Library.

The lynching of Jim Miller in a barn near Ada. Miller is dangling on the left. The other victims are Joe Allen (center), B. B. Burrell, and Jesse West. Courtesy Western History Collections (Rose Collection), University of Oklahoma Library.

Standing, left to right: Elzy and Buster Brown. Seated, left to right: Elzy's wife, Wayne Brazel, and Buster's wife. The photograph was taken in Phoenix, Arizona, about 1914. Courtesy Jack Carter.

Left to right: Jim Lee, Wayne Brazel, and Will Craven, about 1900. Brazel had had his head shaved as a lark, and the boys decided to have his picture taken. Courtesy Hal Cox Collection, University of Texas at El Paso Archives.

273

Mrs. Pat Garrett holding the revolver that Garrett used to kill Billy the Kid. The photograph was taken either in El Paso or in Las Cruces about 1920. Courtesy Tom Kolberson.

The Garrett family plot, Masonic Cemetery, Las Cruces, New Mexico, photographed in 1972. Pat Garrett's grave is in the center foreground. Courtesy Bob McNellis, El Paso.

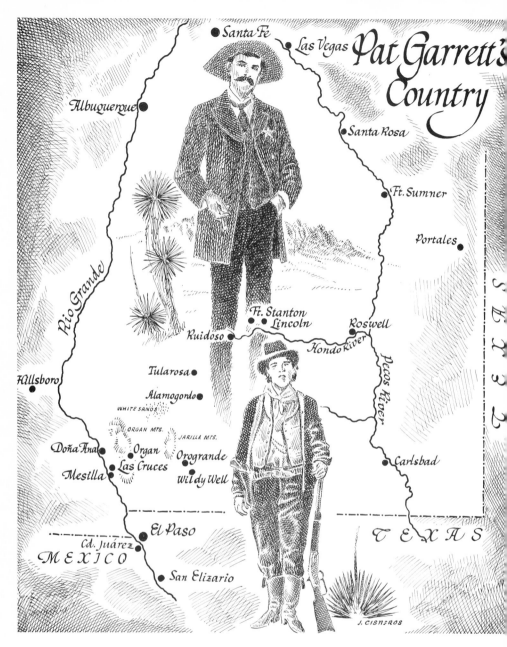

Pat Garrett's country. From a sketch by José Cisneros. Reproduced by
permission.

precisely answered. The pattern of his life indicates that he "intended" to pay his bills, but, like most habitual dreamers and gamblers, he optimistically believed that his fortune lay just around the next turn on the race track or in the mine shaft or in the next deck of cards. He would pay tomorrow . . . if it ever came.

Another reason why Garrett had such problems in repaying delinquent notes was that he was himself a soft touch. His old friend George Curry did not hesitate to utilize Garrett's generosity. As a deadbeat, Curry had few peers. He, along with Tom Catron, who had so piously dunned Pat Garrett, were allegedly notorious for failing to pay their debts. Compared with these two, Garrett was the epitome of fiscal integrity.

On July 12, 1890, the Albuquerque Bank of Commerce lent one thousand dollars in a single lump sum to three borrowers. The first signer was George Curry, just beginning his climb as a significant New Mexico political figure. Directly under his name was John Eubank's, followed on the bottom by Pat Garrett's. The note does not specify whether or not Eubank and Garrett shared equally in the borrowed money or whether they were merely cosigners. The latter would seem more likely, for no collateral was put up, and there was no mention of the purpose for which the money was borrowed.[18] The stipulation was that repayment would be made in six months, but at the end of that time not one cent had been returned. Strangely, the bank did not file suit against Curry or Eubank, both of whom were solvent, living in the territory, and readily available. Garrett had moved to Uvalde.

In 1896, when Pat returned to New Mexico as the Doña Ana County sheriff, the Bank of Commerce asked him to pay the full amount, plus interest. He refused. Therefore, on September 18, 1897, the Second Judicial District Court in Albuquerque ordered him to appear and explain why he had refused to make payment. Garrett ignored the summons, and in December was slapped with a civil suit demanding damages, interest, and the full amount of the note. The bank acknowledged that seven years had passed since the contract was signed but claimed that the statute of limitations was still in force because Garrett had been out of the territory. Garrett replied that he had never been a "nonresident" of the

---

[18] The Bank of Commerce has long since gone out of business and its records have not been found. However, the note is part of the court records. See 2d Judicial District Court, Case No. 6557, Bernalillo County, New Mexico State Archives, Santa Fe.

territory and that the statute of limitations was indeed in force. He asked that the case be dismissed.

The judge threw out his plea and ordered him to appear before the bench. When Garrett failed to appear, the court ruled on January 28, 1898, that the bank collect the full sum of the note, the interest, court costs, attorney fees, and damages of $977.92. The figure, with revisions, totaled $1,733.18. Garrett's personal property was ordered seized and sold at auction. José R. Lucero, probate clerk of Doña Ana County, was ordered to carry out the judgment. On February 7, Lucero returned the cause unserved because Garrett had no land at the time to confiscate and his personal property, which amounted to $565.65, was already mortgaged to Martin Lohman and W. W. Cox.[19]

Thus matters rested for the next few years. In the meantime, Garrett had become the owner of two ranches and had mortgaged them to Martin Lohman for $3,567.50. What happened to the money no one knows. Some of it undoubtedly disappeared at the gambling tables and race tracks, but part of it also financed the acquisition of several fine Steeldust horses and Cleveland bays.[20] Lohman had a mortgage on the ranches, the fixtures and improvements, thirty head of cattle, and 150 head of horses. The note stipulated repayment within twelve months.[21]

Two years went by, and Garrett did not pay Lohman a cent. On April 9, 1904, Lohman rewrote the mortgage in exactly the same language and for exactly the same amount.[22] On April 13, 1905, when another year had rolled around and it was obvious that Garrett could not or would not pay anything, Lohman discounted the note to W. W. Cox for two thousand dollars.[23] Cox had no better luck collecting, and, rather than take Garrett's property, he extended the note himself on May 26, 1906.[24]

Meanwhile, the Bank of Commerce had been active. In September, 1904, the bank once again secured judgment against Garrett and tried to take his ranches, but was unable to do so because of the mortgages held by Lohman and Cox. Undaunted, the bank

[19] *Ibid.*

[20] Willis Walter, interview with author, Lordsburg, N. Mex., January 30, 1968. Walter recalls seeing these horses on the Garrett ranch.

[21] Chattel Mortgages, Record Book 3, 228–29, recorded April 9, 1902, Doña Ana County, N. Mex.

[22] Renewal of Chattel Mortgages, Record Book 1, 139, Doña Ana County, N. Mex.

[23] *Ibid.*, 156; *El Paso Herald*, March 2, 1908.

[24] Renewal of Chattel Mortgages, Record Book 1, 170, Doña Ana County, N. Mex.

lawyers finally convinced the judge that their firm had first rights on the Garrett property based on the 1898 decision against Garrett. The court agreed with the bank, and on May 14, 1906, José Lucero (now the Doña Ana County sheriff) was ordered by New Mexico Supreme Court Associate Justice Ira A. Abbott to take possession of both Garrett ranches, its buildings, and its livestock and sell everything at auction. Lucero delayed two weeks before serving the papers. This delay gave W. W. Cox enough time to transfer most of the Garrett stock to San Augustine Ranch, ten miles south of Garrett's place. Subsequently fewer than twenty of Garrett's animals were rounded up by the sheriff.[25]

On July 28, J. H. Bonney and J. C. Thompson, two of Garrett's neighbors, were ordered by the court to appraise the Garrett ranch. The buildings and 160 acres of land were judged to be worth approximately $225. Garrett's Spring was valued at $250. No appraisal was made of the Bear Canyon Ranch or of the animals on either place.[26] After satisfying all the legal requirements (including a month's notice in the *Río Grande Republican*), Lucero auctioned off Garrett's ranches and livestock on August 4. The high bidder was the Albuquerque Bank of Commerce for one thousand dollars.[27] Territorial laws restrained the bank from taking immediate possession. Garrett had one year to make restitution or vacate the premises. Apparently he was able to satisfy the bank, although the records do not say how. He continued to live on the ranch for the remaining two years of his life.

But Pat Garrett was not out of the financial woods. He had lived on his property (or at least owned it) for approximately six years—and had not paid a cent in taxes. He now owed the county $922.72, and the Doña Ana commissioners published newspaper notices in August, 1906, that Garrett's stock would be sold to meet his tax assessments.[28]

This was too much for Cox. He decided to keep the Garrett livestock. On August 17, to make the transaction as legal and binding as possible, he forced Garrett to sign a bill of sale "for one dollar and other valuable considerations."[29] When the sheriff came calling at the Garrett ranch, all the deputies found were a few strays that

[25] Case No. 6557, Bernalillo County, New Mexico State Archives, Santa Fe.
[26] *Ibid.*
[27] Miscellaneous Deed Records, Book 1, 18–19 (certificate of sheriff's sale), Doña Ana County, N. Mex.
[28] *Río Grande Republican*, August, 1906.
[29] Miscellaneous Deed Records, Book 1, 17, Doña Ana County, N. Mex.

Cox had missed, plus some horses which Garrett considered to be personal property and immune from auction.

The county rounded up everything, including Garrett's personal possessions, and on September 4 auctioned it off for a total of $650. That was all they could get, and so the commissioners called it square and dropped their tax claim.[30]

The county's tax action infuriated both the Albuquerque Bank of Commerce and Pat Garrett. According to the *Río Grande Republican*, the bank filed suit against the commissioners, claiming that they had sold property belonging to them.[31] There are no court records relating to this report. Garrett filed a lawsuit against Sheriff Lucero, claiming that he had sold property "exempt from execution," specifically a Jersey cow with a suckling calf, valued at $40, a bay stallion called Gray, valued at $150; a sorrel mare called Skip, valued at $50; and a dun mare valued at $50 that belonged to his wife. Garrett asked for $100 damages, court costs, and the return of his property, or $290 to compensate him for his loss. The case dragged on into 1908, when it was dismissed after Garrett's death.[32]

During these turbulent times Garrett continued to correspond with Emerson Hough. Pat always addressed him "Dear Mr. Hough," while Hough replied sometimes with "Dear Mr. Garrett" or, more frequently, "Dear Pat." Usually their discussions centered on *The Story of the Outlaw*. On January 12, 1906, Hough commented that portions of the manuscript would soon be ready for Garrett's criticism.

In early February, Garrett was in Chicago on undisclosed business and telephoned Hough. The writer was not at home, but from the tone of Garrett's voice the maid gathered that he was very distraught. Hough wrote him on February 7, apologizing for being absent, and asked Garrett what was troubling him. Garrett replied on March 8, commenting that he had indeed been in Chicago recently and had tried to contact Hough. Failing to do so, he had caught the Golden State Limited for El Paso. Pat did not say why he wanted to talk with Hough but closed in this remarkable manner: "You will please pardon the unintelligent manner in which this letter is written from the fact that I am suffering great distress of mind and soul."[33]

[30] *Río Grande Republican*, August 24, September 14, 21, 1906. There are no extant court records relating to this case.
[31] *Ibid.*
[32] Civil Court Records, Case No. 2680, Doña Ana County, N. Mex.

Hough answered immediately: "I believe that the best thing you can do is write me privately and fully and tell me what it wrong." Hough claimed that he could guess the circumstances, but he did not want to "make any wrong statements." He closed with the reassuring words, "Surely you will not lose your nerve, and if a man holds his nerve and tries to do what he knows is right, you can't keep from winning out in the end."[34]

In the same correspondence Hough mentioned that he had switched to Outing Publishers and had rewritten "nearly the entire book for the new outfit." Garrett's reply was that he hoped the book would sell well. He also asked about royalties for himself. On June 29, Hough confessed that he had received an advance of three hundred dollars and was asking the Outing Publishers to send Garrett two hundred dollars. A financial statement would be sent too, stipulating that in case the book did not sell well the two hundred dollars would be returned. Hough complained that he had already spent over one thousand dollars in book expenses but added that, "while perhaps this book will never make the success you think, and while its changed arrangement makes it general in application and not applicable to any one locality, it may surprise me by making some more money, in which case I think you can depend that I will do the right thing by you."[35] Hough also mentioned some Chicagoans who had turned down one of Garrett's mining ventures, saying that the capitalists were "rather shy about investing in Mexico. There is no use dealing with pikers if you can get in with the real goods."[36]

On February 8, 1907, Garrett made more comments about his ranch: "I am fixing to plant about one half acre in a garden. I never saw such fine vegetables and mellons grow any where in my life. We have sufficient water . . . for we had a mild winter with a great deal of rain." Pat then drifted into his financial troubles: "Everything seems to go wrong with me. I was sold out last fall by the sheriff. I went on a note with a friend [George Curry] and a bank got judgment against me. But we have our ranch and a few stock left and I am going to stay here and build up again."[37]

Hough answered on February 12: "I suspected that something

[33] Emerson Hough Collection, Iowa State Department of History and Archives, Des Moines.
[34] *Ibid.*
[35] *Ibid.*
[36] *Ibid.*
[37] *Ibid.*

was wrong with you in a business way . . . and I am heartily sorry you got in such deep water. Keep your nerve, for money is made now quicker than it ever was, and I have no doubt that it will come your way."[38]

Garrett's final letter was written on July 2. He made no further mention of his troubles, but noted that he had received several copies of *The Story of the Outlaw*. "I have read the work and am well pleased with it as a whole," he said, "but there are some parts of it that are not up to what I expected. When I see you I will discuss these points in detail."[39]

Perhaps Garrett's outspoken opinions ruffed Hough's feelings, for this letter abruptly terminated their correspondence.

[38] *Ibid.*
[39] *Ibid.*

22

The Trail Ends

The last two years of Garrett's life were desperate ones. He belonged nowhere. His enemies hated him, and his friends did not understand him. He was quarrelsome and insulting, brawling drunkenly in the streets and on the open range. With a double piece of rope he threatened to lay open the back of Emmett Isaacs for objecting to the way Garrett drove a few head of thirsty stock away from a waterhole.[1] Pat traded punches with Frank "Pancho" Amador, whose father had built the Las Cruces Amador Hotel, and was shamefully thrashed by the much smaller man.[2] Following this altercation Garrett reportedly fought with big Jim Baird, a neighboring rancher, and banged his Colt .45 across Baird's head.[3]

But Garrett's most deadly feud was with his neighbor on the south, W. W. Cox. The lean old cowman, who habitually included

[1] Emmett Isaacs, interview with author, Las Cruces, N. Mex., October 29, 1967; Bill Isaacs, interview with Mrs. Katherine Stoes, Las Cruces, N. Mex., November 7, 1963, Sonnichsen Papers, University of Texas at El Paso Archives.

[2] Frank Amador may have been a slight man, but he worked as a drayman for the railroad. Perhaps this heavy labor strengthened his sinews to a point where he could compete with taller and heavier opponents. See A. B. Fall to Eugene Rhodes, February 2, 1910, Rhodes Collection, University of New Mexico Library, Albuquerque; G. A. Feather to author, October 27, 1970.

[3] Robert N. Mullin, an authority on Lincoln County, does not believe that the alleged fight between Garrett and Baird ever took place. Mullin says, "Baird was a very tough hombre, and would have killed Garrett had Pat ever tried to pistol whip him." Mullin, interview with author, El Paso, Texas, August 7, 1970. There was bad blood between Garrett and Baird, although it may never have ended in a street brawl. When Garrett went to Las Cruces in 1896, the two men became good friends. But as sheriff Pat was ordered to sell the possessions of one Nathan Spatcier for back taxes, which amounted to $150. As Garrett began his duty, Spatcier tried secretly to sell seventeen tons of hay to Baird at a large discount. Upon learning of the transaction, Garrett declared the sale illegal, repossessed the hay, and resold it to satisfy the county's lien. Baird's vociferous objections were ignored, and he sued Garrett in civil court. The sheriff's actions were approved. See Civil Case No. 2178, Book D, Doña Ana County, N. Mex., March 15, 1898.

"sons of bitches" in almost every sentence, kept Garrett's cattle where Pat could not regain control. He refused to return them until Garrett paid off the mortgage, and Garrett could not pay off the mortgage until Cox returned the livestock. The dispute simmered.

Pat moved his family to Las Cruces, where his children could more easily attend school and where he could wait for George Curry, named by President Theodore Roosevelt to be the next governor of New Mexico, to appoint him as the new superintendent of the territorial prison at Santa Fe, replacing Holm Olaf Bursum.[4] However, after weeks of anticipating a telegram that never arrived, Pat sent his son Poe to watch over the ranch, left the rest of his family in Las Cruces, and joined H. M. Maple and Company, an El Paso real estate firm.[5]

He moved in with a Mrs. Brown, "a common prostitute," according to many El Pasoans. Whether she was widowed, divorced, or separated is of little consequence. They became a well-known couple around town and a familiar sight as Pat's high-stepping horses picked their way through the sandy streets and along the river backroads.[6] Few details of their relationship are known. Many knowledgeable people believed that, because of her, "Garrett went to the bad," that he lost his respect and his government job, that he stumbled deeper into debt, and that he began quarreling with his friends and neighbors.[7]

While Garrett was drinking and carousing in El Paso, Poe was signing papers and making agreements in his own name. On March 11, 1907, he leased for a period of five years the Bear Ranch (called by him the Rock House and Stinking Springs Ranch) to a local cowboy, Jesse Wayne Brazel.[8]

Much mystery and controversy hovers over Brazel, born in 1876 at Greenwood City, Kansas. For a while his family lived at Eagle Creek, near Lincoln, New Mexico, until his father, Jesse M. Brazel, moved them to Gold Camp. These Brazels were not involved in the Lincoln County War.[9]

---

[4] *Río Grande Republican*, April 27, October 5, 1907.

[5] *Ibid.*, August 31, 1907.

[6] Mrs. Hugh White, interview with author, El Paso, Texas, June 3, 1968. As a little girl Mrs. White and some of her friends often followed Pat Garrett and Mrs. Brown as far as the thickets lining the Río Grande.

[7] *Willis Skelton Glenn* v. *The Comanche Indians and the United States Government*, National Archives, Washington, D.C. Many witnesses spoke of Garrett and "his common prostitute," although no details were ever cited.

[8] Miscellaneous Deed Records, Book 1, 65, Doña Ana County, N. Mex.

Since Gold Camp bordered San Augustine Ranch, Wayne practically grew up as a Cox cowboy, although he and Cox were not
related, as many have thought. Cox took an early liking to the blue-
eyed, good-natured boy who wore his wide-brimmed sombrero
pulled tightly down across his ears. Cox admired Brazel's dependability and especially his loyalty. Wayne worshiped Cox. He would
have died for him, and—if necessary—would have killed for him.

Wherever he went, Brazel always found employment. He was
honest and did not drink, and so he often worked part time in the
Las Cruces Cowboy Saloon.[10] He could handle the toughest chores
without complaint, and Cox often employed him to break horses.
It was a harsh life, as evidenced by a long scar jutting from the right
corner of his mouth.

Eventually Wayne moved into the Gold Camp home of A. P.
"Print" Rhode, Cox's brother-in-law, where he met Olive Elizabeth
Boyd, a tutor for the Rhode children and a teacher in the Organ
District School of Gold Camp. She was eighteen, pretty, unmarried,
and the only girl with whom the thirty-one-year-old Wayne ever
went steady. In 1907 they made marriage plans, and Brazel sought
new sources to supplement his income.

Brazel and Rhode planned a goat-raising venture, an endeavor
despised by most cattlemen because the animals cropped the grass
too close to the ground and thus ruined the range for steers. But
for the partners the lure of fast money was strong, and goats were
good profitmakers. The men chose Bear Canyon as their site. It
was remote, unused, sheltered from weather extremes, and near
Gold Camp. To obtain the land they had to get around the objections of Pat Garrett. He hated Print Rhode with a bitterness
dating back ten years to the killing of Norman Newman in the San
Augustine ranchhouse. He also hated goats.

To get around these obstructions the partners dealt secretly with
Poe Garrett and said nothing about goats. Rhode remained a silent
partner. On March 11, Poe and Brazel went to Las Cruces where
the lease terms were drawn, specifying that each July for five years
Wayne Brazel would deliver to Poe Garrett ten heifer calves and

---

[9] There are two accounts of Wayne Brazel's life, both by the same biographer:
Robert N. Mullin, *The Strange Story of Wayne Brazel*; and "The Strange Story of
Wayne Brazel," *Panhandle Plains Historical Review*, Vol. XLII (1969), 23–59.

[10] Frank Brito, interview with author and Dale L. Walker, Las Cruces, N. Mex.
November 9, 1970. Brito is a one-time Rough Rider who worked for several years
as a Doña Ana County deputy sheriff under Felipe Lucero. He knew both Pat Garrett and Wayne Brazel.

one mare colt. Brazel further promised to keep up the annual assessment work, make necessary improvements as required by law, and peacefully return the land at the expiration of the agreement.[11]

Nothing happened for months. In July and August goats began arriving at Bear Canyon after being driven past the front door of the Garrett home ranch. When Pat learned the news, he came charging home and vowed that he would soon get rid of the animals. His task would not be as easy as he thought. He found out that Print Rhode was a partner of Brazel's. He also found out that, on June 29, Cox had lent Brazel $574 to begin the operation.[12] Garrett tried desperately to prove that a verbal agreement existed between the two parties which excluded goats. Brazel denied it, and an argument erupted between him and Poe Garrett. All the parties and their attorneys took a long look at the contract. It definitely omitted any mention of how Brazel intended to use the land, although Pat argued unsuccessfully that payment in cattle and horses was an implied admission that only these animals would be grazed in Bear Canyon.

Garrett next evoked an old New Mexico law making it illegal to herd livestock near a residence, a reference to the small rock house in Bear Canyon which his family had occasionally used. He swore out a complaint with Organ Justice of the Peace Charles M. Anthony, who refused to serve the warrant because he feared Rhode's nasty temper. As Anthony wandered around the wooden, flimsy shacks of Organ, avoiding the pigs and the heavy buckboards, he bumped into Hence Rhode, Print's brother.

"Would you like to make a few dollars, Hence?"

"You bet," Rhode replied.

"You might not like making an arrest I want," said Anthony.

"Doesn't matter. You tell me who he is and I'll bring him in dead or alive."

"It's your brother Print and Wayne Brazel. I can't get anyone to arrest them."

"Don't worry. I'll bring him and Wayne both in," Rhode said.[13]

As Hence Rhode carried the warrants up the canyon toward his

[11] The lease terms say that the land belonged to Poe Garrett. There is no mention in the contract that the land belonged to Pat. However, there are also no Doña Ana County deed records proving in fact that Poe did own the land.

[12] Case No. 3387, Book 5 Civil Dockets, Doña Ana County, N. Mex., March 13, 1913.

[13] Sterling Rhode (brother of Print Rhode), interview with Herman Weisner, Organ, N. Mex., undated.

brother's residence, Wayne saw him coming and was suspicious enough to wait behind cover until Hence had passed. Brazel continued on into Organ, heard what was happening, and turned himself in to await developments.

Early the next morning Hence Rhode peacefully drove a buckboard into town carrying both Print and his wife. Pat Garrett was notified, and the unique trial got under way shortly before Christmas, 1907.

The trial was scheduled for the afternoon, and by then a large crowd had gathered in the muddy streets. Walking around fully armed were Brazel and Rhode, giving Garrett looks which dared him to do something. Finally Pat complained to José Lucero, and the sheriff ordered both men disarmed. It was disarmament in name only. Hence stuck their guns inside his belt and walked between them for the rest of the day so that their weapons would be handy if needed.[14]

Since Organ had no courthouse, Anthony held the trial in the Cox butchershop. Before opening the hearing he removed the window screens, explaining that he "wanted to be the first one out if trouble started."[15] The doors were closed because of the cold weather, and the lack of ventilation made a few of the women spectators ill. Up front, Garrett stomped and swore, impatient for the proceedings to be over. His frustrations were not eased by the continuous taunts of Print Rhode, who repeatedly challenged him to a fist fight.

An impartial jury could not be found, but Anthony refused to act as an arbitrator. He had to live in Organ after the trial ended. Finally, in the hope that time would cool some tempers and that everything would naturally work itself out, he recessed court until the following spring.[16]

In January, 1908, James P. Miller, better known as "Killin' Jim" or "Deacon Jim," arrived in El Paso. His career had begun in east Texas, where he had killed his brother-in-law, although he committed his most notable murder in September, 1896, when he blew former sheriff Bud Fraser's brains all over a Toyah, Texas, saloon wall. Miller's favorite weapon was a shotgun, and with it he had allegedly killed between twenty and forty men, most of the killings paid murders.[17] Now he and Carl Adamson, relatives by marriage,

[14] *Ibid.*
[15] *Ibid.*
[16] *Ibid.*
[17] For two good histories of Miller's murderous career see Glen Shirley, *Shotgun For Hire*; and C. L. Sonnichsen, *Ten Texas Feuds*, 200–209.

reportedly had over a thousand head of cattle in Mexico awaiting shipment to a ranch in Oklahoma. First they wanted to bring the cattle across the border and fatten them up for a while on lush New Mexico grass. They first approached John W. Leatherman, who had a ranch near the mouth of Bear Canyon. When the negotiations fell through, the partners turned to Pat Garrett for assistance.[18]

Garrett and Miller met in El Paso, where Pat explained that a "goat man" would have to be moved off the land. Miller asked to meet this fellow, and Wayne Brazel was summoned to El Paso for a hotel-room conference. Brazel refused to cancel his lease unless someone bought his twelve hundred goats at $3.50 a head. In the end Miller agreed to find a buyer, and a contract between Brazel and Miller was drawn up.[19]

With the goat problem believed settled, Jim Miller offered Garrett three thousand dollars for Bear Canyon Ranch. Furthermore, he hired Pat to drive the thousand head of cattle up from Mexico and hold them until the following November 1, for a fee of one dollar a head. This agreement put Garrett in pretty good spirits. He expected to get out of debt, restock, and spend his old age as a cattleman. On about February 20 he moved his family back to the home ranch.[20]

Then the situation dramatically changed. Brazel notified Garrett that he had miscounted—that instead of twelve hundred goats there were approximately eighteen hundred and that he would not cancel the lease unless Miller promised to purchase the remaining six hundred. Miller frowned on the new figure and doubted that it could be handled. He implied that the entire agreement with Garrett might have to be dropped.

Garrett sank into despair and wrote Governor Curry: "Dear Curry: I am in a hell of a fix. I have been trying to sell my ranch, but no luck. For God's sake send me fifty dollars."[21] A check arrived promptly, and Garrett stuck it in his pocket planning to cash it the next time he went to Las Cruces. It is ironic that Curry thus appeared to be a good Samaritan when Garrett was being forced by the courts to pay one thousand dollars which Curry owed the Albuquerque bank.

---

[18] *El Paso Herald*, March 2, 1908.
[19] *Ibid.*
[20] *Ibid.*
[21] Keleher, *The Fabulous Frontier*, 87; Garrett, *Life*, 40–41; Curry, *An Autobiography*, 218.

On Friday, February 28, Adamson arrived in Las Cruces and rented a top buggy for the four-hour trip to the Garrett ranch. He was greeted that afternoon by Pat and his wife, three of their children, and three cowhands, Frank Adams, Tom Emory, and an unidentified Mexican. Garrett showed Adamson around and mentioned a disturbance the night before, when Adams had been awakened by prowlers. Adams had awakened Garrett, who drowsily told him that it must be the dogs and to go back to sleep. Early in the morning Adams investigated and found tracks of two men and their horses in an arroyo.[22]

Adamson, short and stout, with a boyish, intelligent face, did not impress Mrs. Garrett. He made her nervous, suspicious, and anxious. Pat laughed her fears aside with the remark that the Garretts' financial worries would soon be over. To prove it, he sent Brazel a message to meet him and Adamson in Las Cruces on the following morning.[23]

The next day, in exceptionally good spirits, Pat dressed, chatted good-naturedly with his family, and climbed into the two-horse buggy. As he and Adamson headed across the rough dirt road toward Organ, Mrs. Garrett called to her daughter Pauline: "Quick, get your horse! Your father has forgotten his topcoat."[24] The slender Pauline scrambled onto the back of a mare and quickly caught up with her father. Pat saw her coming and told Adamson to stop the buggy. He climbed down, lifted her gently from the horse, and, cradling her in his long arms, carried her with him to unlatch the gate. Then he kissed her softly on the cheek and said, "Take good care of Mommy, and I will bring you a pretty." That was the last time she saw him alive.[25]

The narrow road stretched past Gold Camp, across San Augustine Pass, through the ramshackle community of Organ, past L. B.

[22] John Milton Scanland, *Life of Pat Garrett; El Paso Herald*, March 2, 1908. Much has been written and said about Scanland's close association with Garrett and that Scanland was close to solving the mystery of Pat's death. A close examination of Scanland's book, however, reveals that he did nothing more than copy newspaper reports—errors and all.

[23] There is considerable confusion about who notified whom to be in Las Cruces the next morning. The Garrett family claims that Brazel came to the ranch that night and delivered a note to Adamson (Garrett, *Life*, 43), but more reliable reports indicate that Garrett sent the message to Brazel (Mullin, *The Strange Story of Wayne Brazel*, 16; *El Paso Herald*, March 2, 1908).

[24] Pauline Garrett, interview with author, Las Cruces, N. Mex., May 17, June 12, 1967.

[25] *Ibid.*

Bentley's grocery,[26] and down to Russel Walter's livery stable, about one-half mile farther. Walter's son Willis was busy unloading alfalfa from a wagon when Garrett and Adamson drove up. The two horses trotted to the water trough.

"Have you seen Brazel?" Garrett asked.

"Yes, he just left," Walters replied, and pointed down the road toward a small cloud of dust kicked up by Brazel's roan roping horse, hanging in the warm, quiet air.[27]

Adamson reversed the team and, chatting with Garrett, urged the horses forward at a brisk but not an especially fast trot. Below Organ the road forked and came together again about two miles from Las Cruces. One route was called the Mail–Scott Road. The other was generally referred to as the Freighter's Road, named for the many ore wagons that bounced across it. Though the Freighters' Road was shorter, most travelers preferred the more comfortable Mail–Scott Road. As Garrett and Adamson entered the junction, they saw Brazel a short distance down the Mail–Scott Road talking to a stranger (a man now believed to have been Print Rhode). The lone rider split off and vanished before he could be identified.

Conversation was sparse when the buggy overtook Brazel. Only a curt nod passed as a greeting between him and Garrett, and for a while it appeared that it would stay that way. Where the road was wide, Brazel rode beside the buggy; when it narrowed, he either loped ahead a few paces or dropped behind a length or two. Adamson finally broke the awkward silence with a jest. "Are your goats kidding yet?" he snickered.[28]

[26] It has been written and said that Garrett met Brazel in Bentley's store and that arguments and threats supposedly passed between them. None of this alleged conversation is borne out by the records or even the newspaper accounts. The source of all these yarns has been Bentley himself, and he told a different version every time he was interviewed. Bentley was one of those characters who lived a long life in which only one significant event occurred, the death of Pat Garrett. Even that passed him by, but, as he grew older and outlived the participants, he placed himself a little nearer the center of the stage. With every discussion he became more involved and more confused about the facts. Mrs. Louis Bentley, interview with Herman Weisner, Organ, N. Mex., undated (taped copy in the University of Texas at El Paso Archives); C. L. Sonnichsen, interview with L. B. Bentley, Organ, N. Mex., November 7, 1953, Sonnichsen Papers, University of Texas at El Paso Archives; Art Leibson, interview with L. B. Bentley, Organ, N. Mex., El Paso Times, October 14, 1958.

[27] Willis Walter, interview with author, Lordsburg, N. Mex., January 30, 1968. Walter claimed that the day was very warm (not cold and gusty) and that Brazel was not wearing a coat on the day of the killing. The extremely warm temperature was further borne out by the memory of Pauline Garrett in her interview with the author. The newspapers reported a high of 72 degrees for the day.

Garrett asked Brazel why he originally said that he had twelve hundred goats and now claimed that the figure was eighteen hundred. Brazel mumbled a reply that he had miscounted. Adamson interrupted, saying that he and Miller could not possibly accept eighteen hundred goats and that the deal might be off. "The facts are that I do not want even twelve hundred goats, but I bought them to get possession of the ranch," he said.[29]

"If I don't sell the whole bunch, I won't sell none," Brazel snapped.

Near Alameda Arroyo, Adamson halted the team and climbed down from the buggy to urinate. According to his and Brazel's later remarks, he handed the reins to Garrett and walked to the front of the buggy. Behind him Brazel was saying that he might keep the ranch lease, and Garrett replied that it did not make any difference whether he did or not. Pat would get him off the land somehow.

Garrett also climbed out to urinate, taking care to pick up his Burgess folding shotgun so that the weapon would not fall onto the floor and discharge its birdshot. Carrying the gun in his right hand, he stepped to the rear of the buggy, turned his back on Brazel, removed his left glove, and unbuttoned his trousers. That was the old former manhunter's position when a bullet slammed into the back of his head.

[28] *El Paso Herald*, February 29, March 2, 1908; *Río Grande Republican*, March 7, 1908.
[29] *Ibid.*

23.

Who Killed Pat Garrett?

The death of Pat Garrett is an even more controversial subject than the slaying of Colonel Albert Jennings Fountain. Five suspects share the attention, and a fairly credible murder case can be established against each of them: Wayne Brazel, Carl Adamson, W. W. Cox, Print Rhode, and Jim Miller. The Garrett family believes that Adamson pulled the trigger.[1] Historians almost unanimously point their finger at Jim Miller. Of late, new evidence has focused suspicion on Cox and Rhode. Practically no one, ironically, believes that Wayne Brazel killed Pat Garrett, and yet Brazel alone confessed to the crime and was tried for it.

In the Tularosa, Mesilla, Río Grande, and Pecos valleys few comments will start an argument quicker than an emphatic statement about who shot Pat Garrett. There are as many "experts" on the matter and as many shades of opinion as there are testifiers. Seldom have so many said so much and known so little. Official inquest and trial records were not preserved. Only the newspaper versions are available.

According to them Adamson turned at the sound of the shots and saw Garrett fall over backward. Brazel sat on his horse, a smoking .45 in his hand. As Adamson rushed to examine the body, Brazel dismounted and handed him his weapon. "This is hell," Brazel said. And on the ground the unconscious Pat Garrett groaned, stretched out, and died. Adamson covered the corpse with a robe and left it on the ground.

With Brazel's horse trotting behind the buggy, he and Adamson hurried into Las Cruces, where Wayne surrendered to Deputy Felipe Lucero. Years later Lucero related that he was preparing lunch when Brazel shoved the door open and blurted out, "Lock

---

[1] Garrett, *Life*, 47; Jarvis Garrett, interview with author, Albuquerque, N. Mex., October 20, 1967.

me up. I've just killed Pat Garrett." Pointing to Adamson, Brazel said, "He saw the whole thing and knows that I shot in self-defense."[2] Lucero placed Brazel in a cell, gathered together a coroner's jury, and rode to the death site. After a preliminary examination there by Dr. W. C. Fields, Garrett's corpse was moved to town.

On Tuesday, March 3, in Manuel López' justice of the peace courtroom, Brazel was asked to plead to the charge of murder. For a moment he did not answer and stared blankly into space. "What's that?" he suddenly asked. When the question was repeated, he replied firmly and quietly, "Not guilty," and resumed his vacant staring.[3]

That afternoon a hearing was held. Asking questions for the territory was Mark Thompson, prosecuting attorney for Doña Ana County, assisted by New Mexico Attorney General James M. Hervey. The attorney general and Governor George Curry had come down from Santa Fe to attend the funeral and to assist in the investigation. Attorneys Herbert B. Holt,[4] William A. Sutherland, and Edward C. Wade conducted the defense, assisted occasionally by A. B. Fall, who did little except lend his name.

According to the March 7 edition of *Río Grande Republican*, Carl Adamson took the stand while Brazel remained silent.

Hervey: "Now tell to your best recollection what happened?"

Adamson: "I stopped the buggy to urinate and as I got out Mr. Garrett reached over and took the reins. And while I was standing there I heard Mr. Garrett say 'Well, damn you. If I don't get you off one way, I will another,' or something like that."

"Where were these people in relation to you?"

"Mr. Garrett was in the buggy and Brazel was on the horse. They were at my back."

"So you didn't see Garrett standing upright at all?"

"I think when I seen Garrett, the first shot had been fired and he was staggering."

"Did he fall to the side, to the front, or the rear of the buggy?"

"About two feet from the side."

"Where was the defendant at this time?"

"He was on horseback, about even with the buggy. He had a six-shooter in his hand."

[2] *New Mexico Sentinel*, April 23, 1939.
[3] *El Paso Herald*, March 3, 1908.
[4] During the last years of his life, Garrett had considered Holt his personal attorney.

"Who fired the second shot?"

"One of my horses started to run and I grabbed the lines and wrapped them as quickly as I could around the hub of the wheel and went back to where Mr. Garrett lay."

"How about the defendant?"

"He was still on his horse and in about the same place."

"Did Garrett speak?"

"No, when I got to him he was just stretching out. He did groan a little."

After the conclusion of Adamson's statements Dr. Fields testified to finding Garrett's body in a six-inch sand drift about four miles from town. He swore that Garrett had no driving glove on his left hand, that his trousers were unbuttoned, and that he was obviously urinating when death came. Two .45-caliber bullets had killed him, the first crashing through the back of his head, driving strands of gray hair into the brain before exiting and tearing away the right eyebrow.[5] The second slug struck Garrett in the stomach and ranged upward into the shoulder, an unusual trajectory that came about only because Garrett was already prone on the ground from the first shot. Fields called the slaying "murder" in "cold blood and in the first degree."

Attorney General Hervey suggested that Brazel's bond be set at ten thousand dollars. Cox, who had been at Brazel's side almost continuously since the shooting, hustled around town and easily raised that amount from cattlemen, citizens, and businessmen.

On April 13 the grand jury indicted Brazel for murder. The trial took place a year later, on April 19, 1909. James Baird swore that Garrett had often plotted to kill Brazel. Wayne himself claimed self-defense, testifying that Garrett threatened him with the shotgun and left him no other alternative except to shoot first. Brazel explained that he fired the second shot as a reflex, because he was too agitated to stop. He denied that Garrett was shot from behind.

The case was prosecuted with appalling indifference and incompetence. Mark Thompson, Herbert Holt, and A. B. Fall were long-time friends, yet Thompson did not remove himself from the case, even though Attorney General Hervey was willing and able to take over. Adamson, the only known witness, was not called to

[5] Since the bullet that went through Garrett's head was not recovered, Dr. Fields could not possibly know for certain that Garrett was shot twice with .45-caliber bullets. He must have assumed, upon recovery of the slug in the shoulder, that both wounds were made with the same weapon. He must have noted also that the condition of the head wound resembled one made by a .45 revolver.

testify. Western Union telegrams sent back and forth by Brazel, Rhode, Adamson, Miller, and Cox were subpoenaed but not produced in evidence. Thompson did not tell the jury that a man such as Garrett, intent on killing an enemy, would have loaded his shotgun with buckshot, not birdshot. He also would have fired from the buggy seat and would not have climbed down first. The prosecutor did not dwell upon the back shooting, nor did he comment upon the obvious irony of shooting in "self-defense" a man who was urinating. Thompson seemed merely eager to get it all over with. At 5:30 P.M. the case went to the jury and the panel took fifteen minutes to find the defendant not guilty.[6]

That night Cox celebrated Brazel's acquittal by holding a barbecue at San Augustine Ranch.

When he learned of Pat Garrett's death, Governor George Curry left for Las Cruces to attend the funeral. With him were Attorney General Hervey and Captain Fred Fornoff of the Territorial Mounted Police. A. B. Fall had been retained to defend Brazel, and since Fall and Thompson were friends, Curry wanted an independent investigation.[7]

Adamson drove Hervey and Fornoff to the site of Garrett's murder and re-explained the events. The two investigators nodded and began examining the scene in detail for additional clues. About fifty feet behind where the buggy had been parked, Hervey picked up a new Winchester shell and wondered whether a bushwhacker had waited there and killed Garrett with a rifle. Both men talked to Adamson again, and back in Las Cruces they questioned Brazel in more detail. The lawmen agreed that Brazel's story did not make sense, and they discussed their suspicions with Governor Curry. Although the three men did not reveal their findings, they did hint at a conspiracy. Hervey said that "Brazel had never been considered a dangerous man,"[8] and Curry seemed equally puzzled about the confessed slayer. Brazel "was the victim of a conspiracy rather than the killer,"[9] the governor said, and he expressed regret that the territory had no money to extend the investigation.

Weeks later Hervey had business to attend to in El Paso, and

[6] Case No. 4112, District Court Records, Doña Ana County, N. Mex., Book C, Criminal Dockets, 525, Doña Ana County, N. Mex., *El Paso Herald*, May 5, 1909.

[7] James Madison Hervey, "The Assassination of Pat Garrett," *True West*, March–April, 1961.

[8] *Ibid.*

[9] Curry, *An Autobiography*, 216–18.

he used the occasion to speak with Tom Powers. The suspicions were explained, and Powers was asked for enough money to hire a detective for a month. Powers smiled and offered his regrets. He was not interested.

Undaunted, Hervey tried to interest Emerson Hough in the proposition. He asked Hough for a thousand dollars, and once again met with failure. Hough backed away, offering the excuse that Garrett had died owing him a lot of money. He warned Hervey that "you will get killed trying to find out who killed Garrett. I would advise you to let it alone."[10] Hervey noted that, after this admonition, "I decided not to be so active."[11]

Hervey did remain interested, however, and he ordered Fornoff to investigate in his idle hours without spending too much territorial money. The captain drifted around El Paso talking to informants and soon heard rumors that a wealthy rancher (Cox) had paid to have Garrett killed. Mannen Clements, part-time law officer and gunman-for-hire, was allegedly the contact man.[12] Clements supposedly met Cox in Fall's El Paso office and collected fifteen hundred dollars. Clements, the story went, would hire Jim Miller to do the job and would pay Carl Adamson to act as witness. Cox would pay the fee and order Wayne Brazel to take the blame.[13]

Fornoff is said to have recorded his findings in a confidential report to Hervey. What happened to this document is not precisely known. It was not introduced at the Brazel trial but seems to have been passed from one mysterious individual to another until it finally came into the hands of Judge Charles R. Brice in Roswell, New Mexico. When Brice died, the document was supposedly burned.[14]

While Fornoff continued to check out El Paso, Hervey sent another investigator to interview Joe Beasley, a Portales, New Mexico, character who had been convicted of several crimes and was at the time working as a foreman on the ranch of Judge Brice and

[10] Hervey, "The Assassination of Pat Garrett," *True West*, March–April, 1961.
[11] *Ibid.*
[12] Clements was a cousin of Jim Miller and also of John Wesley Hardin, who had been killed in El Paso in 1896. Clements spent his life wandering in and out of trouble until he finally reached the end of his line in 1908 at Tom Powers' Coney Island Saloon. Someone shot him in the back of the head, and the case was never solved.
[13] Hervey, "The Assassination of Pat Garrett," *True West*, March–April, 1961.
[14] R. N. Mullin, "The Key to the Mystery of Pat Garrett," *Branding Iron*, Los Angeles Westerners Corral, No. 92 (June, 1969).

Dee Harkey (Harkey was a well-known New Mexico lawman). Beasley made a specialty of perjuring himself in court for wanted criminals, and he told the investigator that Jim Miller went through the Portales area early on the morning of the Garrett slaying, said that he intended to kill Pat Garrett, and asked to borrow a horse. According to Beasley, after Miller rode to Las Cruces and on to Fort Worth, his alibi would be a telegram to Beasley, thus recording his whereabouts as six hundred miles from Las Cruces.[15]

Dee Harkey and Judge Brice accepted their foreman's story; with some embellishments Harkey repeated it in *Mean as Hell*,[16] the story of his experiences as a lawman. Brice confined his comments primarily to personal correspondence. While, oddly, making no mention of the aforementioned Fornoff report, he wrote a California admirer in 1958 that he had known Miller for many years before the Garrett slaying. In a five-page letter devoted mainly to Miller's early career, Brice repeated the tale of Miller's horse borrowing and subsequent wild ride.[17]

In the meantime, throughout the Southwest there were rumors that the Garrett killing was more involved than had been previously thought. Within two years after Pat's death scarcely a man in Texas or New Mexico did not believe that a giant conspiracy was involved and that Jim Miller had committed the slaying.[18] Even the newspapers hinted at Miller's involvement.[19] John Scanland, an El Paso newspaperman who claimed a close friendship with Garrett, wrote in his *Life of Pat Garrett* that "there is a mystery about this tragedy, and it may never come to light. The theory advanced . . . is that there was a plot to kill Garrett."[20]

[15] Hervey, "The Assassination of Pat Garrett," *True West*, March–April, 1961.

[16] Dee Harkey, *Mean as Hell*, 183–89.

[17] Brice told how Tom Coggins, a shady individual who underwrote many of Miller's arrest bonds, had allegedly spoken to Miller about the Garrett killing. Miller told a hair-raising tale about how Garrett had almost killed him before being gunned down and referred to the incident as the closest call he ever had. Charles R. Brice to Lewis Ketring, Jr., Roswell, N. Mex., January 25, 1958, copy in University of Texas at El Paso Archives.

[18] *Willis Skelton Glenn v. The Comanche Indians and the United States Government*, National Archives, Washington, D.C. At least half a dozen witnesses testifying for or against Pat Garrett mentioned a conspiracy against his life and the fact that Miller was believed to have committed the slaying. No specific details were given.

[19] *Río Grande Republican*, June 5, 1909. Without making any accusations, the newspaper printed a long article on the career of Jim Miller and made several references to the fact that Miller was in the area during the time of Garrett's death.

[20] John Milton Scanland, *Life of Pat Garrett and the Taming of the Border Outlaw*, 8.

Writers, historians, and gunfighter buffs almost unanimously agree that the conspiracy began at a secret meeting in the El Paso St. Regis Hotel.[21] How all these "authorities" document their allegations is in itself something of a secret, since many of them cite dead men who meant to talk for the record but never quite made it or quote printed fictional stories which make many insinuations but offer no proof.

Although the names of those attending the meeting vary depending upon whom you read—or whom you choose to believe—those most frequently mentioned have been Oliver Lee, Bill Mc-New, Jim Miller, Carl Adamson, Mannen Clements, Print Rhode, Wayne Brazel, W. W. Cox, and A. B. Fall. The subject of this get-together was Pat Garrett and how to get rid of him. Cox supposedly called this group of Garrett haters together and explained the problem and its solution. He despised Garrett because of the Newman (Reed) killing; he wanted Garrett's land, especially the water; and he feared that Garrett was getting too close to solving the Fountain mystery.

Cox agreed to pay for the shooting but insisted that the murder had to appear as self-defense. Most of the discussion revolved around methods for provoking Garrett, and Lee finally came up with the most acceptable solution. He suggested that Wayne Brazel, an easygoing, good-natured young man who was liked by nearly everyone, lease the unused Bear Canyon Ranch and put goats on it. When Garrett complained—and almost everyone knew that he would—the ensuing dispute would provide an excuse to kill him. Most people could be counted on to be sympathetic to Brazel, and if he took the blame for the killing, a jury would certainly free him. Since Brazel was not a professional gunman and might himself be killed if he tried to shoot Garrett, someone else would have to do the job and guarantee its effectiveness. All eyes turned toward Jim Miller.

There it is, the motive, the conspiracy, and the murderer—enough romance and mystery for a saddlebag full of paperback thrillers. It seems a shame that none of it is true.

Miller's alleged involvement should be examined first. Several

---

[21] Colin Rickards, *How Pat Garrett Died*, 15–22; Shirley, *Shotgun for Hire*, 88–91; Sonnichsen, *Tularosa*, 237–44; Keleher, *The Fabulous Frontier*, 87–101; Hutchinson, *Another Verdict for Oliver Lee*, 8–20; William R. Smith, "Death in Doña Ana County," *English Westerners Brand Book*, Part 1, Vol. IX, No. 2 (January, 1967), Part 2, Vol. IX, No. 3 (April, 1967).

regional newspapers mentioned that he had cattle in Mexico and a ranch in Oklahoma, though no details were published about the location of these holdings. Many writers have subsequently said that the cattle and the Oklahoma ranch were nonexistent, a ruse to permit the imaginative Miller to get close to Garrett. However, no one has ever explained why Miller should find it necessary to invent such a wild tale. One does not need to pretend friendship and offer business deals in order to lie behind a sandhill and kill an unsuspecting traveler.

Investigators Hervey, Fornoff, Curry, and Scanland made no mention in their writings or reports that the cattle and ranch stories might be false. That all of this was a fabrication is more of an assumption and a hope on the part of Miller's accusers than a known fact. If a business arrangement actually existed between Miller and Garrett, then there is no reason for believing that Miller had anything to do with Garrett's death.

Since there is no evidence to the contrary, Miller either brought his cattle across the river and pastured them somewhere else or sold them before or after entering the United States. Regardless of how he handled it, the transaction would have attracted little notice. Hundreds of cattle were bought and sold around El Paso each month, and hundreds more were driven back and forth across the Río Grande. Miller could have leased the ranch rather than purchase it—and it should be pointed out that shortly after Garrett's death Miller turned up in Oklahoma.

As for Miller's wild ride from Portales, this story rests upon the unsupported statements of Joe Beasley, one of the Southwest's most notorious liars. Even Attorney General Hervey admitted that Beasley's testimony would be laughed out of court.[22] It was over two hundred miles of bad road from Portales to Las Cruces, a trip that would have taken Miller across some of the highest mountains and roughest terrain in the Southwest. Such a ride would have been impossible to make in a few hours, and even if he took a day or two, he probably would have required a string of horses and the services of several men, thus making secrecy impossible. From Las Cruces it was still fifty miles to El Paso and six hundred miles to Fort Worth, an impossible horseback trip, especially for a man who had to be in Fort Worth in a hurry to send a covering telegram.

---

[22] Hervey, "The Assassination of Pat Garrett," *True West*, March–April, 1961.

This whole ride, of course, is based on Beasley's talk about Miller's desire for secrecy. According to Beasley, Miller wanted everyone to think that he was in Fort Worth during the killing. Yet people claim to have seen him on the streets of El Paso just before Garrett's death.[23] The *El Paso Herald* remarked that Garrett was going to see Miller on the day that he was killed.[24] And Adamson, rather than indicating that his partner was far away in Fort Worth, said that Miller was waiting in El Paso for the goat deal to be consummated.[25]

An attempt to place Miller at the death site is based on the discovery of a Winchester cartridge case along with horse tracks and droppings in the murder area. How these discoveries implicate Miller is difficult to explain, especially since his favorite weapon was a shotgun. Dr. Fields testified that Garrett died after being shot with two .45-caliber bullets—in other words, with a revolver. All that the rifle case and horse prints and droppings proved was that someone along the road fired a shot at something, sometime. They did not prove that Miller was involved, nor did they prove that Garrett was ambushed. The slug from that case could have been fired at a jackrabbit, a coyote, or a mule deer. The road was one of the most heavily traveled routes out of Las Cruces; horse tracks, droppings, and empty cartridge cases were scattered all over it.

The last link tying Miller to Pat Garrett's death occurred in February, 1909, near Ada, Oklahoma. Miller was once again on a murder-for-hire mission, but he bungled the job, even though the man he shot died within an hour. The authorities tracked him to a farm where he had left his horse, and it was not long before Miller was under arrest and being extradited from Fort Worth. At two o'clock on the morning of April 19, 1909, Jim Miller and three associates were removed from the Ada jail and lynched from barn rafters. Legend has it that, with the rope tightening around his neck, Miller confessed to the slaying of Pat Garrett. But like the other tales, this one has no truth in it either. Walter Gayne, the jailer, says that Miller made no mention of Garrett or any confession before he died. "I ought to know," Gayne said, "because I hung him."[26]

[23] Keleher, *The Fabulous Frontier*, 97.
[24] *El Paso Herald*, March 2, 3, 1908.
[25] *Ibid.*; *Río Grande Republican*, March 3, 1908.
[26] Inez Richmond, assistant librarian, Ada Public Library, to C. L. Sonnichsen, June 5, 1953, Sonnichsen Papers, University of Texas at El Paso Archives.

If Miller did not kill Garrett, the question remains, who did. Jarvis Garrett, Pat's son (who was three years old when his father died), is convinced that Adamson pulled the trigger. He interviewed Bill Isaacs, a well-known Doña Ana County rancher who went with Lucero to recover Garrett's body. Bill Isaacs and his brother Emmett never thought that Brazel was the murderer because "Wayne was no killer."[27] Other than that simplistic belief, the Isaacs brothers had no knowledge of Adamson's participation —only the notion that if Brazel did not do it then Adamson was the next logical suspect. The Isaacs brothers believed that Wayne took the blame because Cox wanted him to, and Jarvis Garrett is inclined to accept their theories.

One of the most interesting and intriguing stories has implicated Print Rhode as the trigger man. He had hated Garrett ever since the Newman killing, and the goat argument had only served to inflame relations between the two. Rhode had challenged Garrett to fight on several occasions, especially during the Organ justice-of-the-peace trial, and Rhode is suspected of having been the stranger talking to Brazel shortly before the Garrett buggy overtook them on the day of the shooting. Oliver Lee, Jr., thought that Rhode might have been Garrett's slayer.[28] However, although Rhode's name presents some fascinating speculations and possibilities, the likelihood of his killing Garrett is minimal. Since there was no conspiracy, there would have been no real reason for Adamson to lie for Rhode and no real reason for Brazel to take the blame for something his partner did.

Yet another yarn about who killed Garrett comes out of Denver, Colorado. The late W. T. Moyers, a lawyer who practiced in New Mexico for several years, reportedly did some research relating to Garrett's death. His investigations led him to believe that Cox himself ambushed and killed Garrett. Brazel was supposed to have been so horrified to see the old rancher rise up from the sandhills that he insisted on taking the blame for the killing. Brazel believed that he could get a better break from a murder jury than Cox could. Moyer allegedly handed this strange story to Fred M. Maz-

[27] Garrett, *Life*, 47; Jarvis Garrett, interview with author, Albuquerque, N. Mex., October 20, 1967; Bill Isaacs, interview with Mrs. Katherine Stoes, Las Cruces, N. Mex., November 7, 1953, Sonnichsen Papers, University of Texas at El Paso Archives; Bill Isaacs, interview with C. L. Sonnichsen, Las Cruces, N. Mex., September 15, 1954; Emmett Isaacs, interview with author, Las Cruces, N. Mex., October 29, 1957.

[28] Oliver M. Lee Jr., interview with a historian who prefers anonymity, Alamogordo, N. Mex., September 14, 1954.

zulla, a Denver attorney whose hobby is the collection of frontier photographs, with the stipulation that "Mazzulla write the story and sell it for a good stiff price."[29] This "good stiff price" was five thousand dollars. Mazzulla reports that he may also "release on a record the true story of who killed Pat Garrett."[30]

The details of how Cox blew out the brains of Garrett are not significant because, whatever were Cox's shortcomings—and there is evidence that he had plenty—he did not kill Pat Garrett. Nor did he hire someone else to do the job. The trend of thinking in the Southwest has been that Cox paid to have Garrett shot, and this allegation has been generally accepted with no serious questions concerning motives. It is now time to examine these motives before proceeding further with identifying the slayer.

The most commonly stated assumptions are that Cox wanted revenge for the Newman shooting and that he wanted the Garrett land, especially the water. Neither of these charges is true. Cox was not the kind of man to wait ten years before retaliating, and had he desired the property, he could have taken possession at any time. However, Garrett's poverty-stricken ranches held no interest for Cox.[31] All that the San Augustine rancher wanted Garrett to do was pay off the mortgage.

If Cox wanted Garrett "goated" off the land, if he wanted Brazel to take the blame for the killing, obviously he would have borne every expense. But Cox did not *give* Brazel anything. Instead, on June 29, 1907, just a month or two before the goats were pastured in Bear Canyon, Brazel *borrowed* $574.80 from Cox and signed a note to repay it within one year. Less than a year later Brazel was charged with murder and began preparing for his trial. Cox realized that Brazel was in no position to tend his goats, stand trial, and repay the debt. He permitted an extension until Brazel was financially solvent again. On May 15, 1909, Cox *lent* Brazel another three hundred dollars, a sum that probably paid attorney fees. Cox expected both of these notes to be repaid, with 10 per cent interest, within ninety days. When the three months were up, nothing happened. Cox waited patiently until 1913, when, upon learning that Brazel was selling his land and moving on, he instituted a civil suit

---

[29] Rickards, *How Pat Garrett Died*, 114; *Southwesterner*, August, 1962.

[30] Fred M. Mazzulla to author, June 22, 30, 1967.

[31] The *El Paso Herald* of December 1, 1908, noted that Mrs. Garrett had sold the home ranch to Cox. No figures were given, and there are no court records of the transaction. In all probability Cox simply repossessed the property.

and asked for a judgment of $1,506, plus costs. It was too late. Brazel was already beginning to wander from Doña Ana County and in despair Cox finally dropped all legal efforts to collect.[32]

Logic, in the end, returns us to Wayne Brazel. A thorough examination of the many theories, all the evidence now obtainable, leads one to the inescapable conclusion that he was, indeed, the killer of Pat Garrett. He admitted the murder, and he never changed his confession despite the many stories to the contrary. Those who deny that he pulled the trigger invariably cite as their reason the known fact that "Wayne was not the killer type." Curry said it, Attorney General Hervey said it, the Isaacs brothers said it, and the newspapers said it. But none of them ever defined the "killer type." Some of the world's most savage and senseless murders have been committed by "mild-mannered men."

That Brazel's plea of self-defense was not consistent with the facts does not mean that he was lying about killing Garrett; it simply meant that he was lying about *how* he did it. Garrett's death was clearly a case of murder, perhaps not premeditated, but murder nonetheless. Brazel feared the old manhunter and possibly had reason to worry about his safety if the goat problem could not be settled amicably. The two men had argued bitterly, and when Garrett turned his back, Brazel took the safe way out and shot him. Adamson seems to have reported almost exactly what he saw and heard. There were no conspiracies, no large amounts of money changing hands, no top guns taking up positions in the sandhills. It was simply a case of hate and fear erupting into murder along a lonely New Mexico back road.

After Garrett's death and Brazel's acquittal, the young cowboy himself became something of a tragic figure and, in the final analysis, a mystery also.

In October, 1909, he acquired the Harrington Well, twelve miles west of Lordsburg, New Mexico, and immediately homesteaded the 160 acres around it. There he finally married Olive Boyd, and, in 1911, a son was born. Their bliss was shattered less than six months later when Olive caught pneumonia and died. Wayne Brazel never fully recovered from the devastating blow of her death.

Although the ranch was sold in 1913, the transaction did not stop the government from filing perjury charges against Brazel

[32] Case No. 3387, Civil Dockets, Book 5, Doña Ana County, N. Mex.

relating to his former homestead claim. In May, 1914, charges were dismissed, and Brazel, free again, disappeared. Neither his son nor his many friends and relatives know exactly what happened to him. He reportedly died or was killed in one of a dozen places throughout the West.

In 1935, H. L. McCune, an El Paso attorney, was hired by Brazel's son to trace his disappearance and determine the facts. McCune did a lot of checking and in his report concluded that "the probable explanation of your father's disappearance is that he went to South America to try to make a fortune in that country and was there killed by what is known as the Butch Cassidy gang."[33]

[33] Mullin, *The Strange Story of Wayne Brazel*, 26–36.

24

An Era Passes

Apolinaria Garrett stood in the narrow doorway of the Garretts' shack house until the buggy carrying her husband and Carl Adamson disappeared among the arroyos near Gold Camp. For the next hour or so she busied herself with household chores while thinking of the plans that she and Pat had recently and so optimistically made. In the Tularosa Basin they would build a new home, a large house with a special room for the children's schooling. "We will have a good life when all of this is settled," she told Pauline, and she strolled to the doorway as if already anticipating her husband's return along the sandy road. Nothing moved out there, not even a dust devil bustling through the sandhills. She picked up a long, solid-oak board to prop against the door so that any spring breezes might more easily relieve the stuffy atmosphere inside the house.

Near noon, for no apparent reason, the heavy door prop tipped up and over, slamming into the floor with an ear-shattering noise. "Something has happened!" Mrs. Garrett screamed. "I don't know what it is, but something has happened!"[1] At that very moment, less than twenty miles away, her husband was being murdered.

Apolinaria could not be calmed, and the young children finally put her to bed. With a tin cup gripped tightly in her small hands, little Pauline ran back and forth from the bedroom to the water barrel, wiping away tears and crying, "Mamma, Mamma, everything will be all right!" But Mamma could not be consoled, and her anxieties were not relieved by the unexplained howling of the hounds, a racket which began with the falling of the board and continued unabated for almost twenty-four hours. Finally, about midnight, the terrified and frantic family received word that Pat Garrett was dead.[2]

[1] Pauline Garrett, interview with author, Las Cruces, N. Mex., May 17, 1967.
[2] *Ibid.*

The grieving Apolinaria and Pauline went to Las Cruces the next day and saw, to their horror, Pat Garrett's corpse lying stretched across five chairs in Strong's Undertaking Parlor. No locally available casket was long enough to hold him, and a special box had to be ordered from El Paso.

The news had already spread across the United States, and people were reacting with shock and amazement. President Theodore Roosevelt sent a telegram offering condolences, as did other Washington friends and acquaintances. New Mexico and Texas political delegations came by or wired to pay their respects. Pat's brothers arrived from Haynesville, Louisiana. Governor George Curry came down from Santa Fe.

To the end Garrett remained an agnostic, and long before he had requested that there be no religious rites at his funeral. Since Curry was the highest-ranking dignitary present, the Garrett family asked him to read the graveside eulogy that the famous agnostic Robert G. Ingersoll had delivered for his dead brother. Curry promised that he would do so but quickly reconsidered when he thought of the possible political consequences.[3] Agnostics were not popular anywhere in the country, and the new governor decided that he had enough troubles without adding unnecessary new ones. He declined to read the oration, leaving it to Tom Powers, who had no popular standing in the religious community. Tom picked up the paper, squinted his one eye, and recited the entire text, intoning:

> Life is a narrow vale between the cold and barren peaks of two eternities. We strive in vain to look beyond the heights. We cry aloud and the only answer is the echo of our wailing cry. From the voiceless lips of the unreplying dead there comes no word; but in the night of death hope sees a star and listening love can hear the rustling of a wing.

Pat was laid to rest on March 5, 1908, in the shabby, overgrown northwest corner of the Las Cruces Odd Fellows Cemetery. In 1957 he and those family members who lay beside him were transferred to the Masonic Cemetery across the road. On a large granite stone is inscribed the single word: GARRETT. One can search across all of New Mexico, and indeed the entire Southwest today, and find no other monument to his memory.

[3] Mrs. Tommy Powers Stamper, interview with author, July 10, 1968, Virden, N. Mex.

Epilogue

Walter Noble Burns, author of the exasperatingly popular *Saga of Billy the Kid*, is credited, with considerable accuracy, with being the principal force behind the legend surrounding the life—and more particularly the death—of the incorrigible young man whose violent end brought Pat Garrett momentary fame, long-lasting rue, and a dubious distinction that can almost be compared to that of the "dirty little coward" who shot Mr. Howard and laid Jesse James in his grave. Perhaps more than any single person, other than the Kid himself, Burns, in his romanticized *Saga*, flagrant with error, distortion, and misinterpretation, became Garrett's nemesis. This vastly popular book served to haunt and cast dishonor upon the lawman long after his mutilated corpse was laid to rest in the Las Cruces cemetery.

The *Saga* became an overnight bestseller, and since 1926 has gone through many printings. However, unknown to most casual readers with no particular expertise concerning southwestern history, the book aroused dismay and wrath among Lincoln County historians. Almost to a man these scholars disputed Burns's contention that Billy the Kid was a knightly hero and that those who opposed him deserved to be sent to the wall.

It is therefore ironic, in view of the uproar, that Burns himself took further cognizance of his notes and interviews[1] and, in response to the outcry, wrote a perceptive evaluation of Pat Garrett's accomplishments. Writing outside his usual fictionalized historical style, Burns gave a cogent statement on this subject in 1928, when he wrote to Maurice Garland Fulton, one of the most knowledgeable students of the Lincoln County War and its brutal history. Burns wrote:

[1] Burns went to Lincoln County and interviewed many of the war's survivors. His papers are now in the possession of the University of Arizona Library, Tucson.

307

I have heard Garrett damned up and down . . . in New Mexico as a coward and a cold blooded murderer. But . . . Garrett carried out the job he undertook with courage and determination . . . when we take into consideration all of its difficulties and dangers. In my estimation Garrett was a brave man—he must have been a brave man to do what he did—and what he did, it seems to me, resulted in a new era of law and order for New Mexico.[2]

Reinforcing Burns's unpublished opinions of Garrett's accomplishments was Eugene Manlove Rhodes, who was sympathetic to the Tunstall–McSween–Billy the Kid faction but nevertheless recognized that a brave and honorable Patrick Floyd Garrett had been seriously slandered. Rhodes treated Burns's *Saga* with sarcasm and wrote that with the election of Pat Garrett as sheriff of Lincoln County came the "appalling discovery that the new sheriff intended to observe his oath of office." The book was described as no history but a fiction in which Billy the Kid was the hero and Pat Garrett was the heavy. Rhodes said that

reading the *Saga* you will get the impression that Billy got shabby treatment all along the line; that it was inconsiderate of the sheriff to molest him; that it was unsportsmanlike to search for him in his own country, right where he lived, among his devoted adherents; and that it was positively discourteous and unfair that Garrett did not let Billy the Kid kill him at the last.[3]

Rhodes furthermore demolished several of the more damaging charges made against Garrett by many of the Kid's biographers and idolaters. Rhodes admitted that Garrett killed a former friend, but argued that everyone knew everyone in those days and that it was unjust to damn the sheriff because "he did not let friendship interfere with his duty." With respect to Garrett's bravery, Rhodes said that Pat kept up a daily pursuit of the young outlaw, knowing that "there was no rock or ridge or tree but death might lurk behind it." As for the oft-repeated statement that Garrett unfairly killed the Kid, Rhodes retorted that Billy would have taken the same advantage had the opportunity presented itself. "There was only one thing [for Garrett] to do and he did it. He shot Billy through the heart. I cannot imagine any man doing otherwise; I cannot imagine any other thing to do."[4]

[2] Walter Noble Burns to Maurice Garland Fulton, January 21, 1928, Fulton Papers, University of Arizona Library, Tucson.
[3] Eugene Manlove Rhodes, "In Defense of Pat Garrett," quoted in W. H. Hutchinson (ed.) *The Rhodes Reader*, 305–16.
[4] *Ibid.*

To his great credit, Pat Garrett had no illusions about what others would think of him after his death, nor did he worry or concern himself about his place in history. That evaluation he left to others. Though this question is still being answered, one view that can be given considerable weight is that of Theodore Roosevelt, who, although he failed to renew Garrett's position as El Paso customs collector, followed the former sheriff's career with great interest. Garrett's death saddened him, and he spoke briefly of the matter to Patrick J. Hurley, secretary of war during Herbert Hoover's administration and later United States ambassador to China. Hurley recalled this conversation in a letter to Oscar Garrett on December 9, 1950:

> When your father was killed, President Theodore Roosevelt made a statement . . . to the effect that Pat Garrett was not the man who upheld the arm of law and order in New Mexico, he was the first man to introduce law and order. In my time and yours, I hope that we will be able to see that justice is done to the character of the greatest New Mexican, Pat Garrett.[5]

[5] Patrick J. Hurley to Oscar Garrett, quoted by Jarvis Garrett in *The Authentic Life of Billy the Kid*, 48.

Bibliography

Books and Articles

Adams, Ramon. *A Fitting Death For Billy the Kid.* Norman, University of Oklahoma Press, 1960.

Ball, Eve. *Ma'am Jones of the Pecos.* Tucson, University of Arizona Press, 1969.

———. *Ruidoso,* San Antonio, Naylor Company, 1963.

Bartholomew, Ed. *Jesse Evans: A Texas Hide Burner.* Houston, Frontier Press of Texas, 1955.

Black, Reading W. *The Life and Diary of Reading W. Black.* Uvalde, Texas, Calithump Press, 1934.

Bonney, Cecil. *Looking over My Shoulder: Seventy-five Years in the Pecos Valley.* Roswell, N. Mex., 1971.

Burns, Walter Noble. *The Saga of Billy the Kid.* New York, Grosset and Dunlap, 1926.

Blazer, Paul A. (as told to Eve Ball). "The Fight at Blazer's Mill," *Arizona and the West,* Vol. VI, No. 3 (Autumn, 1964), 203–10.

Charles, Mrs. Tom. *More Tales of the Tularosa.* Alamogordo, N. Mex., Bennett Printing Company, 1961.

———. *Tales of the Tularosa.* Alamogordo, N. Mex., Carl Hertzog, 1954.

Cook, John R. *The Border and the Buffalo.* Chicago, Lakeside Press, 1938.

Coop, W. E. *Billy the Kid: The Trail of a Kansas Legend.* Kansas City, Mo., Kansas City Westerners, 1965.

Curry, George. *An Autobiography.* Albuquerque, University of New Mexico Press, 1958.

Dykes, Jeff. *Four Sheriffs of Lincoln County.* Washington, D.C., Potomac Westerners, May, 1965.

———. *Billy the Kid: The Bibliography of a Legend.* Albuquerque, N. Mex., University of New Mexico Press, 1952.

Fall, Albert B. *The Memoirs of Albert B. Fall.* Ed. by David B. Stratton. Southwestern Studies Series, Vol. IV, No. 3, Monograph No. 15. El Paso, Texas Western Press, University of Texas at El Paso, 1966.

311

Fenley, Florence. *Oldtimers of Southwest Texas.* Uvalde, Texas, Hornby Press, 1957.

Fugitives from Justice in Texas, 1878. Austin, Texas, State Printing Office, 1878.

Fulton, Maurice Garland. *History of the Lincoln County War.* Ed. by Robert N. Mullin. Tucson, University of Arizona Press, 1968.

Garrett, Pat F. *The Authentic Life of Billy the Kid.* Intro. by Jarvis P. Garrett. Albuquerque, N. Mex., Horn and Wallace, 1964.

Gibson, Arrell M. *The Life and Death of Colonel Albert Jennings Fountain.* Norman, University of Oklahoma Press, 1965.

Hail, Marshal. "The San Augustine Ranch House," *Frontier Times,* September, 1969.

Hertzog, Peter. *Little Known Facts About Billy the Kid.* Santa Fe, N. Mex., Press of the Territorian, 1964.

Hervey, James Madison. "The Assassination of Pat Garrett," *True West,* March–April, 1961.

Hough, Emerson. *The Story of the Outlaw.* New York, Outing Publishers, 1907.

Hoyt, Henry F. *A Frontier Doctor.* Boston, Houghton Mifflin Company, 1929.

Hutchinson, W. H. *A Bar Cross Man: The Life and Personal Writings of Eugene Manlove Rhodes.* Norman, University of Oklahoma Press, 1956.

———. *Another Verdict For Oliver Lee.* Clarendon, Texas, Clarendon Press, 1965.

———, and Robert N. Mullin. *Whiskey Jim and a Kid Named Billie.* Clarendon, Texas, Clarendon Press, 1967.

Jones, Fayette. *Old Mines and Ghost Camps of New Mexico.* Fort Davis, Texas, Frontier Book Company, 1968.

Keleher, William H. *The Fabulous Frontier.* Albuquerque, University of New Mexico Press, 1962.

———. *Violence in Lincoln County.* Albuquerque, University of New Mexico Press, 1957.

Kenner, Charles L. *A History of New Mexican–Plains Indians Relations.* Norman, University of Oklahoma Press, 1969.

Klas, Virginia, and Opal Wilcox. "The Bob Fitzsimmons–Peter Maher Fight," *Password* (El Paso, Texas, Historical Society), Vol. X, No. 2 (Summer), 1965.

Klasner, Lily. *My Girlhood Among Outlaws.* Ed. by Eve Ball. Tucson, University of Arizona Press, 1972.

Lake, Stuart. *Wyatt Earp: Frontier Marshal.* Boston, Houghton Mifflin Company, 1931.

Lingle, Robert T., and Dee Linford. *The Pecos River Commission of New Mexico and Texas.* Santa Fe, N. Mex., Rydal Press, 1961.

McCarty, John L. *Maverick Town: The Story of Old Tascosa*. Norman, University of Oklahoma Press, 1946.

Metz, Leon C. *John Selman: Texas Gunfighter*. New York, Hastings House, 1966.

———. "Pat Garrett: Another Look at a Western Gunman," *Montana: The Magazine of Western History*, Vol. XXI, No. 4 (Autumn, 1971), 70–78.

———. "Pat Garrett: El Paso Customs Collector," *Arizona and the West*, Vol. II, No. 4 (Winter), 1969, 327–40.

Mullin, Robert N. *The Boyhood of Billy the Kid*. Southwestern Studies Series, Vol. I, No. 1, Monograph 17. El Paso, Texas Western Press, University of Texas at El Paso, 1967.

———. *A Chronology of the Lincoln County War*. Santa Fe, N. Mex., Press of the Territorian, 1966.

———. "The Key to the Mystery of Pat Garrett," *Los Angeles Westerners Corral*, No. 92 (June, 1969), 1–5.

———. "Pat Garrett: Two Forgotten Killings," *Password* (El Paso County Historical Society), Vol. X, No. 2 (Summer, 1965), 57–63.

———. *The Strange Story of Wayne Brazel*. Canyon, Texas, Palo Duro Press, 1969.

———. "The Strange Story of Wayne Brazel," *Panhandle Plains Historical Review*, Vol. XLII (1969), 23–59.

———, ed. *History of the Lincoln County War*. Tucson, University of Arizona Press, 1968.

———, and W. H. Hutchinson. *Whiskey Jim and a Kid Named Billie*. Clarendon, Texas, Clarendon Press, 1967.

———, and Philip J. Rasch. "New Light on the Legend of Billy the Kid," New Mexico Folklore Record, Vol. II (1952–53), 1–5.

Neal, Dorothy Jensen. *Captive Mountain Waters*. El Paso, Texas Western Press, University of Texas at El Paso, 1961.

———. *Cloud Climbing Railroad*. Alamogordo, N. Mex., Alamogordo Printing Company, 1966.

Nolan, Frederick W. *The Life and Death of John Henry Tunstall*. Albuquerque, University of New Mexico Press, 1965.

O'Neal, James B. *They Die but Once*. New York, Knight Publications, 1935.

Otero, Miguel. *My Nine Years as Governor of New Mexico Territory*. Albuquerque, University of New Mexico Press, 1940.

———. *The Real Billy the Kid*. New York, Rufus Rockwell Wilson, Inc., 1936.

Parrish, Joe. "Hanged by the Neck until Dead," *Password* (El Paso County Historical Society), Vol. III, No. 2 (April, 1958), 68–75.

Poe, John W. *The Death of Billy the Kid*. Boston, Houghton Mifflin Company, 1936.

Poe, Sophie. *Buckboard Days*. Caldwell, Idaho, Caxton Printers, 1936.

Prichard, Walter, ed. "The Parish of Claiborne," *Louisiana State Historical Quarterly*, Vol. XXI, No. 4 (October, 1938), 1110–1215.

Rasch, Philip J. "Clues to the Puzzle of Billy the Kid," *English Westerners Brand Book*, December, 1957, January, 1958.

———. "The Hunting of Billy the Kid," *English Westerners Brand Book*, Vol. II, No. 2 (January, 1969), 1–10.

———. "The Hunting of Billy the Kid (Conclusion)," *English Westerners Brand Book*, Vol. II, No. 3 (April, 1969), 11–12.

———. "John Kinney: King of the Rustlers," *English Westerners Brand Book*, Vol. IV (October, 1961), 10–12.

———. "A Man Called Antrim," *Los Angeles Westerners Brand Book*, Vol. VI (1956), 48–54.

———. "More on the McCartys," *English Westerners Brand Book*, Vol. III (April, 1957), 3–9.

———. "Prelude to War: The Murder of John Henry Tunstall," *English Westerners Brand Book*, Vol. XII, No. 2 (January, 1970), 1–10.

———. "The Trials of Lieutenant Colonel Dudley," *English Westerners Brand Book*, Vol. VII, No. 2 (January, 1965).

———. "The Twenty-one Men He Put Bullets Through," *New Mexico Folklore Record*, Vol. IX (1954–55), 8–14.

———. "War in Lincoln County," *English Westerners Brand Book*, Vol. VI, No. 4 (July, 1964), 2–11.

———, and Robert N. Mullin. "Dim Trails: The Pursuit of the McCarty Family," *New Mexico Folklore Record*, Vol. III (1954), 6–11.

Rhodes, Eugene Manlove. *The Rhodes Reader: Stories of Virgins, Villains, and Varmints*. Sel. by W. H. Hutchinson. Norman, University of Oklahoma Press, 1957.

Rickards, Colin. *How Pat Garrett Died*. Santa Fe, N. Mex., Palomino Press, 1970.

Rister, Carl Coke. *Fort Griffin on the Texas Frontier*. Norman, University of Oklahoma Press, 1956.

"The San Augustine Springs Incident," *Nike News* (White Sands Proving Grounds, Alamogordo, N. Mex.), December, 1967.

Scanland, John Milton. *Life of Pat Garrett*. El Paso, Texas, Southwest Printing Company, 1952.

Shinkle, James D. *Fifty Years of Roswell History*. Roswell, N. Mex., Hall-Poorbaugh Press, 1964.

———. *Fort Sumner and the Bosque Redondo Indian Reservation*. Roswell, N. Mex., Hall-Poorbaugh Press, 1965.

———. *Reminiscences of Roswell Pioneers*. Roswell, N. Mex., Hall-Poorbaugh Press, 1966.

———. *Robert Casey and the Ranch on the Río Hondo*. Roswell, N. Mex., Hall-Poorbaugh Press, 1970.

Shirley, Glen. *Shotgun for Hire: The Story of "Deacon" Jim Miller, Killer of Pat Garrett.* Norman, University of Oklahoma Press, 1970.

Siringo, Charles. *A Texas Cowboy.* New York, J. S. Ogilvie, 1886.

Smith, Pearl. *Historic Claiborne.* Homer, La., Claiborne Parish Historical Association, 1962.

———. *Historic Claiborne '65.* Homer, La., Claiborne Parish Historical Association, 1965.

Smith, William R. "Death in Dona Ana County: A Study of the Facts and Theories in the Fountain and Garrett Murder Cases," *English Westerners Brand Book,* Part 1, Vol. IX, No. 2 (January, 1967), Part 2, Vol. IX, No. 3 (April, 1967).

Sonnichsen, C. L. *Pass of the North.* El Paso, Texas Western Press, University of Texas at El Paso, 1968.

———. *Roy Bean: Law West of the Pecos.* New York, Devin-Adair, 1958.

———. *Ten Texas Feuds.* Albuquerque, University of New Mexico Press, 1957.

———. *Tularosa: Last of the Frontier West.* New York, Devin-Adair, 1963.

———, and William V. Morrison. *Alias Billy the Kid.* Albuquerque, University of New Mexico Press, 1955.

Strickland, Rex W., ed. "The Recollections of W. S. Glenn: Buffalo Hunter," *Panhandle-Plains Historical Review,* Vol. XXII (1949), 16–54.

Newspapers

Alamogordo (New Mexico) *News.*
Albuquerque (New Mexico) *Review.*
Cimarron (New Mexico) *News and Press.*
Claiborne (Louisiana) *Guardian.*
Eddy (New Mexico) *Argus.*
El Paso Daily Herald.
El Paso Daily Times.
El Paso Evening News.
El Paso Herald.
El Paso Herald-Post.
El Paso Lone Star.
El Paso Times.
Grant County (New Mexico) *Herald.*
Las Cruces (New Mexico) *Rio Grande Republican.*
Las Cruces (New Mexico) *Semi-Weekly.*
Las Vegas (New Mexico) *Daily Optic.*
Las Vegas (New Mexico) *Gazette.*
Lincoln County (New Mexico) *Leader.*
Mesilla (New Mexico) *Independent.*

Pat Garrett

Roswell (New Mexico) *Daily Record.*
Roswell (New Mexico) *Register.*
Santa Fe New Mexican.
Santa Fe Weekly New Mexican.
Southwesterner (New Mexico and Texas).

Manuscripts

Cecil Bonney Autobiography (typescript). University of Texas at El Paso Archives.

Thomas B. Catron Papers. University of New Mexico Library, Albuquerque.

W. W. Cox Papers (San Augustine Ranch). University of Texas at El Paso Archives.

James H. East Papers. University of Texas at Austin Archives.

A. B. Fall Papers, Alamogordo, N. Mex., University of New Mexico.

G. Y. Falls, "A Study in the Development of Town Government in Hagerman, New Mexico, 1905-1948." M.A. thesis, Eastern New Mexico University, Portales, 1951.

G. A. Feather Papers. Mesilla Park, N. Mex.

Albert J. Fountain Papers (typescripts). University of Oklahoma Library Archives, Norman.

Colonel Maurice Garland Fulton Papers. University of Arizona Library, Tucson.

Pat F. Garrett Papers. Private collection in possession of Jarvis Garrett, Albuquerque, N. Mex.

Skelton Glenn Papers (typescripts and microfilm). University of Texas at El Paso Archives.

W. A. Hawkins Papers (Southern Pacific Collection). University of Texas at El Paso Archives.

Emerson Hough Papers. Iowa State Department of History and Archives, Des Moines.

National Archives, Washington, D.C. and New York:
Azariah F. Wild, special Treasury agent, investigating counterfeiting in New Mexico, 1880, Record Group 56.
Board of General Appraisals, New York, August–December, 1902, Federal Record Center, New York.
N. A. M. Dudley to Acting Assistant Adjutant General, November 8, 9, 1405, AGO, 1878.
Willis Skelton Glenn v. *The United States and the Comanche Indians,* No. 1892–1893, United States Court of Claims.
Treasury Department Records, Record Group 56.
New Mexico State Records Center and Archives, Santa Fe:
Corporation Records.

Court Records for Bernalillo County (Albuquerque).
Territorial Papers and Sheriffs' Accounts.
Panhandle–Plains Historical Museum, Canyon, Texas. Oral and hand-written "old-timer" interviews relating to Texas and New Mexico history.
Lee A. Riggs. "A Short History of the Customs District of El Paso." Type-script in possession of the author.
C. L. Sonnichsen Papers. University of Texas at El Paso Archives.
Lew Wallace Papers. William Henry Smith Memorial Library, Indian-apolis, Ind.
J. R. Webb Papers. R. N. Richardson Collection, Hardin-Simmons Li-brary, Abilene, Texas.
Herman Weisner Papers (primarily oral-history tapes). Organ, N. Mex.

Letters to Author

It would take many pages to record every letter received that related to the Pat Garrett biography. Only those referred to in the text are listed below.

Eve Ball, May 18, June 1, 1967.
H. H. Dow, January 24, 1967.
Jeff Dykes, August 5, 1967.
G. A. Feather, October 27, 1970.
Fred M. Mazzulla, June 22, 30, 1967.
Robert N. Mullin, July 26, 1969.
Joe Smith, Jr., July 4, 1969.
J. J. Smith "Jack," July 21, 1967; December 2, 1970.

Courthouse Records

Chaves County (Roswell, N. Mex.). Deed and mortgage records.
Claiborne Parish (Homer, La.). Deed, mortgage and probate records.
DeBaca County (Fort Sumner, N. Mex.). Deed and mortgage records.
Doña Ana County (Las Cruces, N. Mex.). Civil and criminal records, probate, deed, mortgages, mining, etc.
Eddy County (Carlsbad, N. Mex.). Corporation, deed records.
El Paso County (El Paso, Texas). Deed and civil records.
Lincoln County (Carrizozo, N. Mex.). Deed records.
Otero County (Alamogordo, N. Mex.). Deed records.
Sierra County (Truth or Consequences, formerly Hillsboro, N. Mex.). Criminal records.
Uvalde County (Uvalde, Texas). Deed and mortgage records.

Pat Garrett

United States Census Records

Claiborne Parish, La., 1860–70.
Fort Sumner, N. Mex., 1880.

Interviews with Author

Eve Ball, Ruidoso, N. Mex., June 22, 1968, May 14, 1969.
Frank Brito, Las Cruces, N. Mex., November 9, 1970.
Butler Oral "Snooks" Burris, Rumsey, Calif., February 23, 1969.
James Cox, San Augustine Ranch, N. Mex.
G. A. Feather, Mesilla Park, N. Mex., March 2, 1969.
Helen Garrett Fitch, Las Cruces, N. Mex., August 31, 1970.
Arthur Fountain, Mesilla, N. Mex., August 26, 1970.
Jarvis Garrett, Albuquerque, N. Mex., December 14, 1967, November
    18, 1968.
Jarvis P. Garrett, Haynesville, La., August 31, 1967.
Pauline Garrett, Las Cruces, N. Mex., May 17, June 27, 1967.
Emmett Isaacs, Las Cruces, N. Mex., October 29, 1967.
R. L. Madison, El Paso, Texas, February 28, 1967.
Cliff McKinney, Carlsbad, N. Mex., October 9, 1969.
Robert N. Mullin, El Paso, Texas, October 5, 1968, December 9, 1969,
    August 7, 1970.
Allan Rhodes, Eugene Manlove Rhodes gravesite, New Mexico, June,
    1970.
James D. Shinkle, Roswell, N. Mex., August 8, 1968.
C. L. Sonnichsen, El Paso, Texas, September 1, 1967, June 23, 1968.
Mrs. Mary Ellis Wright, Redrock, N. Mex., April 23, 1968.
Willis Walter, Lordsburg, N. Mex., January 30, 1968.
Mrs. Hugh White, El Paso, Texas, June 3, 1968.
Mrs. Rose White, Portales, N. Mex., November 1, 1967.
Mrs. Mary Ellis Wright, Redrock, N. Mex., April 23, 1968.

Index

319